D0935421

THE OTHER PARETO

THE OTHER PARETO

Edited by PLACIDO BUCOLO
Translated by Placido and Gillian Bucolo
with a preface by Ronald Fletcher

St. Martin's Press   New York

ISBN 0-312-58955-7

Library of Congress Cataloging in Publication Data

Pareto, Vilfredo, 1848-1923.
  The other Pareto.

  Bibliography: p. 2
  Includes index.
  1. Economics – Collected works. 2. Sociology –
Collected works. 3. Europe – Politics and government –
1848-1871 – Collected works. 4. Europe – Politics and
government – 1871-1918 – Collected works. I. Bucolo,
Placido. II. Title.
HB177.P32 1980   301   79-24588
ISBN 0-312-58955-7

Contents

Genealogical table   *vii*
Preface by Ronald Fletcher   *ix*

PART ONE *Economic & political freedom*

Introduction: The beginnings   3
 1 Proportional representation 1872   6
 2 Universal suffrage 1872   19
 3 On the logic of the new school of economics 1877   24
 4 Whether it is worth establishing by law a minimum wage and a
   maximum margin of profit 1886   31
 5 Socialism and freedom 1891   41
 6 The future of the liberal side 1892   54
 7 Introduction to Marx's *Capital* 1893   61
 8 Socialism and the duty on grain 1894   69
 9 The ethical state 1894   74
10 The university 1895   78
11 For and against socialism 1896   80
12 Course in political economy 1896   83
13 The new theories of economics 1897   100
14 The dangers of reaction 1898   107
15 The sentiment of freedom 1899   112
16 Liberals and Socialists 1900   115

PART TWO *Sentiments & aristocracies*

17 The danger of socialism 1900   121
18 An application of sociological theories 1900   128
19 Justice 1900   135
20 A little social physiology 1901   139
21 Socialist systems 1901   143
22 Can the bourgeoisie rise again? 1904   166
23 Strikers in France 1904   169
24 Humanitarians and revolutionaries 1904   171

25 Regarding happenings in Russia 1905 173
26 Manual of political economy 1906 176
27 The moralistic myth 1911 189
28 The treatise on general sociology 1910–16 195
29 Conflict between races, religions and nations 1914 225
30 War and its principal sociological factors 1915 229
31 The supposed principle of nationality 1918 234
32 Hopes and disappointments 1919 238
33 Utopias 1920 242
34 The collapse of central authority 1920 246
35 Fascism 1922 251
36 Today and a century ago 1922 254
37 Russia 1922 257
38 The phenomenon of fascism 1923 260
39 The war goes on 1923 265
40 Freedom 1923 268
41 A few points concerning a future constitutional
    re-organisation 1923 272

PART THREE *Conclusion*

I   Pareto and his contemporaries 279
II   Pareto and his critics 288
III Reading Pareto 298

Select bibliography 304
Index of names 306

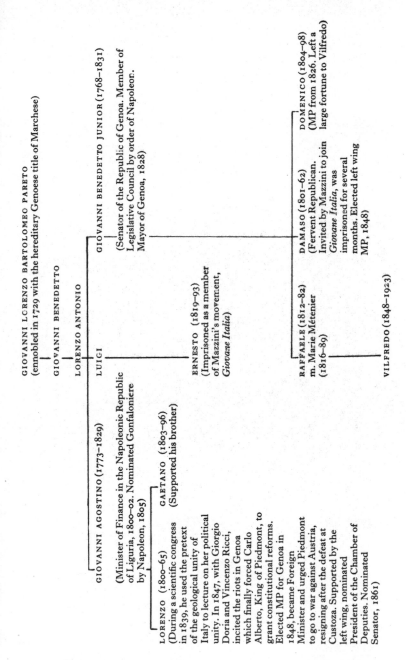

GIOVANNI LCRENZO BARTOLOMEO PARETO
(ennobled in 1729 with the hereditary Genoese title of Marchese)

GIOVANNI BENEDETTO

LORENZO ANTONIO

GIOVANNI BENEDETTO JUNIOR (1768–1831)
(Senator of the Republic of Genoa. Member of Legislative Council by order of Napoleon. Mayor of Genoa, 1828)

LUIGI

GIOVANNI AGOSTINO (1773–1829)
(Minister of Finance in the Napoleonic Republic of Liguria, 1800–02. Nominated Gonfaloniere by Napoleon, 1805)

GAETANO (1803–96)
(Supported his brother)

LORENZO (1800–65)
(During a scientific congress in 1839, he used the pretext of the geological unity of Italy to lecture on her political unity. In 1847, with Giorgio Doria and Vincenzo Ricci, incited the riots in Genoa which finally forced Carlo Alberto, King of Piedmont, to grant constitutional reforms. Elected MP for Genoa in 1848, became Foreign Minister and urged Piedmont to go to war against Austria, resigning after the defeat at Custoza. Supported by the left wing, nominated President of the Chamber of Deputies. Nominated Senator, 1861)

ERNESTO (1819–93)
(Imprisoned as a member of Mazzini's movement, *Giovane Italia*)

DAMASO (1801–62)
(Fervent Republican. Invited by Mazzini to join *Giovane Italia*, was imprisoned for several months. Elected left wing MP, 1848)

DOMENICO (1804–98)
(MP from 1826. Left a large fortune to Vilfredo)

RAFFAELE (1812–82)
m. Marie Métenier (1816–89)

VILFREDO (1848–1923)

Preface
Ronald Fletcher

The title of this new book on Pareto is immediately intriguing, and a preface can do no better than dwell – and comment – on it.

After the juncture of Hume and Kant in the history of philosophy – making necessary the effort to achieve a new science of man, society, and the development of human societies in history – all those scholars who turned their attention to the satisfactory formulation of such a science, since the end of the eighteenth century, trailed great storms of controversy in their wake. In treating as problematical elements of human nature long taken for granted; in questioning long-established assumptions about the basis of society and the significance of these for the interpretation and explanation of events in history and the clarification of human destiny; in questioning the boundaries of the several human sciences as they emerged and developed, proposing new perspectives of theory and judgement, new rules of method for observation, classification, comparison, and the testing of theories, and in rejecting earlier methods as incorrect and insufficient – they antagonised theologians, metaphysicians and historians, and even scholars in the so-called 'natural' sciences and the 'special' social sciences. Some also aroused anger and criticism in their proposals for the reform (or retention) of modern industrial capitalism – the evils of which, despite its great promise of increased material welfare, lay at the heart of their concern. Comte with his (supposed) 'consensus' of imposed authority; Marx with his revolutionary message and fervour; Spencer with his detailed defence of '*laissez-faire*'; Durkheim with his cry for a new moral code appropriate to the new conditions of 'specialisation' . . . these and many others raised the ire of critics, intellectuals and men of affairs alike. Much of this antagonism to sociology and sociologists, of course, continues – but of no one theorist is this more true than of Pareto. Intellectually, ethically, politically, Pareto – ever since his reputation began to take form – has been intensely disliked by many.

His work has not, perhaps, been as well and as widely known as that of other theorists. (When trying to get books published on Pareto – like the present one, for example – I am told by the market researchers of British publishers that Pareto is 'not on the reading lists' and is 'not taught' in current courses on sociological theory in the universities!). In some quarters, however, it has exercised a much greater influence. Long known as an economist, he certainly played a considerable part in the development and formulation of modern economic analysis. The full translation of *Trattato di sociologia generale*, however, was not published until 1935. Yet it was this which exercised one of the most powerful influences on contemporary American sociology – in particular at the hands of the well-known seminar set up at Harvard (including Henderson, Homans, Parsons, and Schumpeter among its members) to study Pareto's system. It was, of course, one of the most immediate and considerable influences in Talcott Parsons' book, *The Structure of Social Action*, which was responsible for one of the most dominant American perspectives after the 1939–45 war.

Pareto, however, drew coals of fire of criticism upon his head for some quite specific – though perhaps not justifiable – reasons. First, his sociology itself was unpopular and controversial, strongly emphasising the power of 'unreason' in society, and stressing the predominance of 'non-logical' action in bringing about equilibrium or disequilibrium among the collective conditions of society. It asserted the perennial existence in the human mind of certain dispositions of motivation – instinctually rooted 'residues', manifesting themselves in established 'sentiments' – and made the analysis of the distribution of these among the élites of society the crucial ground for explaining sequences of social stability and social change. It stressed the power of these 'residues' even in intellectual theorising, arguing that though theories and ideologies had practical utility and causal force in society, it was not their truth or intellectual validity which mattered, nor was it any conviction about their truth or validity which formed the ground of motivation of those whose actions rested on them. On the contrary, such motivation lay, really, in the underlying 'residues' themselves. All this, besides

emphasising the power of the non-rational and the irrational in
human nature and society, also smacked of relativism and cynicism, seeming to abandon all belief in the actuality of any 'progress' in history, or the possibility of 'progress' in any future
society, and, indeed, any firm ethical and political ground for
any projected effort whatsoever. It confined the sociologist's
concern simply to the analysis of the equilibrium-disequilibrium
conditions of society. Those humane concerns, those ethical and
political commitments clearly evident in the work of the other
major sociologists, seemed decidedly lacking in him. His sociology itself, then, provided, for some, reasons for distaste and discontent, quite apart from grounds for intellectual disagreement
– of which there were many. But two other features of his reputation (in so far as these were known) led many to dislike him.

The first was his independence and *apparent* dilettantism.
From a certain point in his life, he enjoyed independent means,
could stand aloof from institutionalised scholarship, and lived
an essentially private life, pursuing his own private tastes and
discriminations among his favourite and favoured Angora cats –
a brilliant, egotistical, Machiavelli-like commentator on economic and political affairs. *La vie engagée* seemed not for him.
But second – and a consideration of much greater importance –
he seemed, towards the end of his life, to lend positive support
to fascism in Italy, and, even more particularly, to the power
and policies of Mussolini. He appeared, therefore, not only to
have adopted and advocated a directionless 'relativism' in his
analysis of society, but also to be prepared to move in expedient
fashion in his political allegiances.

None of this, it is fair to say, led scholars either to disregard or
to underestimate his sociology as such. He has always been
recognised as one of the most significant thinkers of the early
decades of this century in the making of the new science of
society. His name stands on a par with those of Tönnies,
Durkheim, Weber and Simmel. His entire system has commanded the respect of serious criticism, and has been very fully
considered. His analysis of élites, and of the 'cyclical' fluctuations
of power within and among them in the institutionalised inequali-
ties of societies, has attracted much more attention – especially
in political sociology, together with the ideas of Michels and
Mosca. Many elements in his work, too, have been seen to

contain important insights which have not, even yet, been given sufficient attention. His analysis of the operation of the 'nonrational' in human experience and behaviour, for example, and of the mental mechanisms involved, compares in very interesting fashion with that of Freud, and this has, even now, not been sufficiently explored. His emphasis upon the conflicting growth of plutocracy on the one hand and the extension of democracy on the other in the development of industrial capitalism (a feature also mentioned by Weber) clearly underlies much disputation and conflict in our present day economic and political affairs, and could well be a much more fruitful avenue of enquiry than the exaggerated attention given to theories of 'stratification' and the 'class struggle'. At the same time, his system does also contain elements which call for radical criticism – some of which has been voiced, some not. Pareto never denied the actuality of social evolution, or the use of a structural-functional model of the social system for the analysis of its nature and directions, but he nevertheless proposed a quite different model (one of 'atomistic' individual units and motivations – much more akin to that of economic analysis) for the equilibrium-disequilibrium analysis of collective conditions, and this is much open to criticism (as moving, incidentally, in the analysis of social systems, from the analogy of an 'organic' system to that of a 'mechanical' system: a highly dubious change which has also occurred in some American – that is, Parsonian – thinking). Similarly, his very sharp conceptual distinction (and empirical social division) between 'logical' and 'non-logical' action has called for, and has received, serious criticism – though it still requires much more. In short, his sociology has been, and continues to be, accepted and influential in part, and attracts, too, much seriously concerned criticism.

This leaves the crucial criticism of Pareto on the subject of his political allegiance – in short, in his support of fascism, and his general cynicism and relativism. This is the one Pareto we all thought that we knew, and it is here that Professor Bucolo's title – The Other Pareto – demonstrates its true relevance. Was Pareto as black as he has been painted in this respect? And – whatever the truth of his political allegiance – how was the gradual movement towards it related to the development of his ideas?

A considerable literature has grown up around him – the
details of which are very usefully covered in Professor Bucolo's
'Conclusion' – and though, in all this, there have been few *books*,
these few have been of high quality: Borkenau (1936), for
example, and Finer (1966). Finer, especially, offers an excellent
account (with selected readings) of Pareto's ideas. Never before,
however, has there been a study like the one provided here.
Professor Bucolo has gone to great lengths in his new and
widely representative selection of his great compatriot's works,
to trace the detailed development of Pareto's views from the
time of his first public address – very significantly on proportional representation – to that of his later leanings (just before
his death) towards fascism. He has taken great pains to uncover
little-known and unknown newspaper articles and public
addresses, as well as to consider the better-known academic
essays and books, and a glance through the list of contents will
show the very full and consistent chronological treatment
covering publications through almost all the years of Pareto's
working life. It provides a fascinating and revealing story –
showing that Pareto began with no less a position than that of
English liberalism, when it was men like John Stuart Mill who
were his models. From that time onwards, we see the gradual
filling out and development of his views, with the growth of an
increasing political disillusionment and a deepening realism in
his appraisal of the political movements of war-torn Europe –
socialist, bolshevik, fascist alike. It was within this context –
seeing essentially the same pursuits of power, with the same
mental mechanisms at work, whether in socialist or in fascist
movements – that his cynicism grew. It is significant that at the
end of his study, Bucolo finds himself able to argue that Pareto's
work 'no longer seems like the manual of the man who wants to
rule, but begins to look like the handbook of the good citizen'
and that, aspiring to power, he was also ready '. . . to surrender
what little power he had rather than to barter it for his integrity'.
He can claim, too, that Pareto's 'way of life was as single-minded
as his writings' and agree with Zuccarini that his opinions
'always remained liberal and in favour of a system of democracy'.

Clearly, every reader will re-assess the work of Pareto for
himself in the light of this biographical picture of his development, but one thing seems sure: the events, the developments

of thought and action, which we are now witnessing in the politics of every country in Europe, indeed in the world at large (the so-called 'socialism' in present-day Britain, among the trade unions and the Labour party alike, is a prime example!) are such as to make us sympathise a good deal more than we might at one time have done with Pareto's cynicism; to see that there are good grounds for it; to see that what happened under his nose to change his own judgements, is happening in very good measure under ours; and, perhaps, to lead us to reconsider seriously what he has to say in this direction.

There is one final point. During our own twentieth century, we are passing through a very mixed and vexed period of scholarship in sociology, when various 'perspectives of theory' are being hotly declaimed and pursued, even whilst the full contributions of important theorists in different countries (and different languages) are only gradually becoming generally available in translation. International agreement concerning the nature, scope, and methods of the new science is still in a condition of painstaking growth. Major contributions of the recent past are being ignored, going unstudied, and being *apparently* superseded by fashionable 'innovations', 're-formulations', or 'contemporary schools' or 'paradigms,' even as they are being more deeply clarified. A kind of fleet of busy 'professional' boats, all decked out in conspicuous flags, banners and exhibitionist bunting, is being sailed flamboyantly by contending 'professional' crews over an ocean already there, but whose depths and main currents are as yet insufficiently plumbed and charted. A re-orientation of concern and study is required. In the particular case before us, we are, as yet, little more than forty years from the first translation of Pareto's main sociological treatise, itself a highly complex work, and few can yet be said to have assessed his system fully. But here, for the first time, is a fresh and original translation of a selection of his works which clearly demonstrates the development of his thought and opinions throughout his life. This is a book therefore, which contributes significantly to the much needed growth of international awareness and clarification, and which could well lead us to quite fundamental re-appraisals. As such, it is warmly to be welcomed.

Southwold, Suffolk

PART ONE
Economic and political freedom

Introduction
The beginnings

Vilfredo Pareto was born in Paris on 15 July, 1848, of an Italian father and a French mother, Marie Métenier. His father, Raffaele, a hydraulic engineer, was an exile in France for political reasons. A Republican and convinced supporter of Mazzini, like all his family, he had had to escape from Genoa.[1] We do not know exactly when Raffaele Pareto was allowed to return to Italy; we only know that Bousquet tells us: 'It must have happened between 1848 and 1854.'[2] The young Vilfredo was attracted by these ideals and also felt profoundly Italian. In a letter to Signora Peruzzi he considers the fact that he was born in France to be an 'unfortunate circumstance'.[3]

By 1858, he had returned to Italy where later, in Turin in 1869, he took a degree in engineering. In 1870, he was employed by the Florence branch of the Rome Railway Company. Here, in Florence, he was emboldened to present his earliest ideas on political problems to the Accademia dei Georgofili, where he gave a lecture which was to bring him notoriety and, more important, the friendship of the Peruzzi family. For more than half a century thereafter, he was to carry on his widening idealistic and political struggle.

These were the greatest years, both socially and politically, for the nations of Europe. But they were also the years which bred and brought about the degeneration of democracy into plutocratic demagogy and rhetoric. They were the years which marked the realisation of many of the ideals of the Civil War in England and later the French Revolution, but which also ended in the cruel barbarity of two world wars. Only if we bear in mind this parabola of the maximum ascent and rapid descent of Europe is it possible to interpret and explain Pareto's sometimes disturbing and contradictory work. In reality, Pareto's drama is the drama of Europe, which – an impotent witness – watches its own destruction, ready to resign the mastery of the world and become the slave of its passions – the living ghost of the once prosperous, industrious artisan. It decays from the condition of a freeman to that of an instrument, more and more powerless in the face of an arrogant bureaucracy. Speaking of his visit to Pareto's home at

Céligny (called 'Villa Angora' after the many Angora cats which were his life-time companions), Papini reminds us that 'in those days one could go all over Europe, with the exception of Russia, without passports, visas, date-stamps and permits'.[4] 'Happy men want their fellows to be happy too', says Pareto in *Les Systèmes socialistes*, in melancholy mood, evoking times past and justifying the humanitarianism of his youth.

From 1870 to 1914 Europe enjoyed the longest period of peace and well-being in her history. It was the Europe of the freedom of the individual, which respected the human being and demanded the division of powers: legislative, executive and judicial. The point of reference was the English Parliament. Using this as a model, Europe tried to find its own unity after the French Revolution, but the miserable living conditions of the working and peasant masses were to continue to be the dramatic, internal contradiction to the system's successful working. The masses, who by the sweat of their brows had made the industrial, technical and economic advancement possible, had received very little benefit from it. Was a juridical, formal equality to be enough for them?

The entire nineteenth century was to labour over this question of equality. The end of the eighteenth century had seen the Enlightenment and Rationalism triumph over the prejudices of the Middle Ages and breed a neo-Renaissance based on formal equality and individual freedom like that of classical civilisation. But, as in the Classical Age, the fact that some were more equal than others (it must not be forgotten that slavery still existed) had caused a general feeling of protest – of which not only philosophers, but also emperors, were the interpreters, opening their doors to Christian egalitarianism. In the nineteenth century there was another wave of egalitarianism which was to lead to Marxism. The law was equal for all, but as all men are not equal, its application was unequal.[5] This observation, made as far back as Aristotle, was the starting point for the various supporters of the various types of socialism and communism of the nineteenth century to whom Pareto was to dedicate many of his essays.

When he made his maiden speech to the Accademia dei Georgofili with his lecture on 'Proportional Representation', he certainly felt the economic and perhaps even the moral necessity (although he always spoke with irony of this latter term) of interesting more and more people not only in matters of material production but also in social decisions. From this point on, much of his early work was to be de-

voted to the question of 'force or persuasion' in the taking of decisions
and the shaping of effective social policies.

NOTES

1 G.H. Bousquet, *Pareto, le savant et l'homme* (Lausanne 1960), p. 21.
2 *Ibid* p. 24.
3 See V. Pareto, *Lettere ai Peruzzi (1872–1900)*, ed. T. Giacalone-Monaco
(Rome 1968).
4 G. Papini, *Autoritratti e ritratti* (Milan 1962), p. 872.
5 This debate is not yet concluded, as Morris Ginsberg showed in *Justice in
Society* (London 1964).

1 Proportional representation

This lecture marked the beginning, not only of his fame, but also of his concern for problems in the methods of reasoning. It can be said that 'engineer' Pareto closed his career here, and that the political philosopher, sociologist and adversary of every type of metaphysics – including Comte's positivism – took over.

Rationalism interested him at first: 'In order to reason adequately about the lesser or greater good of the principle of proportional representation, it is necessary that we should first have a clear, distinct conception of what we consider the best and most perfect representation ...' Truth springs up *a posteriori*, rather than *a priori*, in the sense that it must already be clear in the abstract, logical form of reasoning. There is only one form of reasoning – direct inference. What remains to be examined and weighed up is only why men's *premises* are different. But the weighing up must be done in a democratic and consensual way. The legislator must do no more than give a juridical form to those principles about which the population has been convinced through persuasion: 'The great liberal reforms that England has made in recent years have been obtained by first persuading the people of the justice of them; so legislative power did no more than dress up in a suitable form a concept that was held by the masses.' Later on he affirmed: 'it is not force which must be the basis of society, it is not the prison or the gallows that must make opinion triumph'. His faith lay in the strength of persuasion, the only thing which guarantees that man will not relapse into the barbarity of physically eliminating his enemies. He believed in the good will of truth; that the eternal light of its principles is capable of uniting men. If deceit and force have already failed many times, why not change our tactics and trust in truth? 'Truth shines so righteously that whoever defends it can be certain of not being disappointed in his hope that men will have to accept it in the end.' To those who put all their hopes in force, he asked, 'Who assures you that it will always be yours, and will never be able to pass into the hands of your adversaries?' But if truth is one, it will be the work of education to acquire an ever growing acknowledgement of it. Despotism – even that of the more educated and intelligent, like that desired by Comte and Gioberti – is, above all, harmful because, by preventing citizens from discussing matters, it prevents real progress, that is, the knowledge and realisation of truth. Every citizen must choose not only the candidates, but also the programmes of the candidates. Citizens do not need *guardians* but *delegates with a mandate*.

But are these innovations subversive? Certainly not, because society must maintain itself through its traditions, customs and habits, though not indiscriminately. The question is always: 'What do you want to keep in a world that is being transformed and changed?' No change can be brought about without respect for the past together with knowledge of it. Here begins the search for a point of equilibrium between conservation and innovation, old and young, past and present. The present is what it is, but it is derived from the past, and can also be affected by what we would like it to be, namely by our aspirations. Here what is needed is not only a knowledge of what has regulated the laws of the past, but also a freedom to regulate the relationships of the present and to prepare those of the future. Therefore no one man, under any circumstances, can dominate others under the pretence of being the arbiter of a fate common to all. Everybody can be right or wrong in similar ways.

Many of Pareto's future themes are touched on in this essay. The main theme is the right to individual freedom in expressing one's opinion, even if such an opinion is a minority view and apparently unreasonable, as 'mistakes need darkness – truth the light'. His speech was not only *on* the minority, but also *for* the minority, interpreted as a cultural élite. Though these statements, made before a gathering consisting mainly of people opposed to the introduction of universal suffrage into Italy, were to attract some sympathetic support – like that of the Peruzzi family – above all, they aroused enmity. This is a testimony to the courage of 'the impertinent youth' and to a certain aristocratic indifference he entertained towards the judgements of others. This last characteristic was one which would remain unchanged for the rest of his life.[1]

FROM A LECTURE GIVEN TO THE ACCADEMIA DEI GEORGOFILI, 29 June 1872. Published the same year in *Atti* of the Accademia.

Gentlemen – I hope that I shall not be accused of being too

arrogant, in asking you who have listened to eminent scholars of economic science, now to listen to me. The very theme of this lecture urges me to speak to you, because consideration of the problems of minority representation should be a good reason for you to be indulgent towards me, and to listen patiently and sympathetically to one who belongs to the minority, partly for my opinions, perhaps, but mainly because I am the only unknown among men of established reputation. For many years almost only one method of philosophical reasoning (namely, synthetic reasoning) has been employed in the search for truth. This method is based upon the belief that from a few fundamental principles it is possible to deduce an infinity of particular truths – making all the sciences at one with mathematics, which has been able to build up an enormous number of theories on a few axioms. However, the sciences which we call positive (I do not know if this term is appropriate) have always shown themselves reluctant to adopt this method, and their rapid, splendid progress had its beginnings in the period in which the analytical method was used – which is called the experimental method by the moderns. You know better than I do that this selects particular truths by direct observation, co-ordinates them, and from those that present a common character, formulates partial theorems from which it deduces other more general theorems: thus gradually progressing towards the general principles which underlie the universality of things.

Political economy receives life and progress from this experimental method. Small wonder therefore if it uses this method again, as, in fact, is the case for the theme that is the subject of my talk. Continually operating such a method can however sometimes bring us up against a brick wall, but a wall which is a product of our mind rather than of the method itself. And this brick wall consists in the fact that, in studying particular problems, we often forget to examine those more general principles from which one could deduce them as logical consequences. So, in our case, it seems to me that in order to reason adequately about the lesser or greater good of the principle of proportional representation, it is necessary, first, for us to have a clear, distinct conception of what we must consider the best and most perfect form of representation; and thence to deduce the best means of achieving our aim. It is a common observation that men usually make mistakes, not from any defect in the logic of their reasoning, but rather because their premises are false.

Similarly one can say that when men reach different opinions, this is not because each man has a different way of reasoning, but because men hold different propositions as the basis of their judgements. One can also add that generally each of the opposing sides takes that principle which forms the basis of its opinion as an almost unquestionable axiomatic truth. So it becomes indispensable to examine these principles meticulously in order to go on to reason about the consequences that everyone wants to deduce from them.

In our case we must first discover the characteristics of a perfect form of representation. Men's opinions about government and representation are varied. To enumerate all, or even some of them here, would be both difficult and tiresome; but I believe that as far as the student is concerned and in respect to our problem they can be classified in a few categories. I say as far as the student is concerned because, as usually happens, the followers of extreme opinions are few, whereas those who have intermediate opinions are more, and they themselves differ from one another very slightly.

In my opinion there are three things to consider when studying the conditions which must be observed by the best and most perfect form of representation. They are: the role of the government, the origin of its power, and the limits of this power.

On the first point some want the government to be essentially active, procuring good, and guiding the people along the path of good. Others instead want the government simply to be passive, limiting itself to being an obstacle to evil.

The supporters of the former have always demanded greater intelligence and industry in government than the supporters of the passive theory. So they, more than the others, should be supporters of the doctrine of proportional representation, defined as that which is the best suited to produce a parliament composed of the most cultivated and intelligent elements in the entire nation. On the other hand, for those who would restrict the action of the government by the passive theory, the problem of proportional representation loses some degree of importance, even if it still remains, while another problem of greater importance must be the object of their attention: that is, how to find a practical way of preventing the government or the representation from overstepping the established limits. In practice it is possible to find opponents of proportional representation even among those who say that they are ardent supporters of the active theory and in no way wish to diminish the executive authority of the government; and so you have heard the eminent speaker who preceded me argue against the representation of the minority. Now, it seems to me that despite all he has said there is a fact which cannot be denied: the cultured part of the population has always been a tiny minority, and even if it grows every day, it is certain unfortunately that for a long time to come it will continue to consist of a relatively small number. It is therefore absolutely essential to find a way for the minority to be able to send representatives to the legislative assemblies unless we wish these assemblies to be composed of men who, besides sometimes being of mediocre intelligence, share the same prejudices and errors of judgement as the uneducated majority of which they are the worthy representatives.

Here the eminent Professor Luchini observes that in elections one should pay attention to the *act* of justice more than to the *form* of justice, and then adds: 'When we put into practice any principle, should we perhaps open schools in order to persuade the masses of its goodness and justice?'

Well, gentlemen, I am not in the least afraid of answering this question in the affirmative, but before proceeding to set out the this opinion, let me draw your attention to the way in which my affirmation, let me draw your attention to the way in which this question has been answered by a people which have been, and perhaps will be for a long time yet, masters of liberty.

The great liberal reforms which England has made in recent years have been obtained by first persuading the people of the justice of them; so legislation did no other than provide a suitable dress for concepts already held by the masses. If Cobden's Free Trade League did not open schools in the real sense of the word, it held numerous meetings and lectures which in another guise most effectively served as schools; and it is due to this active propaganda that the flag of economic freedom was raised in England, and the theories of the Manchester economists were accepted. By similar means the League for Electoral Reform has a similar effect, not to mention other examples of lesser political importance.

It seems to me that there are only three ways of inducing others

to do something: force, deception and persuasion. If you decline
the last and in so doing renounce teaching the masses your principles, there remains only the choice between the first two.
Which will you seize? Unfortunately it must be recognised that
up to now these two forms have been used promiscuously; but
practice, as much as morals, has condemned them severely. If
you resort to deception, besides confusing all notions of good and
evil, justice and injustice, what can you find to oppose those who
wish to compete with you and try to deceive the people with
dangerous sophisms? Truth shines so righteously that whoever
defends it can be certain of not being disappointed in his hope
that men will have to accept it in the end; and whoever consciously denies it will, in the end, find himself a disarmed cham-
pion, even in front of one who, in his turn, brazenly uses lies and
deceit. But if, in order to avoid these dangers, you put your hope
in force, allow me to ask you: what assurance have you that yours
will always predominate and that it will never be able to pass into
the hands of your adversaries? Nay, force should be on their side
because they are more numerous; and when they have this force
and when the tables are turned and they are the oppressors and
you the oppressed, with what right, with what justice, can you
fight and banish those who do no more than follow your example
– turning against you the same arms which served you for such
a long time to their disadvantage?

I believe it is useless, gentlemen, to waste time proving something of which you are already convinced, and that is, that deception and force are worthy of a barbarous or corrupt civilisation,
while education and persuasion remain the only means of civil
progress. But my illustrious opponent will perhaps object that he
does not reject the use of persuasion: he only wants to use it, not
to convince the voters of this or that principle maintained by the
candidate during the elections (in this the elections would be considered the act of justice), but rather to convince them that a candidate is capable of public administration according to the rules
of law. Here I shall observe that this doctrine involves complete
abdication by the voters, and leads to personal government and
despotism in its primal form: that is, that which takes its origin
from the irrational will of the populace . . .

If I have correctly interpreted my honourable opponent, he
wants the voters to choose from among the candidates the one

whom he considers better fitted to carry out the rules of justice and honesty, without, however, bothering about the candidate's opinions. He reproaches the system of proportional representation for not guaranteeing us the best elected candidate and for being, at the most, capable of providing the *act* of justice in the way in which the election takes place. So it is easy to understand why the illustrious Professor Luchini places himself among the opponents of our theory, since whoever does not care whether the elected representative represents the opinions of the voters or not, certainly does not need to care about looking for the way in which these opinions can be represented. It seems to me that with this argument not only is proportional representation destroyed, but also the very foundations of representative government; for in elections under such a system the voters do not choose a representative, but rather a guardian. The fertile clash of parties, which is the principal basis of representative government, ceases; and by means of an inexorable logic we are taken towards a personal type of government that has its origin in a plebiscite, through which the entire nation chooses a man who offers the maximum guarantee of the sword of justice in order to entrust their destiny to him . . .

Having spoken about the mission of government, I shall now go on to reason about the origins of its power.

Some think that it is divine, and with these it is impossible to reason about representations, about majorities or minorities. Others think that it is a direct expression of the will of the majority, whatever it may be. These, even if they do not want to be supporters of it, should at least accept the principle of minority representation in order to correct in some way or other whatever may be too absolute (and frequently wrong) in the unthinking will of an often prejudiced majority – unless they find themselves in agreement with Rousseau, when he maintains that the general will cannot err. This group, however, should seriously think about looking for arguments to support its thesis, because up to now many arguments have been brought against it, and not one in its favour. There are those who see the origins of government in the simple mission entrusted to it by the citizens, to guarantee the freedom of each of them, permitting the government to take all those measures necessary to prevent anyone from causing any type of harm – harm which is immediate, direct and definite.

The supporters of this theory think that proportional representation is useful as the means by which, all opinion being represented in the legislative assemblies, the desires of the various parties
can be better known and, in so far as they are right, satisfied. They
also think that, by conforming to the needs of the citizens as a
whole, proportional representation eliminates the possibility of
someone making people believe him a martyr and arousing dangerous public agitation.

Another school would like power to be concentrated in the
hands of the best and wisest citizens, thus dreaming of a state
similar to that of Gioberti's primacy of the best. Among those
who think in this way we find the followers of the French school
of positive thinking. Their leader, Auguste Comte, saw the ideal
government as an absolute despotism which, in my opinion, even
if exercised by the more intelligent, educated part of the nation,
would be odious to the citizens and ruinous to human progress.
Positivist doctrine passed over to England; but there it was considerably modified, receiving the mark of that lively and everlast-
ing spirit of individual freedom that forms one of the best qualities
of the Anglo-Saxon race. The most illustrious representative of
English positivism, Mill, both wished to give a pre-eminent
place to the more cultured classes of the nation in the government, and to respect the freedom of the individual; and he put no
limit on this except that of not injuring the freedom that others
with the same rights enjoy. While Auguste Comte thought that
detailed rules had to be dictated for every act of human life until,
in both action and in opinion, nobody differed a great deal from
the generality of his fellow-citizens, Mill, in his splendid essay
On Liberty, gives unbounded praise to originality and individual
initiative, seeing in these the greatest factors for social progress.
He was one of the most ardent supporters of the system of proportional representation, which he saw as being useful and beneficial
because the representatives of the more cultured part of the population were admitted into the legislative assemblies, and because
an opportunity for dissemination was given to those opinions
which, although not being universal and therefore not having
many supporters in the country, were perhaps no less good or
right. It is necessary to observe that the legitimate influence of
the majority is not reduced – nay, it receives greater guarantee
than that which it has at the moment. In fact, when parliament

represents all the opinions of the citizens in their right proportions, it is certain that its decisions, taken by a majority of votes, will correspond with the majority of voters. The benefit that minorities receive from the system that we are defending is completely moral and consists in the fact that they are permitted to hear their own voices and to illumine the decisions of the legislative assemblies.

It seems to me that the surest origins of governmental power are to be found in the necessity to provide for the conservation and progress of human society, and that the aim of representation must be that of studying the best ways of taking us to these goals. Now, as these goals are far from being known to us all, I cannot agree with Professor Luchini in the comparison he makes between the magistrate and the representative. The former must apply principles already established. The latter must look for and, sometimes, create these principles. Under this aspect the need increasingly arises for legislative assemblies to be formed of the deepest thinkers and the best representatives of the most varied and original opinions, so that animated discussion may spark a light to illuminate the complex questions that social science often poses. Finally, it remains for me to speak about the limits of the power of government, or of the representation of which it is the product.

For some there are no limits. The power of the representative body, similar to an emblematic snake which winds round itself, finds in itself its beginning and its end. For these all that is legal is right. However, others observe that the eternal principles of justice and morality are above any power and that there must be limits and barriers to the will of the majority. Here I shall not discuss the practical ways by which this can be achieved; but as an example to clarify my thought I should refer to an institution, perhaps the only one of its kind, that is the Supreme High Court of the United States of America, which has the power to amend those laws of Congress recognised as harmful to the constitutional rights of the citizens and the States of the Union.

Professor Luchini, too, admits that the principles of justice must be recognised above any power, and I hoped that from that he would deduce what seem to me the logical consequences of this doctrine: that is, a way must be found to erect a barrier against the tyranny of the majority which tries to invade the field of individual liberty, thus destroying every principle of justice. Instead, I have heard words which, to me, ring – permit me to use this word – with despotism. He speaks bitterly of sects, blaming the system of proportional representation for making it easy for these sects to reach parliament. But I ask him, by what criteria can you distinguish sects from parties? Unfortunately, the majorities have very often damned as sectarian those whose only fault was that of having strayed from the opinion of the generality of mankind. Almost all great things have been proclaimed by men who have been persecuted because of them. Even in Athens, which could be called the motherland of freedom, a man like Socrates was condemned to death: a man who, in a society based on slavery, had realised for the first time that all men must have equal rights. This sublime Utopia was proclaimed and began to come into being through the Christian faith which then, however, was no more than a sect and as such was persecuted in the very Roman world from which you now derive your definition of justice. No, your justice is not mine. It is not force which must be the basis of society. It is not the prison or the gallows that must make opinion triumph. That justice, in the way you have defined it – which in order to give each man what is his (subtly interpreting this possessive pronoun) gives back to the master the slave that has run away, and becomes accomplice to every abuse if it is carried out under cover of legality – is not mine.

Most of the political parties began as sects. It was a sect that, in the period of the first French Empire, dreamed of a German nation, and it was a sect that, not many years ago, hoped for an Italian nation.

I recognise that there are sects that profess principles in which it is very hard to discover anything which could be considered right and true. But for these sects too the principle of proportional representation will be useful. Mistakes need darkness – truth the light. If sectarian leaders are hidden and mysterious they can make the people believe that their doctrines are something different from the vain dreams of a sick mind. Instead, drawn to expound them in Parliament, where the flower of intelligence of the whole nation is united, you will see these theories, when subjected to scientific discussion, dispersed like mist before the burning rays of the July sun.

Against the system of proportional representation held by us, it has often been observed that it is not true that in the existing system minorities have been sacrificed – because, in the elections, they influence the majority to a compromise, and the majority sends men to Parliament with opinions which are less absolute. But in my opinion this observation has justly been answered by the first writers who interested themselves in this problem: saying that if majorities compromise they do so to the detriment of the candidate. There is not a man of striking individuality in politics who has not provoked hatred. Only men who are worthless are allowed to avoid it by living without infamy and without praise. Now it is precisely from among the latter that the majorities more often than not choose their candidate, who for this reason is more easily accepted by those who make up the party.

Gentlemen, it now remains for me to discuss an argument against proportional representation which seems to me partly valid.

All the systems suggested for the practical application of proportional representation present – some more, some less – a certain complexity in the counting of the votes. As this must necessarily be put into the hands of specially chosen clerks, the probability of bribery and corruption at elections increases . . .

In a country in which the parties are strong and well-organised there is a chance that, since each guards itself against the others while fighting for the same objective, the necessary guarantees of scrutineers who are morally sound and absolutely independent will be obtained; but it is clear that these guarantees would disappear were a single party so organised and constituted above the rest as never to need worry about them.

Although Italy does not appear to have these much-discussed inconveniences in the same way as her Latin sisters – Spain and France – it cannot however be said that she lacks them completely, particularly since properly constituted and organised parties are almost non-existent.

It is true that there was a time when it seemed that a ray of light was about to illuminate our political horizon and this occurred when the formation of a great conservative-liberal party was discussed. I believe that our country would have reaped great benefit had this idea been realised. The opposition parties, even the more radical ones, would have had to applaud, as in the end we should have freed ourselves from the fetters of an obsolete empiricism and would have had a scientific basis for discussion. And then we could have hoped to see the rigorous principles of the social sciences applied by those elected geniuses, of which our country has no small number. But, unfortunately, such a hope has been dashed, and we still await the constitution of a party which is coherent within itself and follows the political principles that it maintains, instead of falling into that abyss of expediency abhorred by scientific reason.

I have paraded before you some of the arguments brought forward by adversaries of the system of proportional representation, and I have done my best to show you that they are unfounded. There are few who are rationally opposed to this system but most people are against it simply through inertia. They recognise the weakness of our electoral arrangements but they are frightened by the thought of having to study in order to introduce changes to them. They prefer to let things go their own way without thinking and discussing, and pronouncing themselves for or against the aforesaid reform. And they call themselves conservatives! Perhaps they are, in the etymological meaning of the word, but they certainly do not belong to the party which bears this name. The real conservatives are not those who want to keep everything which is good or bad, but rather those who, before destroying anything, either good or bad, want to substitute something better; and in this respect their party manifests itself as not only a useful but also an indispensable factor of civilisation and progress.

I should like to ask those who call themselves conservatives: what do you want to keep in a world which is being transformed and changed? Heat is movement, light is movement, life itself is movement, and immobility means darkness and death. The hardest rocks are eroded and eaten away. The mountains are flattened and form fertile valleys. Continents and seas change their appearance. Here life is strengthened, there it is weakened. Nations rise and fall, and humanity advances further and further along the way of civilisation and progress. In the midst of so much change do you believe that only you will be allowed to remain immobile? Only you will be allowed to violate with impunity the eternal principles that support creation? Only you will be allowed to stop progress, to assign a limit to intelligence and the activity of the human species and to say to society: 'You will stop here and you will not try to cross the immutable frontiers which I have assigned'?

Ah no! Nature despises such mad attempts and her powerful hand throws you back into the whirling eddy that destroys, confounds, transforms and creates . . .

Here, gentlemen, I end my speech, thanking you for your sympathetic attention. I have not wanted either to set forth or validly to defend the principles on which the system of proportional representation is based; I have only wanted to state what seemed to me good and true about this problem.

NOTES

1 See, *Vilfredo Pareto, riflessioni e ricerche*, ed. T. Giacalone-Monaco (Padua 1966), p. 43.

2 Universal suffrage

'It is necessary for us to have at first a clear, distinct conception of what we must consider as the best and most perfect form of representation.' This was the main problem in the first essay, which dealt with the need for all minorities to be represented. Pareto brought to the notice of the opponents of proportional representation that if the principle of non-representation of minorities were to be accepted, they themselves would soon be banished as they were no more than a small minority, being the educated part of the nation.

The problem brought to the fore in this second essay is complementary to the first, but substantially bolder. It not only condemns the ultra-conservatives, but also those who, by manipulating the electoral constituencies, ensure that the number of members of parliament is not proportional to the number of electors who vote for them. Remembering that this question is still cause for debate and that Liberals in England still fight against single-member constituencies, one realises how relevant this still is after more than a hundred years. After having reaffirmed that 'light is born from discussion' and having ridiculed those who 'see, in the rich, a superior class which must legitimately have the right of government of public affairs', he then goes on tactfully to support the need for compulsory primary education, thus anticipating by a century the realisation of compulsory schooling in Italy.

To those who held universal suffrage to be unrealisable owing to the large numbers of illiterates, he proposed the elimination of illiteracy and the extension to all of education – until then the jealously guarded privilege of the select few. Driven on by his youthful, generous enthusiasm for the weak, he also put limitations on the concept of individual freedom for which he had fought so fiercely in the beginning: 'Asking that a father have the freedom of not letting his son attend school is like saying that he should have the freedom of letting his son die of hunger, or the freedom of prostituting his daughter.' The discussion makes its way from the abstract to the concrete: 'With this misuse of the word freedom, every crime could be justified.'

FROM *Gazzetta del Populo,* 12 November 1872.
To the most illustrious Marquis Trivulzio Pallavicino.

Dear Sir,

Kindly permit one of the humblest followers of the party for freedom to make some observations about your ideas on universal suffrage published in this newspaper. It is not that I dissent substantially from you in this argument; but, being persuaded that light is born from discussion, I am emboldened to set forth my views in the hope that, if I am wrong, it will become apparent where and how far from the truth I stray.

Your observation is correct. The number, unfortunately great, of illiterates in Italy, would endanger, if not perhaps destroy, the establishment of universal suffrage in our country. Nor would it help to exclude the illiterate, because, as you say, merely knowing how to read a primer and write one's name is no proof of being educated, nay, it is a sign of ignorance. (Though I cannot help observing that paying a certain sum in direct taxes, a condition required by our law in order to be a voter, is an even less certain proof of wisdom and culture.)

In my opinion the mistake made both by those who want the immediate and absolute application of universal suffrage, as well as by those who want the quality of voter linked to wealth, arises from the fact that they have considered the electoral vote to be a right rather than the exercise of a necessary duty for the good working of civil society. So, according to the former, every citizen, on coming of age, must enjoy this right; for, as they justly observe, on coming of age the citizen takes part in the defence of the mother-country and through indirect taxes pays his part of public expenses. The latter bring forward the thesis that only those who support public expense should enjoy the right of taking part in government, and, erroneously applying this principle, they limit the electoral right only to those who pay direct taxes.

I shall not mention those who see, in the rich, a superior class which must legitimately have the right of the government of public affairs, and who deliberately create those distinctions of caste and privilege condemned by the times.

For myself, I believe with Mill that the exercise of the electoral vote must be one of the functions of the state. It seems to me, therefore, that whoever is called to carry this out must, as a first

and essential quality, possess that culture and that knowledge
necessary to fulfil his task adequately, quite apart from wealth.
So I should exclude the illiterate from voting, and I should also
like it to be the right, if possible, only of those who have completed elementary school with good results.

To ensure that those rights which legitimately belong to every
citizen are not harmed, it will be necessary for everyone to receive
this elementary education. Thus universal suffrage will no longer
be an empty word, but rather a beneficial reality.

I can only praise those words which you approvingly reproduce
from the newspaper *Il Secolo*: 'And so it is a rigorous duty to
demand compulsory education for all.'

Afterwards you go on to say: 'We respect, not idolise, the principle of individual freedom; the cult of a principle must not extend as far as crime . . . '; and here I should like to make an
observation.

It does not seem to me that compulsory education offends in
the least the principle of freedom. Instead, I believe that it
should be demanded in the name of freedom. First and foremost,
words need to be understood. What is freedom? For myself I
accept the definition originally given by the men of the first
French Revolution, and slightly modified by the illustrious
English economist of whose name I reminded you a little while
ago: freedom is the faculty of doing everything which in a direct
and immediate way does not harm others. It is clear that compulsory education should be called freedom of education; since the
parent who does not educate his son greatly harms him in a direct
way. Education should not be called compulsory. Asking that a
father have the freedom of not letting his son attend school is like
saying that he should have the freedom of letting his son die of
hunger or the freedom of prostituting his daughter. With this
misuse of the word freedom, every crime could be justified, and
thieves could, with this reason, ask for the freedom of stealing.

The newborn son is a citizen to whom the law owes guardianship and protection. This is in fact the principle which prevails
in the modern legislation of all civilised peoples, in which the law
protects the child during his life, inflicting severe punishment for
infanticide, for endangering the life of a newborn child, and for
ill-treatment; and the law protects his property, even taking away
from the father the faculty of disposing of his entire estate in his

will. In virtue of what principle, I ask, must this guardianship, which is recognised for material goods, cease when it deals with that other patrimony – education – which is indispensable to all and especially those – and these are the majority – who have no other patrimony?

I hope therefore, illustrious sir, that you will agree with me in recognising that one can have a boundless devotion to freedom and, at the same time, be an ardent supporter of compulsory education. I have this devotion and I believe that, in any question, the principle of freedom always gives us the best and right solution.

Before finishing these lines, let me speak about something which has a close connection with every electoral law – I allude to proportional representation.

This principle, which at first was inexactly called the principle of the representation of minorities, consists in this: that it is in apparent conformity with justice for every shade of opinion to have in parliament a number of representatives in proportion to the number of its followers in a country. So, for example, if there are 100,000 voters in a country belonging to one party and 50,000 belonging to another, the former have 100 representatives and the latter 50. I do not need to remind you that in practice the opposite can happen and, in fact, often does; and it is common knowledge that the Second French Empire abused the faculty that it gave itself of modifying the electoral constituencies, in order to alter popular suffrage and its representatives in parliament.

A practical way of implementing the system of proportional representation has occupied many distinguished economists and statesmen, among whom it is sufficient for me to remind you of Mill and Hare in England. Andrae introduced this system into Denmark, Morin and Naville introduced it into Geneva, and many other illustrious men have devoted themselves to it.

In our Italy, an association which proposed to study an application of this system has also been founded. In Florence, the Accademia dei Georgofili had made it the theme of a conference . . .

It would be extremely desirable that all those who love liberty and progress should not neglect this question which is, in my opinion, very important; and it is for this reason that I have taken the liberty of setting forth my opinion and I shall be happy if it can obtain the approval of such an authoritative person as yourself in the Liberal party.

3 On the logic of the new school of economics

After his lucky encounter with the Peruzzis, whose busy *salon* gave him the chance of meeting many of the important cultural figures of the time, Pareto left the unsatisfying work at the Rome Railway Company in 1873, and moved to San Giovanni Valdarno to work for the iron industry. This new work strengthened his interest in politics and sociology and 'among iron-workers and miners he soon became involved in their poverty and the way in which they were exploited'.[1] It was during these years that the problem of the relationship between economics and sociology was to arise. The idealistic Pareto – exuberant, optimistic, impulsive and passionate – became more reflective, more sceptical and questioning, translating his dissatisfactions into irony and sarcasm.

His favourite theme was still that of individual freedom, but the horizons of his interests widened. He was interested not only in political and judicial freedom, but also in economic freedom, as he considered the three indissolubly linked. In the five years following his first lecture to the Accademia dei Georgofili he simplified his style and made it more sure – as much in his controversy with Comte as in the ceaseless fight, from then on, against 'vague, indeterminate, cloudy expressions'. One by one, he confuted all the accusations which the supporters of the new school made against the supporters of the classical school of economics. First of all, he underlined how Comte's statement, that classical economy is in a metaphysical state, was not founded scientifically and was therefore unjustified. He then passed on to contest the concept of contingency in economic science, which puts forward the notion of the relativism of economic concepts to the degree of economic development of the people. Pareto was not against every type of historicism – provided one did not expect 'Florence and Peretola [a village near Florence] to have the right to a special economy'. Once more he sought the middle way between two extremes and put forward the first premise for what would become the theory of equilibrium. In the same way as he had tried to bridge the gap between conservation and innovation and between social organisation

and individual freedom, he now repeated the process between historical structure and social, dynamic structure. To those who opposed the
economic theory of *laissez-faire* and would have liked a more organised
state in order to regulate – with the aid of inflexible laws – every human
activity, he pointed out that 'absolute power, which had dominated
and extinguished brutal instincts contrary to human society, was replaced by that type of government which Bagehot calls "government
by discussion" '.

In Pareto's opinion social laws, like economic laws, change slowly
and people have the job of inserting themselves into this cycle at the
right moment. If, in some remote age, 'our ancestors, more like beasts
than men, had a greater need than the savages of our times of a more
strongly constituted power to discipline their souls and dominate their
ferocious instincts in order to start progress', then today, the historical
conditions having changed, the laws of human society need to establish more flexible boundaries. The guarantee of a new development
lay in the inventiveness of the individual. The state, as an organically
centralised power, could not think about anything because 'the great
law of the division of labour' is contrary to its doing so. But leaving the
initiative to the individual could not mean '*laissez-faire* murderers and
laissez-conduire thieves' – Pareto had already said that a parent should
not have the freedom of letting his son die of hunger, or of prostituting
his daughter.

Once more, it was individual freedom, discussion and education
which, in the uncertain future of man, allow progress.

FROM A LECTURE GIVEN TO THE ACCADEMIA DEI
GEORGOFILI, 29 April 1877.
In the controversies that have taken place in Italy in recent years
on the interference of the state and on the extension of its functions, both the opposing parties have slipped back to those principles that are the basis of public economy. While some doubt or
utterly deny them, these principles are called in by others as a
support for their own thesis . . .

The new school of economics which has arisen in Germany
often employs the vague, indeterminate, cloudy expressions that
one sometimes encounters in the works of most German philosophers. I must confess that I cannot understand them. Unfortunately those illustrious Italians who introduced us to this
new science, translated the words but, perhaps owing to the lack

of time, did not give an Italian form to the thoughts ...

The accusations against classical political economy are also formulated in a clear, precise manner by Auguste Comte, who in this can deservedly be called the precursor of the modern German school. Nobody admires more than I do the powerful genius of the founder of positivism, and nobody recognises as much as I do how much human knowledge is indebted to him. It is for this that I am going to explain why I am not convinced by his reasons for attacking economic science.

The principal objection made by Auguste Comte is that the method followed by the economists possesses the more dogmatic characteristics of concepts which are purely metaphysical, and that this is enough to condemn economic science beyond hope of redemption. In fact, having already established the principle that sciences evolve by passing through three stages – theological, metaphysical and positive – it turns out that political economy is still at an inferior level and must radically change its system in order to acquire the dignity of a true science ...

The second objection of Auguste Comte concerns the contingency of economic science. The fact that the development of human societies proceeds according to fixed and determinate laws like those which physics has given us, did not escape the great genius of the French writer, as Vico had already grasped before him. Certainly among Comte's claims to fame not least is that of the direction that he gave to historical studies, in this way inspiring the masterly work of Buckle.

To speak of the contingency of economic science is perhaps inexact: it would be better to apply the word to the *tasks* of economic science. The theorems of science are always true, but if the conditions that they take into account come to an end, the very object of science ceases to exist. It is evident that it is not possible to discuss the distribution of wealth in a people ignorant of private property. In the same way optics would be without object if there were no light. These are two extreme examples, but certainly nobody would think about applying the political economy of civilised peoples to the aborigines of Australia or to our prehistoric ancestors. So, a more general science exists, whose propositions have, as very particular cases, the theorems of political science as we know them ...

Comte's objection seems still more true and more widely applicable to the modern doctrines of evolution, even without admitting the variability of the species and admitting only that of race, and it really seems impossible to deny this. How can it be claimed that modern, civilised man is identical in his faculties to his prehistoric ancestor? And then, is it not evident that in changing the subject of economic science, the science too must change? But let us be careful not to blunder. If present-day man is different from prehistoric man it does not mean that he is not almost perfectly similar to man of a few centuries ago; and if the thought processes of an Englishman are essentially different from those of a native of the Fiji Islands, it does not necessarily follow that the thought processes of the Italians must be different, especially in economic matters. Let this doctrine recognise, then, the economy of peoples and states, but do not expect this economy to change with every step. Do not expect Florence and Peretola to have the right to a special economy, so that the propositions true in the period of Adam Smith become false.

As for the laws of the evolution of human society, we do not yet know any that really merit this name. That they exist is something of great importance, and for our century it will be an ever-lasting glory; but at the moment only a few empiric propositions are known and are therefore of limited value. In truth it should not be forgotten that if the development of human societies has occurred in a closed cycle, as Vico believed, and if the same events are repeated, then the observations of past phenomena could provide us with an almost definitive law. This case would be similar to that of a closed curve on which are noted the positions of many points spread along the whole perimeter. In this case, through interpolation, an almost exact equation of the curve can be obtained. Similarly, if this curve is not closed, but between two given points, the positions of the intermediary points can be calculated. This is called interpolation between limits. But, if from knowledge of that section of the curve, one expects to be able to extend it beyond the extreme points, with an interpolation outside the limits, the process becomes very uncertain and often completely fallacious. Unfortunately, this is precisely the way adopted when one tries to deduce the path that humanity will follow in future, from observation of a limited number of historical facts. But to me, a still greater mistake into which the new school often falls is that of confusing the events that prob-

ably *will* follow with those that one *would like* to follow for the
greater good of man or a nation. Time is running short and I will
not linger on this topic to which I shall return later. It is sufficient
to mention that we are here speaking about how free will, as it is
commonly interpreted, can be reconciled with the regularity and
inflexibility of social laws. This is not the moment to discuss such
important questions but, whatever opinion is held, surely one
does not want to deny that man exercises a considerable influence on the development of events, and that therefore, in
deciding, he must consider whether the end at which he is aiming
is in itself good and useful . . .

So, gentlemen, we followers of the ancient liberal school, because there is a new school in name if not in substance, cannot
deny that the cause of freedom is losing ground in Europe, and
we can also foresee that, despite our efforts, we shall have to submit to other controls and an increase in governmental authority.
But must we resign ourselves to remaining inert and letting ourselves be overcome by a type of fatalism, because of this? And
who can say that the resistance of the liberals, even if it does not
prevent evil, may help to lessen it?

Now let us pass on to speaking about the celebrated motto:
laissez-faire, laissez-conduire. Expressing this motto in these days
without anathematising it at once, is almost proof of civic courage. In fact there are daily newspapers which – well done them ! –
suppose that the liberals want to *laissez-faire* murderers and
laissez-conduire thieves . . .

However, it seems to me that we must accept Mill's and
Comte's observations that the doctrine *laissez-faire, laissez-conduire*, far from being absolutely true, needs strict control in its
application. But having said this I should like to stop and see if,
in the very many sides to the art of governing, this practical pre-
cept does not still represent the best maxim towards which human
knowledge takes us. So that, instead of being taken as an *a priori*
basis of political economy, this proposition should be considered
a result, not only of this, but also of all the other social sciences.

When one speaks about the interference of the state one uses a
term not perfectly determined. If for 'state' one meant the complex of the government and the various provincial and municipal
authorities, we should have precise realities before us. Instead, it
sometimes seems that the term 'state' is synonymous with social

organisation: as with the new school when it contrasts its own theories – which it defines as 'organic' – with those of classical economics, which it defines as 'atomistic'. So it is necessary to consider this double meaning of the word 'state' if one does not want to encounter confusion.

Spencer intelligently notes how society (not least for the individual) in order to progesss, needs to have some organisation. Having reached a certain level of development there is no more growth without modification of the organisation. But he then adds that one must believe that after a certain level the organisation is an indirect obstacle – and gives extremely conclusive examples in which some general rules leading to uniformity, at first useful, later become one of the principal obstacles to further progress.

Bagehot's theory on the origins of civilisation maintains this opinion. He begins by noting that in ancient times our ancestors, more like beasts than men, had greater need than the savages of our day for a more strongly constituted power to discipline their souls and dominate their ferocious instincts, in order to start to progress . . .

Most peoples have gone through this preparatory stage. But those which have become civilised have only done so because the inflexible rules governing every human activity have gradually become less and less rigorous – leaving room for freedom and the spirit of inquiry, originality and individuality. That absolute power, which had dominated and extinguished those brutal instincts harmful to human society, was replaced by the type of government which Bagehot calls 'government by discussion'.

The theory of this English author is probably true, but I recognise that in order to be considered certain it would need very many tests that have yet to be made. However, it is sufficient for us that this theory *can* be true to prove that a blind increase in the power of organisation does not always contribute towards human progress . . .

Up to now we have spoken about the organisation of society in general, but we must also consider that organisation can also exist, powerful and useful, outside the action of government.

Truth to tell, it seems to me that there is also another type of organisation worth mentioning, and it is that of private companies created by private enterprise. The institution of the

London and Manchester Clearing House is a splendid example
of this. There is no government in the world that has been able
to obtain with so few and simple means, results of such great
importance. And perhaps, considering these things more clearly,
one could see instead that in most cases of governmental organisation the roles are reversed: in other words that, with great
waste of time and money, extremely modest results are obtained.
So we must ask ourselves whether the organisations that are held
to be necessary for social life should be constituted by governmental or private concerns. Besides this we must consider
whether the functions that some want to give to government
might not be harmful to its mission to guarantee public order and
give justice to every individual citizen . . .

The conduct of public affairs must be distinct from the care of
private matters; or must it not? When the state itself is transformed into a large industrial company, will there not then arise
the strong need for a new institution which will dedicate itself to
those functions to which the new state will not be at the level to
dedicate itself? . . .

Men, under pressure from what modern naturalists call the
'struggle for survival', always try to use to their own advantage
the power that comes from the conduct of public affairs. If this
power is found exclusively in the hands of one class of citizens,
it can be stated that this class will use it consistently to its own
advantage, unless it is qualified by some external force such as,
for example, a strongly hostile public opinion. History offers us
many examples to support this opinion, as we can see now in the
administration of many Italian municipalities . . .

I have tried to show you briefly why the theories of the new
school of economics do not convince me; but do not think that,
because of this, I want to deny this school every merit. Perhaps if
we free-traders were not limited by opposing forces, we could
easily exaggerate, as – vice versa – could happen to our opponents.
State interference and the rights of the individual must have their
followers, and for the good of our country let us hope that the
fight between them is ample, lively and fertile, so that mistakes
are wiped out, and, in the end, only that part which is true in
these various doctrines remains.

NOTES
1 See *Pareto, riflessioni e ricerche*, p. 45.

4 Whether it is worth establishing by law a minimum wage and a maximum margin of profit

Consistently with his affirmation that *laissez-faire* does not mean *laissez-faire* thieves, Pareto fought the exploiters, speculators and those who drew wealth out of the workers through protectionism. From 1890, he continued to work for the Valdarno Iron and Steel Industry and threw himself into the political struggle. In the exchange of letters with the Peruzzis, we find that in 1880 he was parliamentary candidate for Montevarchi and in 1882 for Pistoia. Unfortunately he was defeated both times and his sensitive spirit especially hurt by the underhand goings-on. Maffeo Pantaleoni considered Pareto's defeat fortunate, because otherwise 'politics would have robbed science of a first-rate talent'.[1] He was so hurt by the corruption and the ease with which men are corrupted that he swore never to go through another similar experience. In a letter written to Ubaldino Peruzzi on 16 February 1886, refusing an invitation to stand as a candidate, he wrote, 'I have already had plenty of opportunity of seeing at close hand the cowardice and bad faith of certain people . . . It is enough for me to have the satisfaction of despising them and saying it aloud to everyone.'[2] So the social battle was taken up again on the field which most suited him – that of writing – and which would make him the Cato of Italian politics. This activity, with freely flowing pen, went on without flattery or compromise. His role became that of public prosecutor of minor politicians, accusing them of their misdeeds, stimulating public opinion to react and thus to limit their petty tyranny. In this period he wrote to Signora Emilia Peruzzi: 'I prefer to discover shame rather than be a part of it.'

When he read this paper on a minimum wage at the Accademia dei Georgofili, over fourteen years after he attended his first conference there, his basic position remained that only economic and political freedom could guarantee social justice. Consistent with this principle he begins deriding the false liberals who call upon the non-intervention of the state in work problems only when intervention puts justice on the side of the workers. Hypocritically, they are pleased about intervention when it guarantees their speculation and illicit profits through protectionism. Can the state that denies the freedom to strike but allows the freedom to speculate through monopolies call itself liberal? Can the state which imprisons those who refuse to work for a starvation wage – established, not by the free law of demand and supply, but by the greed of speculators – call itself liberal? Pareto confronted the problem of justice for the first time. It is not an abstract or metaphysical entity, but a social product which must be guaranteed and applied by the liberal state when, in the fight between capital and labour, it must guarantee the survival of both. Consequently, he stated, 'I believe that according to justice there are only two ways: either the state does not interfere in the relations between capital and labour and does its best to keep competition free, or, if it does interfere, it does so impartially, and not in favour of one and to the detriment of the other. Either the state does not protect anyone or it protects all. Beyond this there are only arbitrary acts, injustice and harm to national prosperity.'

In this essay what remains unchanged is his admiration for Mill and the English liberalism which applied this concept of justice: not an abstract principle, but the best practical compromise between extremes. Linked with it we find two others which were to spring up quite often in the future: (1) that of respect for 'the natural conditions of the struggle for survival' and (2) that of equilibrium between the increase in population and means of subsistence. But in this case, too, Pareto thought that the struggle should not go on blindly without human guidance: 'labour, in the sharing out of the product, cannot permanently obtain such a portion as not to leave to capital that amount that is indispensable to it for its reproduction. For the same symmetrical reason it is necessary to recognise that capital cannot have such a share of the product that that quantity capable of assuring the survival of the worker does not remain – otherwise emigration, illness and death would re-establish the balance.' As can be seen, not only must reason respect the laws of nature, but also nature must follow the choice made by man. The state must save the workers before nature, by eliminating them physically, re-establishes a new balance; because a decrease in work corresponds with a decrease in capital. The humanitarian justice of the state ends by being useful not only to the occasional workers saved from hunger, but also to the whole collectivity.

FROM A LECTURE GIVEN TO THE ACCADEMIA DEI
GEORGOFILI, 4 April 1886. Published the same year in *Atti*
of the Accademia.

Dear Fellow-Members,

When Signor Baccarini asked Parliament to pass laws to
safeguard the interests of the workers, followers of the liberal
economic doctrines, until then unknown, turned up from all over
Italy to reject scornfully the proposals of the illustrious scientist,
without even examining them. And they did this only because
these proposals seemed to them to be harmful to the freedom of
contracts and not to conform with those proper rules of the non-
interference of the state in commerce and industry; rules which
in Italy as you know, are rigidly observed.

Whoever has faith in these liberal principles cannot but be
pleased with the sudden love that some citizens have shown towards them. However he cannot but be surprised in wondering
where on earth they were hiding when the tide of governmental
interference was growing; when monopolies of every type were
being created; when citizens were being sent to prison – their
only crime being that of having refused to work for the wage of
one lira a day; a wage that the court held to be extremely just.
Neither did this new love of liberty manifest itself when Parliament discussed and rejected the Strike Law. Only a few Members
of Parliament dared to propose the extension to the rest of Italy
of the rules of the Tuscan Code, held by our legislators to be too
revolutionary and subversive.

It is difficult to understand how those liberal economic principles, which remain unharmed when a citizen – either alone or
in agreement with others – who does not want to work for a lira
is punished, are mortally wounded when this so-called right
salary is imposed, not on the workman, but on the employer.

I believe that in all justice there are only two ways of looking at
the problem: either the state does not interfere in the relations
between capital and labour and does its best to keep competition
free, or, if it does interfere, it does so impartially, and not in favour
of one and to the detriment of the other. Either the state does not
protect anyone or it protects all. Beyond this there are only
arbitrary acts, injustice and harm to national prosperity.

Baccarini did not want to state a principle of abstract science;
instead he mentioned a concrete measure that can be held to be

more or less good according to the concomitant circumstances . . .
Let me remind you that an illustrious scientist, examining the
problem of whether it is convenient or not to establish a minimum
wage, affirms: 'If this social problem could only be limited to the
present generation, if it were only necessary to obtain the forced
accumulation of capital to give lasting employment and an ample
wage to existing workmen, nobody more energetically than myself would be a supporter of such a measure.' He goes on to say
how such measures should not be accepted, because with the un-
controlled increase of population any beneficial effects are
immediately wiped out.

This economist-scientist is Mill, and I hope that he will be
forgiven by those who opposed the Hon. Baccarini in the name of
freedom.

I hold that if the problem is considered in the abstract it is not
useful to the prosperity of a nation and the good of the poorer
classes for the state to regulate wages; and I say this not only for
the reasons expressed by Mill, but also with reference to the fatal
effects that such measures would have in altering the natural
conditions of the struggle for survival. But when it is a matter of
a concrete case of effects that are modified through already existing laws in the country . . . it does not seem to me that one can
decide with the same certainty, and the problem merits closer
examination.

First of all let us establish the terms of the problem . . . the Hon.
Baccarini said that he did not want to bind in the least the contracts of private industries, but only to establish a minimum wage
for workmen employed in those public works put out by the
government to tender. So, only in these limited terms must we
examine the effects of his proposal. They can be divided into
proximate effects – that is considered independently of the increase in population; and remote effects – that is in relation to
this increase. As to the latter I agree with those many economists
who believe that no stable, efficient improvement in the conditions of the poorer classes can be obtained if the number of individuals that is included in them is not limited. Later we shall
examine whether this result can be reached by limiting the number of births, or by emigration . . .

Mill thinks that an improvement in the standard of living of a
people can become stable when it happens suddenly, is of notable

importance, and is capable of enduring for not too short a time – at least the life span of one generation. In these cases the habits of the people change radically and the people, rather than falling back to their old state of poverty, prefer to limit the number of births or to emigrate. I, too, agree with this, but should like to add that here Mill has neglected to take into consideration the law of continuity . . . I am not convinced that the phenomenon that takes place when the conditions of the people improve over a period of say, thirty years, will not take place, to a lesser extent, when the improvement takes place only over a period of twenty, ten, or even five years. In other words, it is not clearly demonstrated why the variable has a discontinuous function.

So I believe that any measure that tends to improve the actual conditions of the people must not be rejected because it is thought that its effects can be annulled by a subsequent increase in the population. In fact, the improvement, even if it is not great, immediate and long-lasting, can have just the same influence, even if very slight, to prevent the phenomena that destroy the effects of those improvements from happening. However, when in doubt, one must not refuse an actual good only because it could come to an end in the future.

We must, therefore, examine the actual, concrete consequences of the proposed measures and from these formulate our judgement.

If we consider the phenomenon of production in a country we shall see that a certain capital, called the wages fund, is spent every year. It is obvious that in order to increase the average remuneration of the workmen either the total wages fund must increase or the number of those among whom it is divided must be decreased. Establishing by law a minimum wage for workmen employed in public works on a level superior to that already existing in private industry will increase the cost of the product. The increase will be directly sustained in part by the government, and I do not exclude the possibility of it being compensated by a decrease in the profit of the contractors, admitting that, as now seems probable, the profits of this investment of capital are on average superior to other investments in Italy . . .

When the profits are above the average they can go down in two ways: either by increasing the cost of production or by the pouring in of new capital attracted by greater profits.

If workmen's wages are not increased, what will certainly happen is that new capital will pour into public works, thus causing costs to become less, with a saving exactly equal to that amount to which profits could have been reduced, and to that amount to which wages could have been increased to the detriment of the profit...

This means that the government, in all, will not spend more, in that the increase in cost for the work can be compensated by a decrease in the quantity of work; so the total cost will remain unchanged.

The modern parliamentary governments of Italy and France are forced to spend in order to constitute and maintain those majorities from which they derive their existence. There is no limit to expense. The only limit is the resistance of the people to the burden of taxation. This resistance is often overcome by loans and other artifices. So, for the love of their country, the people are invited to fill in some space in the national balance made by ministers to ingratiate themselves with their followers. Costs then, would not increase if the work became more expensive, also because any saving obtained would not be of any use to contributors because it would immediately be invested in other public works...

The conclusion is that the proposed measures will leave the wages fund unchanged... varying only the distribution of it.

As to this distribution, the government, spending the same amount but giving higher wages, must decrease the number of those among whom the sum is divided: that is the government will employ fewer men and pay them better.

On the one hand there is an undeniable improvement in the conditions of the poorer classes. But where will those who will now be out of work go? It seems more than likely that the greater part will have to emigrate either temporarily or permanently. It is necessary to remember that the measure proposed by the Hon. Baccarini is not applied to intellectual work, for which, perhaps, competition in Italy has not reduced costs to a minimum, but rather to manual work for which the actual price is inferior rather than superior to the cost of production. It is not even enough to make life bearable, as can be read in the pale faces of those who are living in poverty in the fertile plains of Lombardy and Venetia, and in the faces of those who go to the ports to emigrate

to a less inhospitable country than their own; inhospitable not
because of nature, for nature has been generous to this country,
but because of the erroneous actions of men. And then, the
government is trying to limit the already meagre wages of these
poor wretches. A little while ago several workmen, guilty of not
wanting to work for a wage that was not even sufficient to feed
them, were arrested and brought before the Court of Legnago.
But, thank God, there still are some brave and honest judges left
in Italy who sentence only according to justice and conscience,
and so the Court absolved the accused . . .

As can be seen, then, by the establishment of a minimum wage
for workmen employed in public works, these workmen will live
better and will not make their companions worse off; and neither
will the tax-payers pay new taxes, in that the increase in wages will
be compensated by a reduction in the expenses of the state. Those
who are against the establishment of a minimum wage would be
right only if all the money spent was used to increase the productive strength of the country in order to be a fruitful investment of capital. But this does not happen in reality, to say nothing
about the millions wasted in the sands of Assab and Massawa,
and neither is it possible to understand how the ornamenting of
cities can increase production. For this, it would be more useful
to reduce the heavy railway tariffs instead of wasting money on
certain 'electoral' railways . . . The essence of the problem we are
examining is this: labour, in the sharing out of the product, cannot permanently obtain such a portion as not to leave to capital
that amount that is indispensable to it for its reproduction. For
the same symmetrical reason it is necessary to recognise that
capital cannot have such a share of the product that the quantity
capable of assuring the survival of the worker does not remain,
otherwise emigration, illness and death would re-establish the
balance.

The payment of the workers can swing between two limits: a
minimum profit and a minimum wage. It is only between these
two limits that natural means, or artificial means like trade unions,
can have influence.

The English writers who have dealt with the effects of strikes
were interested in the former of these two – a minimum profit.
This is natural, as in England profits are near the minimum, and
the trade unions, until the recent formation of the Agricultural

League, were principally made up of factory workers for whom there was a sufficiently large margin between the salary they received and the salary that would have been strictly necessary in order to survive . . .

When the state increases, through monopolies and similar means, the profit of a portion of the capital, it simultaneously decreases the profits of the remaining capital. A part of the country's wealth constitutes the wages fund which is divided among the workers. So another part of the wealth, that could be called the profits fund, is divided among the capitalists. And if one part of the total capital receives more than another, the remaining parts must have less, unless the profits fund increases. When profits have already reached the minimum . . . the total quantity of capital decreases both through emigration and no reproduction . . . So, privileged capitalists benefit through those means that assure them a large profit of money, but – in the case when minimum profit has been reached – do not harm other capitalists. Their benefit is obtained by discouraging the formation of new capital that would come to compete with already existing capital, or by provoking the emigration of money; in conclusion, those who pay the expenses are the workers. The form taken by the measures in favour of capital is that of expenses made by what is obtained through the issuing of public debt bonds, securities and similar things.

It is not very important to capitalists whether or not those expenses are productive. What they want is that the state should ensure a convenient interest apart from the capital; thus avoiding having to invest it productively in agriculture, industry and commerce. But as they have the government in their hands, they manage to do just what they want, and the influence they have is such that they never lack people who will to try to convince the country that it is for the good of all if millions are wasted in the desert sands, or if monopolies and privileges of every sort are created.

It is easy to understand that the wealthy classes try to prevent the workers from following a road perfectly similar to the one that is so useful to them, but it is too much to hope to be able to rely on human ignorance, expecting to convince the workers of the uselessness and damage that would come from the Hon. Baccarini's measures, which are exactly similar to those used by the wealthy classes to their own ends...

The Hon. Baccarini's merit lies in the fact that he is interested in the weak and helps them by all the possible means that he considers to be effective. He has always fought so valiantly in favour of justice that he has relinquished power rather than do things which were against his conscience. As he has not been able to prevent the wrong that has already been done, he tries, at least, to compensate in some way, those who suffer.

The real conservatives are men like the Hon. Baccarini: men who try to prevent violent claims, and demonstrate how the people can reach an improvement in their conditions through the law. It is useless to delude oneself. Education is widening every day, and sophisms, by which privileges are to be protected, will fall one by one. Obstinately carrying on defending them could have fatal consequences, provoking a reaction in the opposite direction. And there is no hope of avoiding this reaction except through justice and freedom, since it would be fatal for a civil society to avoid it in other ways.

The measures proposed by the Hon. Baccarini are only a very small part of what can be done for the workers, and he, himself, cannot but see that the effects will not be very great. The only real way to help the working class is that taught us by economic science, which demonstrates on the one hand that it is indispensable to control the growth of the population, and, on the other, that every destruction of wealth and every fruitless use of it is harmful to the workers.

It is strange that this last sentence, even though very evident, is ignored by most people. People are not conscious that every useless, unproductive expense that destroys part of capital is to their disadvantage. They see the immediate effects of the expense, but not the long-term effect. They do not know that all capital, when it is not destined to be destroyed, is born again in the product. Everyone wants the state to spend money on his own borough, without thinking that if everyone does this, the only result is an enormous waste of money. Unfortunately, those who should educate the people cultivate prejudice instead – perhaps even using these prejudices to corrupt and rob them; whereas others, in order to pursue Utopia, neglect the principles of economic science. But the laws of nature, unlike the laws of man, are inevitable, inexorable, and do not tolerate subterfuge and deceit. Whoever transgresses incurs deserved punishment. It is folly to accuse political economy of being cruel. Science is no more than the knowledge of the necessary relationships between things, and this knowledge is always useful, even if it can sometimes be harmful. For this, we have put our faith in science, look to the future with trust, because we know that truth is eternal and that her triumph is certain.

NOTES

1 M. Pantaleoni, *Giornale degli economisti*, Jan–Feb 1924.
2 See *Pareto, riflessioni e ricerche*, pp. 57–8.

5 Socialism and freedom

The years which Pareto passed with the Iron and Steel Company
were no improvement upon those spent working for the Rome Railway
Company. His spirit of initiative and independence often clashed
with the incapacity and inefficiency of the technical manager of the
company, an engineer called Langer. His letters to the Peruzzis during
this period (they had recommended him for this post) are a series of
grumbles and complaints.[1] He felt boycotted and ill-treated, and in a
way he was right: his suggestions for the company's modernisation
were ignored. Mismanagement of the company made the workers in-
subordinate: he nearly had his skull broken by a blow from a spanner
but his knowledge of fencing saved his head – and he escaped, having
dislocated the arm which he used to protect himself. His dissatisfaction did not end when Langer resigned and he himself became General
Manager of the company, which was reorganised and renamed the
Italian Iron and Steel Company.

In 1887, in spite of the short time at his disposal for writing, his
fiery essays in favour of economic and political freedom came to the
notice of the editor of *Journal des économistes*, Gustave de Molinari,
who invited him to collaborate on the journal. Pareto accepted, and
from then on wrote several articles, including one on the new Italian
customs tariffs. This was to introduce him into the circle of the Parisian
liberal economists where he met Yves Guyot whom he was to quote
with fervent devotion in his works. This is the second great turning-
point (the first was in 1872): Pareto abandoned twenty years' work as
an engineer to devote himself to social studies. Having married
Alessandra Bakounine in 1889 he retired to his villa at Fiesole in 1890
where he became completely absorbed in his studies. A lively and
fluent letter-writer, he put himself in contact with Maffeo Pantaleoni,
and so began a long correspondence and his full-time involvement in
the learned world.[2] His essays, once rare, became frequent. Encouraged by Pantaleoni, his main interest was directed towards
economic problems, but there were essays on politics and sociology
as well.

He came under the influence of Napoleone Colajanni, their collaboration being based not only on mutual esteem, but also on the common conviction that the evils of Italy sprang mainly from speculators
turning to their own advantage protectionism and the Treaty of the
Triple Alliance which, in their view, had decisively halted the economic development of the country.[3] During these years Pareto drew
attention to the grave consequences of the customs tariffs of 1887 and
the interruption of commercial intercourse with France. He was so
taken up with this idea that in 1891 he held public meetings for workmen in Milan. Fiorot reminds us that during one of these meetings:
'the police broke it up because they considered Pareto's speech to be
contrary to government policy'.[4]

'Socialism and freedom' certainly has an important place as it is the
first essay in which we see the beginning of the concern with socialism
which would become one of the predominant themes throughout his
life. But which socialism are we talking about? It could be said that
this essay inaugurates the method of classification which is to be the
hall-mark of his future work. Here, too, he does not stop at the abstract
meaning of words. The first observation that he makes is that there
are multiple elements which go under the name of socialism. But what
have they in common? They want 'the intervention of the state to
change the distribution of wealth'. After having made this first observation Pareto raises another consideration which will be another
central point in his thinking: have not Protectionists always wanted
the same thing? Have not citizens been made poorer through 'customs
duty protection, monopolies, public works and public debts – the
prevalence of indirect taxes over direct taxes – war and the armed peace
that follows it'? Is it not perhaps true that 'the origin of most patrimonies can be found in one of these forms of intervention by the
state'? Are we not perhaps in the presence of a bourgeois socialism
which differs from true socialism in that it tends 'to favour the rich
instead of trying to raise the state of the poor'? There is certainly more
than one analogy between this writing and that of 1886. Then, he
complained about the lack of equidistance on the part of the state in
all labour controversies. Now, he underlines the fact that if a bourgeois socialism had been able to transfer more and more wealth towards those made rich through protectionism, monopolies, public
debts, why then could not a proletarian socialism transfer some of the
wealth of the rich to the poor? What right had the old bourgeois
Socialists to condemn the new Socialists who wished to replace them?

How could it be wondered at if a 'deep thinker' like Marx had thought of making use of the old instruments of collectivism and the particularism of the state to favour the workers? Precisely because the means of injustice of the state were ancient: 'Socialists are far less innovative than they think.' The only ones who had the right to oppose the new Socialists were those Liberals who had consistently fought even against the old Socialists in the name of political and economic freedom.

There are relevant points of contact between this essay and that of 1872 on universal suffrage. Then, he condemned the fact that the electors might have given their guardians *carte blanche*. Now, he ridicules those who thought that they were serving 'the good of the people minus the people'. Once more he was of the opinion that without freedom there could not be progress. Here, too, it can be seen how the term freedom is exactly midway between authoritarianism and anarchy. The work of the Liberals was that of rebalancing the scales which were now leaning in favour of socialism. But as the new Socialists were in the front line in the fight against the old Socialists, it was not at all strange that the Liberals accepted their collaboration in this first phase in fighting 'the real and tangible' evils of bourgeois socialism. The real Liberals were those who fought against every prejudice in order to leave the citizens a greater degree of freedom for intervention and initiative. For this it must not be believed that liberalism and parliamentarianism were synonymous. Parliaments had been useful in a phase of static society, that is, when exchange and production were in an embryonic state. Now, instead, in agreement with liberal ideas, a greater number of citizens must be involved in the governmental sphere, and so – 'limiting the power of parliaments has now become as urgent as it was in past centuries to limit the power of the sovereign'.

Analytic research and the desire for novelty are riveted together in the optimistic enthusiasm expressed in these words: 'the human mind has been able to evolve leaving behind dogmas, prejudices, and metaphysical principles which hindered the natural sciences from reaching that dignity which they have now reached. Thus, it is worth doing the same in politics and social sciences, as the whole of society will obtain great benefit from it – greater perhaps than we can ever imagine.' His thoughts and actions were to move along this track for a long time yet, and the foundations were laid for his *Cours d'économie politique*.

FROM *Il pensiero italiano*, February–April 1891.

By the word socialism one usually means the many schools or sects which have a common quality: that of wanting a total renovation of society: changing, especially, the basis of property and also that of the family; increasing the power of the state and diminishing the freedom of the individual, with the aim of favouring the less well-off.

A looser definition could be that socialism wants the intervention of the state to change the distribution of wealth; but other systems of social organisation would go under the same name (for example, protectionism) which, though similar to socialism in common use, are not called by this name . . . So we can group socialists and protectionists under the name of restrictionists, whilst those who want to base the distribution of wealth solely on free competition can be called liberationists . . .

Thus restrictionists are divided into two types: socialists, who, through the intervention of the state, wish to change the distribution of wealth in favour of the less rich; and the others, who, even if they are sometimes not completely conscious of what they are doing, favour the rich – these are the supporters of commercial protectionism and social organisation of a military type. We owe to Spencer the demonstration of the close analogy of these two types of protectionism. This similarity between protectionism and socialism was very well understood by the English liberals of the school of Cobden and that of John Bright and was clarified in the writings of Bastiat.

All those subject to modern governments are – some more, some less – in the hands of restrictionists; and the well-off modify the distribution of wealth to their own advantage, using the labour of the masses to satisfy their interests and pleasures . . .

In modern times the intervention of the state to change the distribution of wealth is always indirect and can be divided into three types: customs duty protection, monopolies, public works and public debts; the prevalence of indirect taxes over direct taxes; and war and the armed peace that precedes and follows it

Customs duty protection and monopolies exist in nearly all civil states – only England is totally exempt, although but recently, and Belgium, Switzerland and other small states are partially exempt. To this must also be added the intervention of the state when it gives money a fictitious value. Thus we have inflation – as in America – and forced currency.

Customs duty protection has two direct and immediate effects. The first is to destroy a part of wealth, making the labour of the protected nation less productive. This loss affects every citizen. The other is that which permits astute capitalists to be paid a tribute by their fellow-citizens. This is a gain for one but becomes a loss for the other . . .

Monopolies usually destroy wealth to a much lesser degree, and if it is not possible to prevent the people being made poorer, it is preferable that it happens through monopolies rather than through customs duty protection. Unfortunately, the latter is tolerated by the people more easily than monopolies – which are more hated, perhaps, because the injustice of robbery is clearer. Of all the means of imposing taxes on certain citizens in order to favour others, protectionism is the most expensive. It brings about a greater waste of wealth, but as it is less evident it is more easily tolerated. The same thing happens for both direct and indirect taxes. For example, the family tax costs almost nothing to collect in comparison to the expenses for collecting duty on consumer goods. However, town councils more readily increase the latter, as an increase in the family tax is immediately recognised by all, while an increase in duty becomes confused with the variations in the normal prices of the goods, and passes unobserved.

Public debts are often the result of the destruction of wealth rather than the direct cause. They are one of the most powerful means by which the rich are assured of a return from their own capital greater than that which they would receive in a regime of free competition, if this capital were to be used exclusively in industry and commerce. The harm which the enormous increase in the public debt causes the poorer part of the people has been illustrated very effectively by Mr E. de Laveley.

Building speculation, subsidised by the state and county councils, brings about a great waste of wealth. Unfortunately, public works useful to the citizens are few, and the greater and greater number of these public works does nothing but satisfy the love of luxury of the ruling classes.

The prevalence of indirect over direct taxation causes a greater weight of public tribute to fall on the poorer part of the people, even if it is true that because of the phenomenon called 'incidence of taxes', part of the indirect taxes ends up by returning to the

rich, who must pay more for labour. In any case, the poor have
the burden of paying these indirect taxes in advance. To know the
effects of indirect taxation a certain political education is needed
and this explains why the ruling classes have been able to abuse
this way of procuring money for their government without having
to face serious resistance from the people.

In this respect, the difference can be shown by contrasting
Great Britain with Italy. The British, by the exercise of great
tenacity in the face of enormous obstacles, were able to free themselves of the duty on grain, while the Italians let themselves be
taxed without even realising it. The Germans, too, resist this
heavy increase on primary goods. Civilised peoples who have the
Italian resignation are few.

War and armed peace are the most expensive luxuries that the
ruling classes enjoy at the expense of the nation. The British must
still pay the debt that the upper classes incurred in fighting the
French Republic and in defending the power of the sovereign
and European absolutism. But now perhaps the people will not
let them take advantage so shamefully of their wealth. The proof
of how little the Italian government cares for its people can be
found in the heavy sacrifices which, with supine patience, the
nation makes by preparing for a war, which, if it is victorious,
can only favour that organisation euphemistically called 'the
Establishment', serving only a small minority. Meanwhile this
war can do nothing but increase the sufferings of the majority.
The vanity of the rich is fed by seeing Italy allied on an equal
footing with the German and the Austro-Hungarian Empires,
but for this satisfaction – in comparison with the rest of the
population – they pay far less than proportionally would be
justified by their wealth. This is because of the prevalence of
indirect taxes over direct taxes . . .

The origin of most patrimonies can be found in one of these
forms of intervention by the state . . . In our country great patrimonies nearly all have their origins in monopolies (tobacco, railways, and so on), in government work given in tender, in other
speculations subsidised by the state or by local councils, or in
industry which enjoys customs duty protection.

The actual condition of civil society, as it is today, is based not
on free competition and respect for private property, but on the
intervention of the state. So the governments of civilised peoples

SOCIALISM AND FREEDOM   47

can be defined as bourgeois socialist, differing from real socialist
in that it tends to favour the rich instead of trying to raise the
conditions of the poor. Those who defend the existing government make a mistake, believing that they are defending the freedom of the individual, and those who fight against the existing
state of society make a mistake believing that they are fighting
against a liberal society . . .
   Every country must resolve its own social problem by itself.
Each has its own history, so each must have its own economy.
This is the key concept for academic economists . . . They have
compassion for the plight of the less-rich, but the only remedy
they can propose is one of hot compresses, which certainly cannot
disturb the dreams of mighty emperors and their powerful chan-
cellors, kings and their ministers and generals – all good people –
who, according to academic economists, have acquired the right
to guide the people and to imprison democrats, who would quite
willingly do without these shepherds.
   This God-State position of socialists of the chair is, to tell the
truth, a little like usury. If it promises to shed its favours on the
people it starts by making them pay a thousandfold. It is true
that Bismarck proposed social legislation to the Reichstag, but
first he had the law on duty on grain and meat passed, by which
the people paid tribute to the landowners. Here at home the Hon.
Crispi, in a famous manifesto, promised to solve the social problem, but since then nobody has heard any more of this programme
– instead, the only news is that of more expenses and more
taxes.
   This charitable solicitude of the state for the people is very
similar to that of the monks – so derided by Boccaccio – who, in
exchange for the enormous wealth which they extorted from the
faithful, distributed a few bowls of soup at the doors of their
monasteries.
   In Italy the friends of the socialists of the chair published
letters showing their compassion for the people of the provinces
of Naples, but once elected to Parliament, helped to weigh them
down with taxes to support the African expeditions, excessive
re-armaments against France and to guarantee German ownership of Alsace-Lorraine . . .
   These faults are not simply of the men themselves but, above
all, of their system, which reproduces the ancient formula of

Caesarism: to do the good of the people, without the people's participation. But the consequences have been the same everywhere, and the less well-off have paid dearly for the honeyed words and flatteries of their authoritarian benefactors.

Marx seems completely different from other socialists – an indomitable spirit, a deep thinker, able to achieve the highest ideals. He saw the childishness of trying to reform society as a whole while retaining those mean prejudices which divide peoples. Founder of the International Workingmen's Association, he showed the poor of all civilised countries that only by uniting could they be saved from oppression. His economic doctrines still inspire the majority of socialists. He holds that capital usurps the remuneration owed legitimately to labour, thus producing a value much greater than the daily wage paid to the worker; and that this surplus goes to the capitalist. While this system lasts it is vain to hope for a gradual improvement in the workers' lot. The progress of industry tends to reduce the workers' wages and to increase the length of the working day. The piece-work system forces the worker to intense effort, damaging his health and strength.

The remedies are to remove the divisions of social classes and to organise production through *collectivism*. This always happens through the intervention of the state of which the workers must become masters. Thank goodness this does not mean increasing the power of governments which are ruling us at the moment . . .

The liberationists, in comparison with the socialists and the supporters of our present government, are in the same position as positivists in respect to the various religious beliefs. This analogy is deeper than it might seem at first sight. For many, socialism is a faith rather than a scientific opinion, and in many ways its growth in our society reminds us of the growth of Christianity in pagan societies. Although one must be careful when making these historical comparisons so as not to be deceived by fortuitous similarities, in this case, however, the analogies are so many that the intimate connection between the two phenomena is completely established . . .

At first Christianity was a religion for the poor and had to be greatly modified in order to allow the rich to join it, and still retain their wealth and their social position. Thus very gradually the religion, which had been the comfort of the poor, became the instrument of their oppression. For many centuries religious and military despotism tyrannised body and soul. Only small rebellions, quickly put down, like those of the Anabaptists, the Quakers and the *jacquerie* in France, showed that the spirit of resistance to oppression was not dead for ever in the people. This spirit exploded in the great French Revolution and let the world know that when the people have the will, they can also find the physical way. Nowadays, when modern society is becoming more and more prosperous through the invention of the steam engine, railways, and the telegraph, social doctrines are becoming more and more widespread and winning fresh adherents. Because of these social doctrines the poor no longer demand the comfort of dreams but of something more tangible – although the happiness that every political party hopes to achieve through the organisation in which it believes, is incompatible with the inexorable laws of the real world. The number of these parties matches the innumerable Christian denominations, and every day some appear and others disappear. This similarity is inevitable since these arguments on how to construct a human society are very similar to theological disputes. The experimental method – the only sure guide of human reason – is lacking in both of them . . . On the other hand, there is no harm in some men having a faith that helps them to arrive where science does not, as in this way, they can fight the present ruling bourgeois socialism and the real and tangible harm which it unfortunately brings. All socialist parties are united in showing this harm, and this is the most positive aspect of their doctrine. They are, however, divided in the remedy they propose – and this is the most uncertain aspect of their doctrine. Socialists are far less innovative than they think. They copy much of the structure of bourgeois socialism, except that they employ it on behalf of the poor – as the French Jacobins copied many aspects of royal despotism on behalf of the Convention . . . .

If you want to reason according to the teaching of positive science, the argument in favour of freedom can be reduced to two fundamental principles: one in respect of the tangible benefits which can be earned through it; the other in respect of the considerations by which freedom is accepted as the lesser evil, given our present ignorance in the fields of social science.

The benefit that freedom can bring us is, above all, to educate men to be able to act vigorously. The physiological law which says that any organ that is not used for many generations atrophies also applies to the intellectual faculties. Social systems which regulate every aspect of individual behaviour cannot produce anything other than the aptitude of obeying – and not the aptitude of governing. And yet the latter is necessary, as the 'state' of the socialists is no more than an abstract word. In reality there must be men of flesh and blood to assume responsibilities to match the tasks imposed upon them by the state. A society organised according to an excessive form of socialism would thus be incapable of producing the men it needs in order to be governed. Once socialist organisation has used up all the men from the liberal organisation which it has replaced, it will fall into decay. The Roman Empire, having used up all the men of free Rome, fell into decay.

Social science is being born now, and not one of its scholars can be so sure of the truth of his theories as to be able to impose them by force. We only know that there are a few laws that are probably true, and only time and experience can tell if they are right or wrong. Given this state of uncertainty, a prudent man, even if he were able to impose what he believes to be good, must abstain from so doing as it could be harmful.

Liberal systems are of two types: (1) *Systems a priori* – which are the products of metaphysical considerations. The principal forms are: those which want to take man back to his natural state, i.e. the nihilist forms; and the anarchist forms. The organisation that Herzen talks about is a society without government and a religion without God. He describes nihilism as the absolute independence from all principles and every traditional prejudice blindly accepted by man up to now. Bakunin declared that he abhorred communism because it was the negation of freedom, and because it gives the state the ownership of the soil and the means of production. Instead Bakunin wants to destroy the state and in his boundless love of freedom, reaches the point of preaching destruction: the destruction of any existing institution in society. The anarchists are not very different from nihilists. One of their most widely read newspapers, the Boston *Liberty*, is very similar in its theories to the political orthodox economy, as was rightly observed in the Paris *Journal des économistes*. I shall not speak here about certain nihilists who are more like beasts than

men. But, in all justice, I must add that the despotism they are
fighting in Russia is so fierce and immoral that one cannot really
blame them. (2) *Liberal experimental systems* – which have, as
their principal character, to derive from experience and history
the liberal organisation that they propose. The experience of our
times has given us a political economy and a history through
Buckle and Spencer and other philosophers of the positive school,
and has shown us how human evolution progresses towards
freedom.

The principal experiments are: (1) liberal conservatives, who
would like to use freedom as a shield against democracy and
against the different systems of political economy which, instead
of seeking to modify our social organisation, seek to justify it; (2)
other bolder systems which, like that of de Molinari, proceed
towards the conquest of freedom, using all the knowledge that is
offered by modern science.

De Tocqueville has masterfully developed the theories of the
liberal conservatives, and his writings are worth careful study for
the many truths and sound observations they contain. But the
error of this school is to see only what is wrong with democracy
and to be blind to the faults of conservatism.

Fortunately economic science has better and more sincere
scholars. Mill is held by the socialists to belong to their way of
thinking owing to the great love that he has always shown for
everything that can improve the plight of the poor. On the other
hand, orthodox political economy, since it is not a dogmatic
science and accepts every type of scientific research, does not
repudiate Mill. He proposed that there should be a fixed limit to
the amount of wealth a citizen could inherit, thus imagining in
some way to limit the creation of excessively wealthy patrimonies.
Economic science recognises the many evils inherent in the right
of inheritance, but neither this modification nor others that have
so far been proposed seems to have the virtue of eliminating the
existing evils without causing other greater evils.

De Molinari goes further than Mill, and anyone reading his
works will soon see that political science is open to every innovation and does not cling to old dogmas. He foresees that private
property will be transformed into a liberal collectivism and that
there will be strong modifications in all social organisations. 'The
day will come', he says, 'when citizens will be able to choose freely

the government that they want without having to emigrate, and political tutelage will disappear in the same way that economic tutelage is disappearing now.'

Others before Mill, like de Molinari, have described the many evils of parliamentary government which was already held to be perfect. In the state of New York efforts were made to remedy parliamentary government, at least in part.

Limiting the power of parliaments has now become as urgent as it was in past centuries to limit the power of the sovereign; and those peoples who are more civilised begin to realise how much corruption is generated by the conflict between the various parliamentary parties for whom the good of the nation is often a very distant consideration.

Restricted suffrage, universal suffrage, minority representation, single-chamber or bicameral legislature, the more or less restricted prerogatives of sovereign or presidential power – none of these seems to have much reforming influence upon a parliamentary regime. In Switzerland the referendum has given good proof of its worth and could perhaps show us the way to obtain better government. This experiment, like that of the township in America, could help us to understand how false is the axiom on which the constitution of parliamentary government is based: that the people are able to choose the men rather than the things that these men must do. So the study of such an important reform must not be neglected, especially for what it could do gradually, and without too many abrupt changes in our systems of government. But it would be an illusion to think that this alone is enough to heal all the ills of parliamentary government – it must undergo more radical reform.

This problem is of the greatest importance and on its solution depends the further progress of our society. The more one studies these problems the more one sees how complex they are and how wrong are the superficial solutions given by certain schools. Proclaiming the abstract principle of collective ownership of the means of production will not help at all if the problems of how to put it into practice are not considered at the same time. And if we want to take seriously all the lessons of history, we must recognise that to give this task to governments such as we have now would be to create very great evils, and the people would be exploited even more than they are now. It is therefore worth investigating every measure that can be considered capable of improving our society. In this examination we must use all the means that the social sciences offer us in order to know the truth. If these means are not sufficient, as often happens, nothing remains but to fall back on experiment, using it carefully on the smallest possible part of society. The Swiss cantons and the U.S.A. do just this. Each canton or state is on the alert as to what is happening in the others, quickly copying anything that has been successfully tested.

The human mind has been able to evolve, leaving behind dogmas, prejudices, and metaphysical principles which hindered the natural sciences from achieving that dignity which they now have. Thus it is worth doing the same in politics and the social sciences, as the whole of society will obtain great benefit from it – perhaps to a greater extent than we can ever imagine.

NOTES

1 See Pareto, *riflessioni e ricerche*.
2 See V. Pareto, *Lettere a Maffeo Pantaleoni*, ed. G. de Rosa (Rome 1960).
3 See S.M. Ganci (ed.) *Democrazia e socialismo in Italia. Carteggi di Napoleone Colajanni, 1878–1898* (Milan 1959).
4 D. Fiorot, *Pareto* (Milan 1969), p. 62 fn.

6 The future of the liberal side

The line which this essay follows is fairly close to that of its predecessor. Here, too, a trace of bitterness at the cowardice of the multitude is compensated by a large dose of messianic optimism in the power of ideas about justice and freedom. There is a foresight of decadence. Corruption and nepotism which had already curtailed economic and political freedom now began to corrode the exercise of justice. Pareto was shocked by the meanness of men, and in their lack of ideals he foresaw the symptoms of a rapid decline. He complained: 'This hurry, this anxiety to obtain something tangible, to aim not at the victory of principles, but at the victory of the individual, ruins and turns all our political life upside-down.' But he was still convinced that it would be enough for a few heroes, a few martyrs, to save freedom in the same way that a few brave men, prepared to make any sacrifice, were enough to save Sparta.

Reading this essay, one has the impression of a Pareto still impregnated with the enthusiasm of the *Risorgimento*. The men whom he criticised – perhaps much too severely – were those politicians who had replaced the right wing party in leading the country and who – the epic period of Italy having passed – were faced by the innumerable unsolved problems of a state united only on the map and divided in many other respects. The language spoken in Turin was not the same as that spoken in Naples or Palermo. There were large gaps in the levels of education and standards of living between the various social classes. The economy was very backward and presented differences between an agricultural south and a north wanting to become industrialised. The agricultural economy and the embryonic industrial economy were too weak to keep up with European competition. Unemployment fed brigandage and social disorder. Once national unity, the goal of the struggle, had been achieved, enthusiasm evaporated: few were satisfied and many were disappointed. The desire for greater social justice had brought the Left of Depretis to power in 1876, where it remained until 1887. Among the points in its programme was the lowering of the wealth limit for voting, and therefore, the widening of suffrage. A second point was a greater intervention of the state in the economic life of the country.

As we have already seen, Pareto had fought for universal suffrage and was partly in favour of the second point, but only to balance the existing intervention of the state in favour of speculators with the intervention of the state in favour of the workers. What left him completely shocked was the total lack of any idealistic imagination on the part of an authoritative and despotic ruling class.

During these years Pantaleoni was forced to resign his teaching post at the Scuola Superiore di Commercio at Bari because he had criticised, in an article, the policy on the customs duty on wine. As de Rosa observes, Pareto was hurt and indignant 'because he considered himself to be partly at fault, even if involuntarily, for the loss of Pantaleoni's job, for having quoted the incriminating article in *Revue des deux mondes*'.[1]

In his sincerity, Pareto did not understand the dark and devious workings of politics, and so began the divorce between himself and the Italian political ruling classes. As a left wing liberal and supporter of a frank, open encounter between the majority and the opposition, he did not appreciate the socialist transformism of Depretis. In this essay therefore, he complains that there is no real opposition, and one is never created. This complaint is similar to the one he was to make in his 'IX Cronaca' in *Giornale degli economisti*, 1 November 1893. Here he wrote, 'Gladstone in government speaks and acts like Gladstone, Member of Parliament. Lord Salisbury can contradict policy today because he does no more than follow the maxims which he used when he was a minister.'

Although Pareto had already had his first disappointment in his dream of an alliance with the Socialists, and expressed it in this essay, he probably did not expect the left to use the same miserable means of transformism already used in the past once they achieved power. In his 'XLIV Cronaca' in *Giornale degli economisti*, 1 October 1896, re-evoking the past, he said that 'Transformism was not invented by Depretis, at all, but was practised as early as 1860, and continues to be the most powerful arm of the ruling classes.' Thus those who think that Pareto's anti-socialist phase had already begun are mistaken.

FROM *Idea liberale*, 28 August–4 September 1892.

It is said that Leonidas did not abandon Thermopylae and went to certain death, because the oracle had predicted the destruction of Sparta if one of its kings did not sacrifice himself.

If we lived in those times perhaps the oracle would say that
freedom would not win unless some men first sacrificed themselves to defend it, and to prepare a triumph that they themselves
would never see.

Economic freedom procures the good of the majority, and
because of this, does not distinguish between friend and foe. It
does not have the means to reward one and punish the other.

Protectionism, by contrast, draws a small sum of money from
many in order, then, to divide it among a few. So it has tepid
opponents and fervent friends . . .

The government, extending its authority over the citizen's
every activity, has a thousand ways of rewarding its friends, while
its enemies find themselves in the position of outlaws.

In France, reliable sources affirm that the power of awarding
the Cross of the Legion of Honour, and the more modern Cross
of Agricultural Merit, helps the different ministries, in no small
way, to obtain favourable election results.

But without going any further afield than our own country,
look at the power enjoyed by certain individuals with influential
connections in Rome! How their friendship is sought after! How
feared they are as enemies! Everyone runs to them for everything
– and many are the things that the government must decide!

It has long been rumoured that weeds have started to grow in
the severe courtrooms of justice, too. Elderly men, who have
experienced the administration of justice under past governments
and that of the present, say that, except for political trials, it was
quieter then than it is now. I cannot say whether this is true or
not. I can only say that everyone can see the undue interference
of political lawyers, and especially ex-ministers, at trials. The
evil seems to have increased owing to wider jurisdiction given to
the Court of Cassation in Rome.

In every age such evils have been blamed on the wickedness of
individuals, whereas they should have been sought in the systems
of government. In Italy, it was once believed that the fault was
that of certain factions. Then the left wing came to power and
there were no changes – or, if they did take place, they were for
the worse. Sugar speculators will go down in history – and they
do not belong to any faction.

But we have tried every sort of government. Half or three-

quarters to the left, we have enjoyed *transformism*; the diluted
right wing with Rudini, and now – what a joy! – we have the Left
again, but not just any Left – a real Left – according to those who
know about such things! But all the changes of face have not
brought about any changes in substance, which slowly gets
worse. So we have more proof of the truth of the theory that
Molinari deduced from very many facts – that it is pointless to
hope for any economic improvement from the present political
parties of the country.

What place have the Liberals among these political parties?
With all their hopes of victory, they have never been able to put
an army in the field! And it is understandable why – they have no
ammunition . . . unable to offer any loot, they can find no soldiers
to follow them and their own chiefs, if they are in the least bit
ambitious, abandon them, make compromises, and act in a way
completely opposite to their doctrines.

The Paris *Siècle*, a Republican newspaper, in the edition of the
eighth of this month, reports how peasants have become supporters of the Republican Government. Some mayors say, in all
sincerity: 'In the end we realise that if we want to get anything
out of the Government, we must not fight it.' Unfortunately, the
Liberals, too, realise in the end that if they want to obtain power
and honour they must stop fighting the petty politicians who
form the government. This explains why Italy has had extremely
authoritative men to defend Liberal doctrines, without these
doctrines having any concrete effect.

Read, for example, Minghetti's book, *I partiti politici e la loro
ingerenza nell'amministrazione*, reminiscent of the works of Mill
and Spencer, without the Italian writer seeming in any way
inferior to these two men. But try to realise, if you can, why he
could be a supporter and protector of the Depretis cabinet, under
which corruption in Italy grew out of all proportion.

Signor Jacini, who was another of our most worthy and valiant
politicians, seemed for a while as if he wanted to raise the flag of
freedom, even if very near that of the Conservatives. In his
Pensieri sulla politica italiana can be found proof of a profoundly
Liberal way of thinking. But a little before his death he was beginning to weaken, and advised his party to choose a different leader
in order to achieve power more quickly.

This hurry, this anxiety to obtain something tangible, to aim, not at the victory of principles, but at the victory of the individual, ruins and turns upside down all our political life.

If Gladstone had been Italian he certainly would only have opposed Salisbury for a couple of years, and then he would have reached a compromise, and England would have been governed by a Gladstone-Salisbury cabinet, which would have been useful to many petty politicians, but would certainly have corrupted not only the principles of each of these two men, but the integrity of the political life of the whole country as well.

All things considered, it seems to me that there is no hope of the Liberals winning by using the arms that the other parties use. We must examine whether there is another way of defending our doctrines, and preparing – at least for those who come after us – for the victory that eludes us . . .

King Frederick of Prussia, explaining to Voltaire the persecution of the Encyclopaedists by the French Government, wrote: 'The Government of Versailles needs money, so it sacrifices to the clergy, who promise it, the philosophers, who haven't any at all, and who can't give any.' And yet, even if the Encyclopaedists lost that battle, at least their ideas eventually won the war. The same thing would happen to the Liberal doctrines if they were defended sincerely. Unfortunately, however, what very often happens is that this defence, which is powerful and strong when it is turned against the weak and poor, itself becomes weak and poor when turned against the powerful. Any abuse which favours the powerful is considered good, and sophisms and excuses are never lacking to demonstrate that nothing different can be done.

How can Liberal ideas possibly win credit if the apostles of these doctrines use them to oppose the requests of the workers who wish to improve their lot, and then forget them when property-owners, industrialists and bankers ask for the intervention of the state for their own ends?

If it is right for the state to pay the iron foundries at Terni twenty-two lire a quintal for railway lines instead of the twelve lire paid abroad, why is it not also right for the state to control the wages of the workers in these foundries?

At Homestead near Pittsburg in the U.S.A. there are the iron foundries of Mr Carnegie who was penniless on his arrival in America, but now possesses thousands. These thousands have been extorted from the people of America, with the complicity of

Congress. Mr Carnegie and his friends think it obvious that, when it is a matter of selling the products of their industry, the law must protect them against competition. They also think it obvious that when it is they who buy the sweat of the worker, nobody must interfere with competition.

But workers do not reason like this. As Mr Carnegie – thanks to protectionism – can ask double the real value of iron, it seems to them that they have a right to a cent or two of that elevated price.

Mr Carnegie trusts in the chicanery of petty politicians. The workers trust in the strength of their cause, and so follow the strikes which the newspapers have been talking about. In Italy, the owners of the rice fields, acting rather like Mr Carnegie and his friends, obtained permission from the complacent government to sell their goods, through customs duty protection, at 30 per cent more than their real value. Driven by hunger, miserable workers earning a few centesimi a day in the rice fields, rose up. They were fired on and those missed by the bullets were imprisoned.

They were accused of violence! Of course, violence should always be condemned. Society would disintegrate if everyone were allowed to do what he liked. But, on the other hand, we must not forget the punishment which, according to Dante, God inflicts on defrauders in Hell. Here, however, the violent receive grave punishment, while defrauders and their friends, the petty politicians, enjoy the tribute that the whole country through chicanery is made to pay.

Now, let us imagine that some Liberals had the courage, the boldness and the virtue to recognise such a truth and to stand firm in condemning any offence against freedom and justice; without caring who committed it, and without giving in to flattery or threats. That firm will, that indestructable faith, would certainly end by enforcing respect, and gaining for Liberal ideas that authority and trust which they now lack. If only the Liberal flag could be raised aloft, those who see the falsity of modern governments would gradually gather round it. Following the road on which we now stand, we should walk faster and faster towards socialism. It only remains to solve the problem of whether or not we can peacefully stop on this slope, or climb up it again, or if we must first undergo a revolution that will completely overturn the existing social order.

We can hope that at the approach of danger, those who realise that it will become greater will do all they can to remove it and to avoid a catastrophe that could take us back to the barbarism of the Middle Ages. The work of isolated individuals is useless, and can be effective only if it is in harmony with common ideas, pure and sincere liberal ideas which, held in common, serve as a means and an end for this desired union.

As in many other things, so in this: once an arduous and wearisome beginning has been made, the going will be easier.

For their ideas to be victorious, the Liberals must always abstain from the chicanery and tricks of petty politicians, who will always win that sort of game. They must hold fast to a doctrine which is organic, sincere, right and honest, paving a way where they cannot be followed by those who have acquired their power by lies and deceit.

NOTES

1 See de Rosa commenting on Pareto, *Lettere a Maffeo Pantaleoni*, vol. 1, p. 143.

7 Introduction to Marx's 'Capital'

1893 was an eventful year for Italy. Crispi became Prime Minister for the second time and his authoritarian policy and his tendency to imitate Bismarck in making Italy a military and colonial power caused more than one violent demonstration. This new authoritarian and anti-popular wave placed more burdens on the shoulders of the poorer classes, already bowed down with taxes and protectionism. It irritated Pareto. He despised the way in which Crispi wasted money trying to make Italy a military power, the more so because Crispi, once a fervent supporter of Mazzini, had been considered a man of the left, though now he infringed civil liberties more than anybody. This was further support for Pareto's embittered view of the common interest of bourgeois socialism and popular socialism in the exercise of power, and of the way in which men change their opinions according to the rôle they play, and not from rational conviction.

1893 was also a decisive year for Pareto. The change in his way of life which began with his retirement to Fiesole in order to study, and his friendship with Pantaleoni came to fruition when in May he was called to succeed Leon Walras in the Chair of Political Economy at Lausanne, where he was to teach for over twenty years. Although this took him into the heart of the European learned world, he was not to lose interest in the social, economic and political problems of his country. Through 'Cronache',[1] a regular feature which he was asked by the editor, Pantaleoni, to contribute to the *Giornale degli economisti*, he never let slip the opportunity to point his barbs against the incapable Italian ruling classes. Although political economy was his main concern in these years, Pareto realised more and more how closely it was linked to social events rather than to abstract, metaphysical phenomena. In condemning the repression of the Sicilian *Fasci*, ordered by Crispi, Pareto wrote in one of his 'Cronache' of that year: 'Signor Crispi and his lieutenants continue to see simple, financial problems where, instead, it is a matter of the economic and social foundations of Italy.'

His 'Introduction to Marx's *Capital*'. too, is an invitation to consider the sociological aspect which always lurks behind the purely
economic one. Observation begins to cool passion, and he reproaches
the socialists in their studies in political economy, for considering men
as they would like them to be rather than as they are. But once again
he tries to find a measure of agreement not only theoretical but also
political and economic with Marxism – considered to be the only one
among the infinite socialist groups having as its basis a scientific conception of society. He finds more than one point in common with
Marxism, from the need to accumulate capital to the fight against the
corrupt petty politicians of bourgeois socialism. He conjectured that
the points of disagreement with Marxism concerned the new, future
society which still had to be built.

Pareto thought that, to socialism, the challenge posed by the liberal
effort to improve the standard of living of the poorer classes, would be
decided by the greater or lesser good resulting from one or the other
system. But, as the result of his analysis showed that socialism would
destroy a large amount of wealth, he reaffirmed his faith in liberalism
which he considered to be the most efficient system of government.
Almost in a hymn to economic freedom, he concluded: 'Any attack,
from any direction, on economic freedom is an evil. Whether this freedom is violated in the name of bourgeois socialism or that of the
people's socialism, the effect is the same – a destruction of wealth
which, in the end, falls on the poorer, more numerous part of the
population, increasing its sufferings.'

FROM Vilfredo Pareto, *Marxisme et économie pure* (Geneva 1893).
Karl Marx's book should be called 'The Capitalist' rather than
'Capital', at least if we want to understand the word in the generally accepted sense of economic goods destined to facilitate the
production of other goods . . .

So, in order not to create confusion, and to keep as close as
possible to Karl Marx's terminology, we shall call the economic
goods destined for the production of other goods, 'Simple
Capital', and the capital which is in the hands of capitalists
'Appropriated Capital'.

Marx's book is evidently directed against the second category;
that is against capitalists. As to Simple Capital, Karl Marx in no
way denies its importance. He affirms that it must not only reproduce itself, but also increase in order to develop 'the productive

forces and the material conditions which are those that form the basis of a new, superior society' [259].*

According to Karl Marx, the capitalist system is not only useless, but also detrimental to the accumulation of Simple Capital. Every year capitalists, their rich fellow land-owners, their vassals and their vassal-governments waste a considerable part of the net annual production. The proportion of wealth which is capitalised is never as large as it should be [267].

Assuredly, if the services that capitalists give could be continued, and the capitalists themselves eliminated, it would be of great advantage to humanity to enjoy the work and eliminate the man who performs it. But is this possible?

Karl Marx may ridicule thrift as much as he likes: yet assuredly it plays no negligible role in the formation of new capital. Ignoring the thrift of the capitalist (clearly, if the capital does not belong to him, neither does the interest which it produces) one has only to think of the money which accumulates in savings banks in order to understand that the thrift of the worker is highly productive. The bank books of the cook, the caretaker, the gardener, the labourer, show sums which really are the product of the thrift of these workers. But would all these people save in the same way if the private ownership of capital were abolished and all capital held in common? There is no evidence whatsoever that these savings would increase . . .

But creating capital is not everything. It must also be employed. Organise society as you like, some human being will always have to decide to what ends capital should be invested. Will government employers decide more wisely than capitalists when observation indicates that men generally look after their own interests better than those of others?

To know whether or not a certain amount of capital must be invested in factory A or factory B to be more profitable for society, is there a more efficient way than that of giving to the bidder who offers the highest interest?

Capital can perish, it can be frittered away. Is it to the good of society for the minority to carry the losses caused by the imprudence of the majority, or is it not better for each to bear the consequences of his own actions?

* The numbers in square brackets indicate the pages of Marx's *Le Capital* (Paris 1893).

The capitalists of our society have a strong tendency to obtain an interest guaranteed them by the state which is better than that which they could obtain on the free market.

A bargain and compact between this bourgeois socialism and a people's socialism made under the auspices of petty politicians is well within the bounds of possibility. In fact, it is being realised, and the day is not far off when we shall see the enormous destruction of wealth which will be the consequence. The fault, however, will not be that of the capitalist system, but of the intervention of the state which arbitrarily modifies the distribution of wealth . . .

Marx says that a government can force the owner of economic goods A to take economic goods B for them, without receiving any interest: for example it can oblige a wine producer to exchange his wine for wheat of the same value without receiving any profit.

However if this capital receives no interest nobody will want to save it. So nobody will cultivate the vineyards if he must exchange his product for goods of the same weight and inferior quality. But Marx replies that the state can abstract from the product of the work of the citizen whatever is necessary to assure 'the simple, progressive reproduction of capital without the intervention of the *grim-looking cavalier* called the capitalist'. We can also say that the state will subtract from the work of the citizen that which is necessary for the cultivation of the vineyard without the intervention of another *grim-looking cavalier* called the peasant.

But is the good of society better served if the reproduction of capital – like the cultivation of the vineyards – is done through *corvées* imposed on the citizen rather than by a regime of free competition? . . .

What a strange state this will be, where everyone, instead of checking up on his own work, will check up on that of his neighbour!

All we know of human nature points to the fact that this state will not greatly favour industrial progress, and that it will soon be forced to pass a law to stimulate the activity of the producers. Thus, if the honest Corporation of Tailors discovers and perfects a way of reducing the time needed to produce a suit of clothes, it will receive a premium from the government. But then the value of the exchange of products will no longer be exactly proportionate to the quantity of work that they contain – as the buyer,

the tax-payer, will have to pay not only the amount of work contained in the suit of clothes, but also his part of the premium that
the tailors receive . . .

What do petty politicians do now when they want to try out
some socialist experiment or the like? They get the government to
give them a loan. Through savings banks they collect the money
of the workers. With the issue of bonds guaranteed by the state
they attract a large amount of capital. What they really do is destroy the greater part of wealth accumulated . . .

The people's socialist state needs to borrow the same or more
than the bourgeois socialist state that we have the good fortune to
have here at the moment! If it does not want to pay anything for
the use of the economic goods for which it asks, its subjects will
not fall over themselves to give them to it. If, instead, it pays
something, the capitalist is born again and takes root in the new
society. He will be better off than in a society where only free
competition determines the distribution of wealth, as, in coming
to an agreement with petty politicians (men of doubtful virtue)
on an artificial demand for capital, he can force up the rate of
interest. On the other hand, this type of capitalist does not run
any of the risks run by the capitalist who is obliged to risk his own
capital in a business venture where he can lose everything –
interest and capital.

It is extremely difficult to abolish the ownership of those economic goods called *capital* if the ownership of other economic
goods is not abolished at the same time. This has been understood
by certain socialist sects . . .

Logically there is a fundamental difference between the
theories which aim to abolish only a certain ownership – that of
capital – and the theories which aim to abolish all types of ownership – even a morsel of bread.

The former come up against innumerable difficulties arising
from the arbitrary distinctions which they seek to establish between the ownership they aim to abolish and that which they
want to keep. The latter avoid these difficulties, but only at the
cost of still greater difficulties which follow the hypothesis that
the powerful sentiment which drives man and animal to possess
the objects which are useful to them can be neglected.

Some sects try to get round these difficulties by stating as a
premise that human nature can become completely different to

what it really is.* If this hypothesis is accepted, imagination can
run riot and create any social system it likes. No objections can be
raised because it will always be possible to imagine a type of
human nature which makes the proposed system possible. But
political economy studies the actions of man as he is, not as we
like to imagine him to be . . .

Karl Marx's book also contains a very important, descriptive,
historical part dealing primarily with English industry. However
the logic of this part seems rather weak, in my opinion.

It is a matter of proving that certain reprehensible facts are the
consequence of the capitalist system. But then, this is a proceeding frequently employed by capitalist schools . . .

Marx quotes a certain Ed Potter who, in 1863, wanted to stop
the emigration of English workmen. This gentleman wrote that
two hundred and fifty-one economists 'encourage, or allow, the
working power to emigrate, and what of the capitalist?' Marx, not
without reason, blames these words. But why, then, does he not
note, at least this once, that among the *sycophants* of the liberal
economy, the 'Ideologists of Capital', two hundred and fifty have
the good fortune to agree with him? The school of *laissez-faire*
considers all the measures aimed at stopping workmen disposing
of their persons reprehensible. G. de Molinari too, has strongly
insisted on the progress that must be made in our society so that
the workman can more and more easily offer his work in the
market which pays the best . . .

Nor should one forget that the protests of the masters who
wanted to stop the emigration of workmen received no support
from an English government inspired by the liberal principles
of Cobden and John Bright. On the other hand, to please their
friends (certain rich land-owners), a protectionist government in
Italy recently passed measures which on the pretext of regulating
emigration aimed to make it more difficult.

The liberal economists agree with Marx on many points: as in
condemning the exploitation of child and female labour by those
who are their guardians . . . This agreement ceases when it comes
to discovering the causes for these phenomena. For Marx it is
solely in the capitalist system; but if this were true, should the

* This is the answer given by an important Milan socialist magazine, *La
Critica sociale*, to certain objections which I had made with reference to the
future action of the socialist state.

effect not disappear with the cause? Instead, what we see is just
the opposite, and women and children are even more badly
treated in primitive societies where the capitalist system either
does not exist or is only in its beginnings, than in our own society,
where this system has had its major development . . .

In any case, it is useless merely to talk about the effects of
poverty, because if there is a way of avoiding it, every man who is
honest and in his right senses will be in favour of it.

Let us return to the problem with which we began: whether to
reach the hedonistic maximum by the play of free competition or
by charging the governmental employers to distribute wealth
among those who produce it.

In order to solve such a problem it is not enough simply to
underline the ills from which our society suffers. First of all we
must distinguish the ills which are the products of bourgeois
socialism – which, thanks to petty politicians, pervades our social
organisation more and more – from the ills which are the consequence of free competition. We must prove that another system
would incur a lesser ill; and this has not been done so far.

The point of view which illustrates the liberal political economy has been admirably expressed by G. de Molinari, and we
can do no more than quote his words:

> Production has increased and wealth has multiplied; interna-
> tional solidarity has spread and war has ceased to be necessary
> in order to ensure the existence of civilisations; but the forms
> of government have not yet adapted themselves to the new con-
> ditions of existence which economic progress has given to
> various societies and individuals. The observance of both col-
> lective and individual rights and duties has not made any
> appreciable progress.* It could be argued that, if it has pro-
> gressed in some directions (for example in tolerance) it has
> regressed in others.
>
> Instead of more exactly adapting positive laws to natural
> rights, governments arbitrarily extend the property and liberty
> of some at·the expense of others, and through monopolies and
> protectionism protect the income of property owners at the
> expense of the workers' wages. This will continue to happen
> until the workers control the government and protect their

* See H.T. Buckle, *History of Civilization in England* (London 1857).

wages at the expense of the earnings of the industrialists and
the incomes of the property owners. Such governments expose
us to a permanent state of instability by now raising, now
lowering, the obstacles they have built against freedom of
labour and free trade. Instead of coming to an agreement to
ensure peace, something which could be had at very little cost,
they burden their people with the expense of war preparations,
waiting to loose on the civilised world a more bloody and destructive conflict than ever before. Everywhere the ruling
classes have one thought – their own selfish interests – and they
use the government to satisfy them, without bothering to know
whether their interests conform with the permanent general
interests of society.*

Political economy shows us that this permanent, general interest can only be assured by free competition, and that every
obstacle against it is an evil; that protectionism is synonymous
with the destruction of wealth; and finally that the majority of the
evils in our society spring – as Professor Todde says** – not
from an excess of freedom, but, on the contrary, from the lack of
certain, necessary types of freedom. All the known facts bring us
to this conclusion, and every new fact confirms it.

Any attack on economic freedom, from wherever it comes, is
an evil. Whether this freedom be violated in the name of bourgeois socialism or that of the people's socialism, the effect is the
same – a destruction of wealth which, in the end, falls on the
poorer, more numerous part of the population, increasing its
sufferings.

NOTES

1 Literally translated means chronicles or reviews.

* G. de Molinari, *Précis d'économie politique et de la morale* (Paris 1893),
pp. 253–4.
** G. Todde, *Note sull'economia politica* (Cagliari 1885), p. 5.

8 Socialism and the duty on grain

Only two years after Pareto had told the puzzled Pantaleoni that the radicals could be more useful to the liberal cause, we can already notice a change in language. Pareto had passed from seeking points of similarity in socialism to challenging it. A long series of scandals, corruptions and bankruptcies in the machinery of the state, made him the unyielding enemy of state intervention, which only a few years before he had accepted as a simple means of holding a balance. Now, he pointed out to socialists who wished to establish a state monopoly for grain, 'If it is your aim to propose an increase in the number of sources from which petty politicians can quench their thirst for plunder you act wisely by adding the grain to the banking monopoly; but if you want to lower the price of bread, making it easier for the people to buy, you are going directly against your aim.' Were the socialists acting in bad faith? Or could they not see the logical connections between their actions and the results they wanted to achieve? These and future reflections led him to make that distinction between logical actions and non-logical actions enforced in his *Trattato*. He developed a new way of observing things: circumspect, disbelieving, sceptical. History, in addition to offering us new facts, repeats itself, and 'the same things will be repeated in the future, only the oppressed will become the oppressors and vice-versa'.

With a deep regret which was not yet resignation, he asked himself, 'Why should history stop? Why have men been able to make progress in natural science, physics, biology, technical discoveries, and yet have not been able to make any progress in social science for two thousand years?' Under the influence of Buckle, the concept of an eternal history began to form in Pareto's mind, and the time seems a long way off when he wrote in his essay 'On the logic of the new school of economics': 'If the development of human societies has occurred in a closed cycle, as Vico believed, if the same events are repeated, then the observations of past phenomena could provide us with an almost definitive law on these.'

FROM *Idea liberale*, 29 April 1894.

Professor Coletti says that whoever is a socialist can easily accept free trade and at the same time desire state intervention to regulate the distribution of wealth.

I myself have no objections to this, as this organisation would not be any the less reasonable than so many social systems that we know . . . But, I do not know why, he quotes *Critica sociale* . . . which, in addition to what he writes, says: 'We in Italy do not have a Socialist party which is so strong that it can seriously propose that the government should possess the monopoly for the importation of grain, as the French Socialist party did through Guesde and Jaurès.'

This organisation which the *Critica sociale* prefers (we will not examine it at the moment to see whether or not it is sound) is certainly not one which supports free trade.

At this point I could let Professor Coletti and *Critica sociale* get on with it and come to an agreement . . . but as Professor Coletti offers other considerations on the distribution of wealth, it seems useful for me to follow his train of thought. He repeats the principle common to the majority of socialist theorists, that the proletariat, 'faced with capitalists and rich land-owners, naturally more powerful than themselves, are driven to seek the moderating intervention of the State to help them in the unfair fight.'

In answer to this, the liberal school maintains two points. First, it denies that the 'capitalists and rich land-owners' can oppress the proletariat in a liberal organisation; and secondly, while admitting that this oppression does exist, the school argues that the intervention of the state will not remedy anything but rather worsen this oppression.

There has been ample debate between liberals and socialists on the first point. But as we are not composing a treatise, we shall leave it to one side.

It is impossible to obtain any answer from the socialists on the second point. If we ask them: 'What will you do for your future state to make it better than the one we know?' they abuse us and accuse us of ignorance. They are quite right about this and it is precisely for this reason that we ignore their reply and insist on asking the question; and those who know are at fault in not answering our question . . .

Although the socialists always talk about the 'historic method' as if they had the monopoly of history, I believe it is right for the liberals to use this method, too. So, if we wish to know the nature of the creature called 'the state', we shall obtain the necessary information both from the study of history and by observing contemporary phenomena. If someone were to tell you: 'I have thought about having a lion as a secretary', you would try to check up on whether or not lions know how to write...

Meanwhile observe that the word 'state' is abstract: only governments are concrete and we must argue from the concrete if we wish to remain in touch with reality. The historical enquiries of the liberals seem to demonstrate that when governments interfere in economic affairs, they have more often than not done so to the advantage of privileged classes, rather than of the proletariat. So the conclusion is, that if the organisation of those governments is not changed radically, the same things will be repeated in the future, only the oppressed will become the oppressors and vice versa ... It only remains to see whether there is a way in which future governments will not resemble past or present governments.

This is not a problem to undervalue. For two thousand years men have been seeking a better form of government – with little result. Wonderful discoveries have been made in science. Oceans are crossed in a few days. Messages are sent from Europe to America in a few seconds. And yet no way has been found for even our god-like Premier Crispi's butler to avoid having to ask the bank for a loan.

It is proposed that the state should have the monopoly of the importation of grain. Let me ask history and the observation of facts what effect it will have ... We shall not say whether it is a good thing or an evil, but let me say that all those Deputies who received favours from the banks will now be able to go to the director of the future grain monopoly, and repeat the same things ... So, if it is your aim to propose an increase in the number of sources from which petty politicians can quench their thirst for plunder you act wisely by adding the grain to the banking monopoly. But if, instead, you want to lower the price of bread, making it easier for the people to buy, you are going directly against your aim. But are these exceptional cases?

Let us see what Thorold Rogers, the learned historian of

agriculture and prices in England says . . . He warns us that the most serious trouble among the English had its origins in the debasement of the coinage by Henry VIII and his successors . . .* Similar facts are to be found in the history of Ancient Rome, France, Germany and Italy.** Similar facts are to be found today, with the difference that, as Molinari so rightly points out, debasement of the coinage has been replaced by the issue of paper-money. So now, we shall no longer say, as the Romans did, *ferrum argento miscere,* but *chartam argento miscere.*

Let us set our statements against what is happening today in Italy. To favour the Tiberina Company and other companies protected by party politicians, our government – not without reason – has often mixed paper and silver, and, as a result, this paper has now lost about 14 per cent of its value and so the prices of oil, coffee, sugar, grain and any other imports have increased at the same rate and perhaps more. But wages have not been increased by the same percentage, and so the lot of the Italian people has got worse. I conclude that for the people to avoid this evil, the government must be deprived of the power to mix copper, paper or anything else with gold or silver.

Equally rich in useful lessons is the history of the Bank of Naples. This bank began in the sixteenth century . . . and went bankrupt for the first time about 1623, because an order of the viceroy reduced the value of the small gold coins called *zannette* . . . History then relates other admirable government actions, which bled the banks of Naples successively, as phylloxera destroys the vine, until at last the Bourbons came to power.

'The first thing that Acton, Corradini and Simonetti did', says Tortora in the History of the Bank of Naples, 'was to charge the wages and pensions of state employees, especially the police, to the bank . . . Next, most of the deposits were commandeered as a forced loan to the Public Treasury . . . then all the banks were forced to violate not only the spirit, but also the letter of their

---

* See Thorold Rogers, *The History of Agriculture and Prices in England 1259–1793,* 7 vols, (Oxford 1865) and *The Economic Interpretation of History* (London. 1888).
** I shall discuss these facts at greater length in my *Corso di economia politica* which will soon be published – if the *imperium* and the *tribunicia potestas* of Crispi or others do not interfere first.

statutes . . . Finally, on 15 and 16 December 1798, the government seized the strong-boxes from the bank, and had them loaded onto Nelson's ships.'

So ended one act of the play and others began. Other thefts followed until the Bourbon government fell and our present government came to power. Just as the Socialists promise us the moon, so, at that time, the new governments made wonderful promises to the people. But as they did not keep them, is it not natural for us to be afraid that the promises which the Socialists are making will meet with the same fate? The government was new only in name, the same old mistakes went on being made. So why should history stand still? It seems to me that the same causes will produce the same effects, and that if one day the Socialists become masters, we will read the same old news . . .

The followers of the historical method should recognise that there is a grain of truth in my predictions. Why can they not see that the lion they want to employ as secretary is a vicious illiterate brute which only knows how to claw and tear men to pieces? If I am wrong, why won't you teach me the secret by which the new state will be so different from those we already know?

The history of the French Revolution proves that the people do not make a better master than the bourgeoisie. So I conclude by saying that it is folly to leave the disposal of public economy to the will of one or the other.

9 The ethical state

This essay, which came out just a few days after 'Socialism and the duty on grain', is completely different in concept. As can be seen, the change in Pareto's way of thought was neither immediate, nor uniform. Sometimes it is easy to find contradictions in the same essay – something which was to baffle many of his readers and which would cause him to be neglected for many years. However, his faith in the liberal system was to remain intact, his inductive method of scientific research remain unaltered, combining with his original rationalism and basing itself on experimental verification. He reproached the metaphysical thinkers as being quack salesmen of beautiful, empty words. He only believed in what he could touch, see and hear. But the roots of what was to be his contribution of the concept of 'sentiment' in men's actions can be found in the anti-fatalist aspect of the essay. His hatred of abstraction, besides being a way of life, became a scientific method. The romantic exaltations, the esoteric doctrines, the metaphysical theories, the inheritance of medieval thought, left him indifferent – it could be said that they frightened him. Some totalitarian theories already manifest in political economy had frightened him for some time. He now feared that this totalitarian wave could also influence social and political organisation as well as philosophy and economy. Thus, he remained a strong supporter of individual freedom and in opposition to those who spoke of a Golden Age or the City of God. He remained a citizen of this world. Well, then, what was Pareto? – a man of the Renaissance? of the Enlightenment? a follower of Voltaire?[1]

There certainly remains the fact of his aversion to idealism – strengthened by the publication of this essay – which was to reach its climax in the anti-Hegelianism of his *Les Systèmes socialistes* and the polemics against Croce which would occupy him in later years. What is Pareto? – a supporter of an individualistic, anti-fatalist voluntarism? Side by side with the purely economic problems he poses another question which he thinks 'goes beyond the limits of economic science: to know what each of us must do. Whoever confuses determinism with fatalism will answer – nothing.' But whichever of the two is the right interpretation, the fact still remains that in this essay Pareto's opinion is that history *does not* necessarily repeat itself twice, 'If we have reached the point where men no longer rob with violence, can we not also hope that they will stop robbing by stealth?' In the previous essay he had said the opposite.

FROM *Idea liberale*, 29 April 1894.

As I like controversy when it is within the bounds of science (in this way I can always learn something) I shall add a few words to those already written on the subject discussed by Professor Coletti.

The illustrious professor says that the liberal state is an ethical state like that of the socialists. He could be right in certain cases. Both have been supported with metaphysical argument...

When one speaks about the state, more often than not one speaks about an entity which does not exist, and we are back in those wonderful days when one talked about a *substance* modified by *accidents*. It was believed that *whiteness* could exist independently of *white bodies*. The state would therefore be something abstract of which governments are the accidents. Thus, everything that is good is the product of the substance – the state – while everything bad is the fault of the accidents – the government. It is easy, then, to demonstrate that the state is ethical and perfect!

Tritschke says that the state is society in its organisation as a whole. But for Stein and Gneist it is the organism of right (*Rechts organismus*). Even after long research I have not been able to discover this organism and I am like Diogenes, who said to Plato: 'I can see the table and the glass but I cannot see the substance of the table or the glass at all.'

In reality I can see men who provide things for themselves in two ways: either by operating directly or by being forced by other men who command either by divine right, or habit, or who are delegated by the people to do so...

... In the social sciences we are a long way from possessing valid general laws and we often content ourselves with empirical laws directly induced by facts. Observing this principle, many capable men, after long, patient research, have demonstrated that in economic affairs one can provide better for one's own affairs directly rather than through others. As Pliny said: '*Et ideo majores fertilissimum in agro oculum domini esse dixerunt.*' To this inductive law is added Walras' deductive demonstration, which, admitting the principle that man tries to obtain most good with least sacrifice in economic affairs, shows that free competition produces maximum well-being.

All this could be wrong. Show us, and we will change our opinion. But it has nothing to do with the ethical state. Instead, people should be shown either that the facts about which I have spoken are incorrect, or that our line of reasoning in deducing the consequences is faulty. This is just the method that I shall use to examine briefly a subject which seems to be the most important for the 'historic socialists' who affirm that, according to an historic law, the economic functions of the state have increased more and more, and so one must not oppose this tendency...

But to admit that the state every day usurps new economic functions is not enough to prove whether it serves to increase or decrease the quantity of wealth produced. And this is the main question for an economist.

On finding the answer another question arises which, in my opinion, goes beyond the limits of economic science: to know what each of us must do. Whoever confuses determinism with fatalism will answer: nothing ... Whereas, whoever thinks that the single actions of every individual are included in the forces that determine the social phenomena, will try to oppose those who misuse economic science. Now, supposing that, as Professor Coletti says, the state is an instrument which the stronger social classes use, what value can the liberalist doctrine have which, while preaching freedom, must recognise that it will never be realised?

... I do not admit that it will not be possible to realise freedom because it is contrary to the interests of the governing classes ... as the dominant class could oppose economic freedom not only through ill-will but also through ignorance ... Robbing a bank is useful when the safes are full of good money, not when they are only full of filthy, paper money...

Once the strong and powerful robbed in the main streets. This type of social organisation destroyed much wealth and it ended. Today, the powerful have less violent ways of stealing from others. In proportion, they destroy less wealth than before but it is still considerable. Why, then, could there not be further evolution? Perhaps we shall not achieve economic freedom at once, and we shall have to submit to some other fraud, less damaging than the existing one, just as this one is less harmful than its predecessor. If we have reached the point where men no longer rob with violence, can we not also hope that they will stop robbing by stealth? As facts are more useful than reasoning in educating man, I should like socialism to win at once, to burden the bourgeoisie with the yoke that it is imposing on the people. I should like the sides to be changed. At this point it will be asked: why should socialism not continue to command if it wins? I would reply that I am afraid that such an organisation will destroy so much wealth that a great part of the population will die in poverty.

NOTES

1 See G. La Ferla, *Vilfredo Pareto filosofo volteriano* (Florence 1954).

10 The university

As we have already said, Pareto compiled his 'Cronache' for *Giornale degli economisti* from March 1893 to July 1897, when Pantaleoni resigned as editor of the journal. During these years and in this column, Pareto not only conducted his fight for liberalism, but also observed and analysed concrete facts, and set them against his theories. In these regular contributions he created a sociological laboratory in which he achieved the ambition which he has so often expressed – of treating social phenomena in the same way as physics. Existing facts were compared with past facts, and those similarities to which he gave a definite systematic classification in his *Trattato* began to take shape.[1] Mongardini says, 'The Pareto who begins writing "Cronache" is an economist immersed in a "sea of doubts". The Pareto whom we find at the end of "LXIII Cronaca" has become a sociologist who has formulated and proved a series of important hypotheses.'[2]

This essay on the university is one of the shortest and simplest, but it is rather useful in throwing further light on the concept of society on which Pareto was working. Its main problem is that of respect for the law. In weighing up the disorderly state of the university in Italy, he affirms that the existing law, whatever it may be, whether just or unjust, must be respected by all. This, too, is a fixed point of all the liberal traditions and yet, for someone who has read Pareto from beginning to end, it cannot be representative of the change in emphasis in his thinking from discussion to authority.

FROM *Giornale degli economisti*, 1 March 1895.
. . . In Italy nobody cares about the law. One has only to consider the state of the universities. Not a year passes without students striking, universities closing, and disorder of every kind. Does it not occur to the Italians to investigate why such things do not happen in England, Germany and Switzerland? Is it not strange that the same young people who make so much noise in Italy, are among the most sedate and studious when they go and study in Switzerland? The crux of the matter is that there they are in a

THE UNIVERSITY 79

country where the law is universally respected.

Why do they not establish once and for all in Italy a time for examinations and then keep to it? Instead examinations are benign concessions which ministers make at their discretion. So, after having obtained certain concessions one year, it is natural for young people to come back and ask for them the following year. The fact is that to them it seems unjust not to obtain the same things that other students have obtained, and so they pile their disorder on the disorder of the authorities. In addition, politics enter where they have no business to be, and the students know quite well why some professors spend more time cultivating ministers than they do cultivating learning.

In Switzerland they have strange ideas about such things! They say that the students go to the university to study, and the professors to teach. They believe that examinations are a test which serves to find out if young people know the subjects they have been taught, and not a favour of the authorities. If the young people want to criticise any regulation, they are listened to, and if they are right, the regulation is modified, and their wishes fulfilled. But as long as the old regulation is in existence, it is observed, and nobody, neither students nor professors nor public authorities, thinks that he can contravene it. It should be noted that Swiss universities are attended by people from all over the world: Germans, Bulgarians, Serbs, Russians, Rumanians, Italians and so on. The cause of the orderly and beneficial progress of the studies in the Swiss university springs, not from the character of the people, but from the practice of freedom and the honest respect of the law. There is no doubt that in Italy similar causes would have similar effects . . .

NOTES

1 See T. Giacalone-Monaco, 'Le "Cronache" politiche e economiche di Pareto', *Pareto e Sorel*, ed. T. Giacalone-Monaco, 2 vols, (Padua 1960–1).
2 See Pareto, *Cronache italiane*, ed. C. Mongardini (Brescia 1965), p. 31.

11 For and against socialism

1896 was another crucial year for Italy. After the disastrous defeat at the Battle of Adowa where the expeditionary force to Ethiopia was virtually annihilated, Crispi resigned. The reactionary forces tried to clamp down on the ever-increasing discontent by limiting individual freedom more and more. Many of the Liberals of the day, either through cowardice or for their own ends, joined the reactionary forces. Only the Socialists (in 1895 they had clandestinely formed a party in Rome) and a few Liberals were left to defend freedom. It was no chance occurrence that the Socialist Deputy, Colajanni, should have stood shoulder to shoulder with Pantaleoni in his courageous denunciation of the Bank of Rome, and have helped him in the investigation which he conducted. As will be remembered Pantaleoni had already carried out similar investigations, personally paying the price. Once again he encountered censorship and the hostility of the press. However, he was not deterred, and for revealing what had gone on behind the scenes at the surrender of Fort Macallé, he was put on trial. Apparently he had discovered that the Italian garrison had been freed after King Umberto I had assumed responsibility for payment of a debt incurred by a certain Ras Makonnen for a consignment of arms. Pantaleoni, who now taught at the University of Naples, was forced not only to resign his post for the second time, but also to leave Italy. As G. de Rosa observes, 'Another illustrious Liberal economist has been obliged to leave Italy owing to a situation which is making the life of honest defenders of the Liberal conception impossible.'[1] On this occasion, paying back a favour which his friend had done for him, Pareto used his influence to ensure that Pantaleoni was offered the Chair of Political Economy at Geneva.

But Pantaleoni was not the only example of political persecution in the Italy of 1896. The hardest hit were the intellectuals and Socialist militants. This new atmosphere drove Pareto towards a fresh feeling of solidarity with the persecuted Socialists who, with a few Liberals, seemed once more to be the only defenders of freedom in the struggle against the authoritarian state and the militarism which squandered

the hard-earned savings of the poorer classes. In considering that –
'if the bourgeoisie wish to fight the Socialists effectively they must do
better than them in order to win' – there is not only the inheritance of
the Marxist conception of the class struggle, but also the insight of the
cyclic succession of the élites.

FROM *Il Secolo*, 20–21 June 1896.
The economic basis of socialism is definitely wrong. Private
property has produced our civil progress and for many centuries
it will remain the fundamental basis of every civilised people.

Socialism, however, has had the great merit of listening to the
complaints of the people who suffer because of the prejudices,
vices and faults of the bourgeoisie. It has scorned those old-
fashioned ways of thinking to which many of the bourgeoisie still
cling. While the ruling classes ceaselessly amass armaments and
turn Europe into a fortified camp and burden the lives of the poor
with heavier and heavier taxes in order to satisfy their vanity and
lust for military glory and bloody conquests, the Socialists – with
undiminished faith – have fully understood the need which the
poor have for peace, and are not afraid of those who say that with
the fall of militarism will also come the fall of political institutions.
By contrast, the timid bourgeoisie shake with fright before this
threat, and if they preach peace in the evening, the next morning
they approve of every expense incurred by the militarists. So the
ruling classes leave the Socialists in isolation to ponder about the
people's need for peace and justice. In Italy the first person who
effectively revealed the horrible bank speculations was Napoleone Colajanni, whereas Crispi appeared as the saviour of all the
speculators and sent the Socialists, who asked for justice and
honesty, to prison. Thus the Italian ruling classes have made
socialism the synonym of honesty . . .

The people believe that there must be justice in this world.
They love, want, and need this justice, and so they go to those
who promise it. Our bourgeoisie promise it with their lips but
deny it in their hearts. They would like to give justice but they
cannot because they are afraid of disrupting political institutions
and hence are unwilling to hurt those who are really guilty. The
people can only turn to the Socialists . . .

But if the bourgeoisie wish to fight the Socialists effectively,
they must do better than them in order to win. One is forced to

conclude that wherever in Europe the bourgeoisie are more honest, right and just, socialism flourishes less. In Switzerland where the bourgeoisie are so, the people reject through a referendum all laws which have only a slight touch of socialism. On the other hand, in Spain socialism flourishes – assuredly not because of a surplus of freedom.

Militarism and protectionism are the two principal sources of socialism. Whoever accepts these two causes must also resign himself to accepting the effects without blaming others.

NOTES

1 Pareto, *Lettere a Maffeo Pantaleoni*, p. 416.

12 Course in political economy

1896 was also the year in which the first volume of Pareto's *Cours d'économie politique* appeared. It was his first systematic work and can be called a pioneering work in that he provided a sociological base for his predominantly economic studies. Man as a citizen – for whose sake the battle of political freedom had been fought for more than twenty-five years – now became the subject of economic study. Political economy must take into account the individual, his tastes and desires. The *Cours* was the first really scientific, elaborated fruit of Pareto's work which not only represented a maturation of his methodology, but also an advance in the political economy of that time.

Before Pareto, economists had based their studies either on the hedonistic hypothesis of personal interest or on an abstract formalism. In both cases neither feelings nor moral or religious beliefs were used as evidence. Pareto was perhaps the first to discover the need to use a concept of psycho-sociological equilibrium in political economy. In giving this credit to Pareto one must not forget that a first synthesis between hedonistic theories and those of the classical school had been tried by Marshall, Cournot, Edgeworth and, in an even more elaborate form, by Walras. But neither must one forget – as de Maria reminds us – that Pareto went further, by affirming the subjective need of inter-dependence 'and by making socio-economic equilibrium the mirror of subjective equilibrium'.[1] The interdependence is a *datum* and, even if subjective, it is scientifically possible to analyse it. It is a subjective *datum* because at the bottom of everything are 'the actions and individual judgements of value which make up economic problems, and not the actions or the judgements of the masses', as Walras thought.[2]

So – Pareto's economic, social system is an unstable system which man tries to stabilise continually through the hypotheses that represent the universal aspect in research, while *values*, like tastes, represent the contingent aspect. In order to understand this concept better, it is useful to remember the controversy between Pareto and Croce which we shall discuss in more detail later. To the latter, who spoke about values in an indefinite way, Pareto wrote, 'I see that you use the term *value*. Could you tell me what precisely this word means in your writing?... The term *value* corresponds to extremely complex feelings in man. The task of science is to get rid of that complexity and study separately the elements of which it is made up. For example, it is said that an object is *valuable* when it *costs* a lot of money ... It is also said that a certain wine costs much but is of little *value*. Here the term value indicates the pleasure that a wine procures for one or more individuals ... It can be said that gold is of great *value* everywhere and this means that everywhere men are looking for gold. Going on talking we could find many examples. You must admit that unless we know exactly what term we are talking about, we are going round in circles ... I suppose that in your writing *value* indicates either enjoyment, or at least something in which enjoyment plays a main part ... Therefore, the concept of *utility*, *value*, *ophelimity*[3] is not "the same economic action in the measure in which it is well conducted" ... but a relationship of convenience between a thing and a man ... so I deny that *value* exists only in the moment of exchange.'[4]

But if the relationship between man and thing is always a matter of convenience, then is the term *value* tied to the term *quantity*? In the same letter he reminds us how, in man, the term *value* simply indicates 'choice of quantity', while in animals it becomes a qualitative choice, as they are attracted by the food which they prefer, even if little. Is the dualism of Pareto's method which we have already discussed contradicted here by economic quantification? It is a problem we shall try to answer later on.

BOOK I: *Personal capital*
As we shall see, the first volume – published a year before the other – was subjected to much criticism, especially by English economists, and is another example of the dualism with which Pareto always faced his problems. Man is examined under the double profile of subject – as an agent, having will, taste and desires – and object – as economic capital. In studying man's presence in the world in relation to space, goods produced, and wealth consumed, Pareto makes us realise that this presence is determined both by genetic force – subjective instinct – and social interest in the increase or decrease of population.

He criticised Malthus' theory because, by using population only on the relationship between economic goods produced and economic goods consumed, Malthus did not take into consideration the subjective aspect represented by the genetic force. The above book set the seal on his hatred of abstraction and metaphysics. The concrete, deductive method which he had applied in his early works (having read Mill) seems to have been put aside. The new theoretical formulation finds its finest expression in the simple, but extremely meaningful sentence: 'a good workman can be recognised by his work'. He used this pragmatic concept as a basis for his analysis. With a kind of sangfroid which many were to consider cynicism, he made it evident that 'only with economic progress do certain men in possession of sufficient capital cease to transform their savings into that personal capital represented by their children'.

To those who considered a return to the natural state to be to a lost Golden Age, Pareto pointed out how life held more sufferings for man in that state than in that of the industrial society of their time. As can be seen, although he criticised metaphysics on progress, it is not true, as some maintain, that he did not believe in progress. This point of the greater unhappiness of primitive societies is enlarged upon in *Les Systèmes socialistes*, and, in an age where it was the fashion to criticise technology, he was to be accused of 'mechanism'. He understood that man was able to express his humanitarian instincts towards children, the weak and the old, only after the accumulation of capital had brought about economic development. So, the individual can make a 'comparison between the economic and moral cost of producing men' and it is only through this comparison that there 'springs the reason which causes this production to be increased or restricted'.

This is another subject on which Pareto could support the thesis of the uselessness and harm of trying to upset the equilibrium between economic object and moral subject in order to impose false behaviour and equilibrium through laws from above. The same concept is expressed in the same period in his essay 'La Courbe des revenus', where he said: 'Classical political economy has been accused of occupying itself primarily with production and neglecting distribution. On the contrary, we see that classical economy is right. There is only one way to obtain a more balanced distribution for the poor: improve production and, in this way obtain an increase in wealth superior to the demographic increase . . . The efforts made by the "socialism" of the state to change such a distribution artificially only have the effect of provoking a destruction of wealth. In other words they achieve a result opposite to the one they intend, that is, they worsen the conditions of the poorer classes instead of improving them.'[5]

Was this a conservative, sceptical turning point in his thinking?

BOOK II: *Correlation in social phenomena*

Another novelty worthy of note in Pareto's *Cours* is the concept of
correlation – by which social phenomena act and react among themselves, and by which every effect is not only produced by the cause,
but by a multitude of causes which meet by pure chance. 'It is sufficient to remember the Athenians', said Pareto, in order to give a better
explanation of this concept of multi-causation. 'The physical conditions of Attica have remained the same throughout the centuries.
However, only once was it inhabited by a wonderful people like the
Athenians.' As Pareto went deeper and deeper into the study of
society, his activism was diluted into a type of descriptivism in an
attempt to avoid the collision between the concept of causality and the
concept of casuality. He had already quoted Mill, de Molinari, Buckle,
Thorold Rogers, Ammon, Bagehot and Delage many times, but now
perhaps he was also influenced by the structuralism of Ferdinand de
Saussure – at least, Busino thinks so, when he says that Pareto was
beginning to examine social phenomena both 'from the point of view
of its historic evaluation (diachronic), and from a synchronic point of
view, as a system of interdependent elements which are in equilibrium
at a certain historic moment'.[6] Influenced or not by Saussure, the concepts of justice and injustice seem to have been suffering an eclipse
behind the expository language of the dispassionate observer.

In the passage from undifferentiation to social differentiation and
from democracy to tyranny, and vice-versa, he confined himself to
pointing out how one or the other can be more useful according to the
historical moment. He said 'It is impossible to express an absolute
judgement on the different social regimes. Their action depends above
all on the particular moment of evolution being considered.' But is
there anything that man can do to improve social organisations besides
economic production? It would seem that the answer is 'no'. In fact,
Pareto affirmed: 'In most cases the best we can do is to retain the
organisations tested by experience, while seeking to improve them as
much as possible.' As if a deep, religious feeling had taken possession
of him, Pareto observed nature and bowed reverently before her
eternity. 'The laws of nature are far above man's prejudices and passions. They are eternal, unchangeable. They are the expression of a
creative power. They represent existence as it is, as it must be, as it can
be in no other way.' Far above the justice of men he saw the nemesis of
history. He noted that the same wealth desired by all 'can be in itself a
source of corruption and decadence'. As if in a mystic ecstasy, but

with firm faith, he said: 'The imperfection of the human spirit makes the division of the sciences necessary – it distinguishes astronomy from physics and chemistry, natural sciences from social sciences. In its essence science is one – it is none other than truth.'

He did not realise that in speaking about the essence of science, he placed himself willy-nilly in the same position as those whom he had so much derided in 'The ethical state' for having spoken about a 'substance modified by accidents' and for believing that 'whiteness can exist independently of white bodies'. Is the inductive method used in the past and also in the first volume of his Cours definitely ousted by the rationalistic deductive method? Pareto would try to give an answer to this in his Manuale di economia politica.

FROM Cours d'économie politique professé à l'Université de Lausanne, 1896.

159 Political economy must consider the composition of the population. One could say that, in general, the individuals from twenty to fifty years of age are those who support the others by their work . . .

184 In France it is observed that two causes influence the movement of the population. If studied carefully, they can be found to have their roots in economics.

Peasants and smallholders, not wanting to divide their property, limit the number of their children. If, for example, new methods of agriculture were to make the subdivision of the already-existing inheritance advantageous, this would be a reason for smallholders to increase the size of their families. On the other hand, the wealthy also limit the number of their children to avoid their falling from the position into which they are born . . .

186 Seeing that an influence of economic forces over the population exists, let us then study the nature of such an influence.

Economic forces are not the only ones which, together with the genetic force, act on the movement of the population (257). The action of the economic forces can be immediate and delayed, and in the latter case this action can be manifested through other forces which must be taken into consideration. If the genetic force were the only one, it would bring about a maximum increase in the population . . .

192 Forces exist which act against the genetic force – limiting the increase in population. This proposition will be proved if we show

that the increase in population would be greater than it really is
if the genetic force were the only force . . .

198 So, we must conclude that in our epoch there have been
increases which there have not been in the past, and which there
cannot continue to be in the future (**211**) . . .

200 . . . According to Malthus, the population is limited by
subsistence. As this increases in an arithmetical progression, such
must be the real progression of the population . . . The population under the command of the genetic force tends to double in
twenty-five years . . . This second thesis could be true but it is
not supported by sufficient proof (**211**); the first is certainly
wrong (**212**).

206 It is often objected against the theory of the limitation of
the population by economic forces, that it would be possible to
furnish means of subsistence to a larger number of men than that
which the earth supports now. Such an affirmation is exact from a
general point of view . . . but man would soon find himself
threatened by lack of space . . .

211 . . . Let us take the data referring to the population of
England and Wales, starting from 1801 . . . We find a curve
which represents a geometric progression with an average annual
increase of 13 per cent . . . We find that if the law of increase
observed from 1801 to 1891 were to continue for another 658
years, there would be an inhabitant for every square metre of
ground. As it is certain that such a dense population could not
live, whatever the economic progress, it is also certain that there
are signs to show that this rate of increase is tending to lessen.

212 We have seen that from 1801 to 1891 the effective population of England and Wales has increased in a geometric progression. It is certain, however, that the well-being of the average
Englishman has not decreased. This springs from the fact that
during this time wealth has increased with a progression more
rapid than the geometric progression. This is sufficient to show
that Malthus' proposition, according to which wealth would
increase in an arithmetical progression, is wrong – at least in this
case . . .

222 Malthus' mistake consists in this: there are a large number
of causes (A), (B), (C) . . . all equally indispensable to the prosperity of the people. For example, to assure prosperity it is necessary: (A) that the population should not increase too rapidly; (B)

that an organisation should exist with the sole purpose of protecting property instead of stealing from the people; (c) that the greater part of the wealth produced should not be destroyed uselessly; etc., etc.. Malthus considers cause (A). It is not difficult for him to demonstrate that this proof is indispensable. He erroneously concludes that the others, (B), (C), and so on have no influence.

The two following propositions are both wrong: (1) The well-being of the people depends exclusively on the action of the government or on certain economic and social measures (free trade, protectionism, socialist organisation), and does not depend on the rate of increase of the population. (2) The well-being of the people depends exclusively on the rate of increase of the population and does not depend on the action of the government or economic and social measures.

The mistakes which are the result of neglecting certain causes of economic and social phenomena are many and frequent (**605**).

225 . . . Extremely complex and partly neglected laws link the birth-rate, the death-rate and economic conditions without it being possible to establish that any *one* of the phenomena is the cause of the others. In a position so nicely balanced, every disturbance of any one of these movements upsets the others. If the economic conditions remain constant, the increase in the birth-rate will make the death-rate increase. One must not forget that in reality these last two phenomena will in their turn act on the economic phenomena. So one must not consider the 'preventive and repressive obstacles' as entities independent of the movement of the population which limit such a movement in a fixed way. Instead one must always bear in mind the mutual dependence of these two phenomena.

226 *Preventive obstacles* can only act in one of the following ways: (a) limiting the union of the sexes; (b) decreasing the number of births in each union . . .

227 There has been much discussion to find out which of these two forms is preferable; and this often accounts for the controversy arising from Malthus' theory . . . This is the work of morals, philosophy, physiology and other similar sciences.

235 *Repressive obstacles* consist of an increase in the death-rate. It is probable that in other times such obstacles had a large influence, and that they still do on those peoples who are outside the main stream of civilisation . . .

239 Economic conditions act on the tastes of men. They also produce a biological reaction. They not only have subjective effects, but also objective effects. The total lack of food assuredly kills men whatever their tastes and habits . . . By contrast, and this is confirmed by statistics, a certain level of well-being favours the longevity of man. It is only possible to drain marshland, provide cities with drinking-water, and, in general, to take the measures necessary to avoid epidemics, at great expense.

244 When an adult can just scrape enough together to live by working, it seems natural for the weak, i.e. children and the aged, to be sacrificed. This conclusion is verified in part by the observation of what happens among the poorer class of our population, and from the many eye-witness accounts of travellers among primitive peoples. Among the classical writers we can find plenty of evidence to make us think that not even our own races have been able to avoid these things happening.

245 Abortion, infanticide, exposure of infants were once accepted by law and morals. The accumulation of capital produced civilisation and has made it possible for the weak to be protected. Stuart tells how an Australian roasted and ate his sick child. In Southern Africa children are put as bait in lion-traps. In the Sandwich Islands a great number of children were killed. In Tahiti at least two-thirds of the children were killed by their parents* . . .

246 In ancient societies abortion and the exposure of infants were frequent and did not incur any moral obloquy **. . . Only with economic progress do certain men in the possession of sufficient capital cease to transform their savings into that personal capital represented by their children.

247 A community cannot subsist if it does not bring up a certain number of children. The same reason does not protect the aged. Some uncivilised peoples put them to death; we have proof that our race, too, has used this system . . .

248 Here is the course that evolution seems to have followed: in the dawn of civilisation the fate of the aged was one of the most horrible; death was often preferable and the habit of killing the

---

* *Polynesian Researches*, vol. I, pp. 334–40.
** The Law of Gortyna, III, 21, 23, legitimises it. For Athens see Aristophanes, *The Clouds*, 531–2; *The Frogs*, 1190.

aged frequent. When man's work became more productive, the population was able to feed the aged and the sick. Then, when man no longer needed to use his physical strength to procure the means of subsistence, the aged were able to contribute to the increase in production. In the end, in our epoch, thanks to the accumulation of capital, it is possible to think about guaranteeing every need of the aged and sick through old age pensions.

256 As compensation for the cost of producing men there are the pleasures and advantages that parents receive from begetting and rearing their children, that is the satisfaction of the reproductive instinct, the moral satisfaction that children give, and finally, the economic profit which the majority of society gains. The influence of this last advantage is very marked. De Molinari says: 'In agricultural production where children are employed from early in the morning, and above all in manufacturing industry where they replace adults in many jobs, it is profitable to multiply them . . . '

257 From the comparison between the economic and moral cost of producing men and the economic and moral advantages which are obtained, springs the reason for broadening or restricting this production . . .

261 John Stuart Mill cites a large number of laws which discouraged marriage in different countries, and which he considers capable of preventing an excessive increase in the population.* He quotes as an example Bavaria, where the law forbade people from marrying unless they could produce evidence of having sufficient means of livelihood. In 1868, this law was repealed, and now it can be seen that it only served to increase the number of illegitimate births . . .

264 Ancient Rome had a wealth of legislation on this matter. Camillus, when he was censor, adopted measures against bachelors . . . Augustus reminds us that from the beginning of the Republic, laws were made to encourage the procreation of children . . . But all this legislation was to no avail. It was incapable of increasing the number either of marriages or of children . . .**

265 In France, too, several laws encouraged the increase in the birth-rate – yet their effect was nil. Lavasseur says: 'Such mea-

* J. Stuart Mill, *Political Economy*, vol. II, Ch. XI.
** Tacitus, *Annals*, III, 25.

sures are fruitless. A husband and wife do not calculate beforehand that for every child that they bring into the world, the
seventh will lower their taxes by nine francs a year.' And he rightly
concludes: 'The progress of nations is derived from causes of a
more intimate nature; unnatural stimuli can cause harm, but do
not help to achieve the desired end.'

268 Even if we confine ourselves to a consideration of economic forces alone, we must still observe that the ophelimity of
parents is not identical with that of their children. The line of
reasoning leading us to demonstrate that free trade guarantees
maximum ophelimity is based on the hypothesis that between
the two parties each is free to choose what he prefers. It is certainly not the son who chooses to represent the transformation of
savings of personal capital. It is his parents who decide for him.
It derives, then, from the necessity for a legislative tutelage of
infants. The consequence is that it is the selfishness of the
parents, who bring more children into the world than they can
conveniently support, which is the greater cause of human
poverty. It is really absurd to expect man to be provident in every
act of life, with the exception of one, which is one of the most
important – that of bringing a human being into the world.

In spite of all the metaphysical theories which have been formulated on this subject, it is quite clear that the greatest ophelimity is only obtained when procreation is proportional to the
needs of society for such personal capital; in the same way as this
maximum ophelimity is attained only if the number of locomo-
tives, sewing-machines, oxen, horses, is in proportion to the
utility that these, as capital, have for society.

605 Forgetting the mutual relationship between social phenomena has caused very many errors. The idea that the economic
and moral well-being of a community depends exclusively or
principally on the form of its government is still widespread.
Reacting against these mistakes, some economists have made the
opposite error of denying that the form of government has influenced the well-being of a people. The two points of view are
equally erroneous. There are also theories which attribute to the
race a pre-eminent influence in social questions. The Ancient
Greeks did not admit barbarians as their equals. Similar theories
in different forms have sprung up again in our day with respect to
the Latin, Anglo-Saxon and German races. If the South Ameri-

can states occupied by the Latin race present differences when compared with those of North America, occupied by the Anglo-Saxon and German races, it can, it is said, be concluded that such differences depend exclusively on the *race*. But why have these races gone to these different countries? If they have gone there it is because they have found favourable conditions. Why, then, can we not admit that physical and climatic conditions have such an important role and such a strong influence on race, as to modify or even completely transform it? The English rule India, but do not people it. If some English families were to acclimatise themselves to India, it is probable that their descendants would lose the characteristics of energy and activity which are typical of their race – as has happened to the Portuguese in Goa. On the other hand, it would be wrong to attribute to the physical conditions of a country the only influence that there is on social phenomena. One has only to remember the Athenians. The physical conditions of Attica have remained the same throughout the centuries. However, only once was it inhabited by a wonderful people like the Athenians. All this is explained by the complexity of the interdependence of social phenomena. The existence of the ancient people of Athens depended on a great number of circumstances. The greater the number of circumstances, the smaller the probability that they should occur together. For this reason we should not be surprised if this phenomenon occurred only once over a period of many centuries.

607 It is often asserted that the religion and philosophy of a people cause its moral conditions. In the same way, such an assertion could legitimately be reversed and it could be said that moral conditions were the cause. It is evident that an essentially immoral people would not adopt either a refined religion or a refined philosophy. In this case one cannot really speak about cause or effect. These are phenomena which interact.

608 Socialist schools consider the distribution of wealth to be the main cause of social phenomena. By modifying the cause, all the effects are changed. Unlike the Evolutionists, they think that a change in human nature takes place rapidly, that is, as soon as the distribution of wealth is changed. The question has been discussed at length by Lombroso on one side and by Colajanni on the other. For Lombroso, a criminal is genetically abnormal. But crime is committed under the influence of other external causes, among which there are economic causes. I do not want to deny the importance of these two causes, but the problem is to see the degree of their importance. For Lombroso, the anthropological factors predominate; for Colajanni, and even more for Marx, economic causes and education act almost exclusively. One could say *both* that economic conditions modify the moral and intellectual qualities of man, *and* that these qualities modify the economic conditions. It is sufficient to observe that improvident and lazy individuals are born as often to the poor as to the rich. The influence of economic conditions resides in the fact that those who are born poor can surrender more readily to the temptation of crime. The influence of vices on the distribution of wealth is proved by the fact that those who are born rich can ruin themselves and fall into poverty. So, it is wrong to affirm both that poverty is always the consequence of vice and that it *never* is.

636 There are things that have survived which have no influence on the capacity of a people to compete in economic affairs and in war – the vestments of Catholic priests, the robes of English judges, much ceremonial, and so on. Sometimes a function is lost and then reappears again. This is a *revival* . . . Compulsory trade unions which some would like to organise in our day are a revival of the medieval guilds, and not a survival.

637 The more useless the surviving institutions, the heavier their burden. It is probable that many aspects of the English, French, Italian, Spanish parliamentary regimes have outlived their usefulness . . . In our day, the same can be said of war.

658 In general a despotic regime, whether that of the monarch or that of the Jacobins, possesses very little differentiation . . . while freedom and obvious heterogeneity are synonymous.

659 The differentiation of human societies generally begins with the formation of an aristocratic class. This is merely a phase of evolution. If the differentiation proceeds, the aristocratic class loses its power. England is more heterogeneous and differentiated now than at the time of the Plantagenets. It is impossible to formulate an absolute judgement on the different social regimes. Their action depends above all on the particular movement of evolution under consideration. Despotism can represent great progress if it is useful in differentiating a homogeneous, but anarchic, society. In its turn the aristocratic regime represents fresh progress, and, as this phase always occurs in evolution, it can be said that people are indebted to the aristocracy for their freedom. In Ancient Greece, tyranny represented a return to a lesser heterogeneity and was thus a sign of decadence. The English barons gave freedom to their country. In France, Louis XI and Richelieu, by emasculating the aristocracy, became the worst enemies of freedom.

660 Despotic governments instinctively and severely forbid their subjects to form associations and these intermediary organisms between individual and state are, in fact, one of the most powerful agents of social differentiation . . .

662 Within certain limits guardianship seems indispensable. Where it is lacking completely it seems that the individual and society perish. As to private wardship one need only remember the minor or the lunatic. As to society, observation teaches us that there exists no people, either barbarous or civilised, which has not some type of government. Anarchists, who want to abolish every type of guardianship, are as worthy of consideration as a fairy story.

663 For private guardianship to represent an effective benefit for the ward, three conditions are necessary: (a) the guardian must be intellectually and morally superior to the ward; (b) the guardian must use his authority in the interests of the ward; (c) the guardian must not prevent the development of those faculties in the ward which enable him to organise his own life.

670 As man has an absolute need to live in society, and as society cannot exist without some kind of guardianship, the individual receives a greater or lesser utility from such guardianship. For a people, the worst of all governments is a lesser evil than no government at all.

672 Given a certain society – the form of government best capable of providing the greatest utility is an insoluble problem in the present state of social science. In most cases, the best that we can do is to retain those forms tested by experience, and seek to improve them as much as possible. To want to change everything – letting ourselves be dragged along by abstractions – is as absurd as to want to keep everything – letting ourselves be guided by a loathing for all that is new. These considerations make us favour economic freedom. If we are ignorant of what is the best form of government, we know, however, that the forms existing now are clumsy and complicated machines . . . Therefore, it is

worth our while to reduce the work of these machines to a minimum.

687 The characteristic of the more civilised, modern peoples
is intellectual, moral and religious freedom of the individual,
differentiation, and lack of any state authority in these areas.
Many think that this has no connection with material and economic progress, and believe that Watt's steam engine could have
been invented in antiquity or in the Middle Ages, if the men of
the period had had the necessary knowledge. This is a serious
error, because you cannot isolate a fact from its environmental
context.

If a man like Edison had invented the telephone in the Middle
Ages, overcoming the material difficulties of application, both he
and his apparatus would simply have been burned . . .

692 The movement which leads to differentiation is so essential to progress that it would probably continue even after the
installation of a socialist regime. If not, society would decline
into barbarism. Even now, parliamentary time is insufficient, and
a great number of bills are waiting to be passed. So, a socialist
parliament would find it impossible to pass the laws designed to
regulate all production. It would, therefore, have to hand over
this work to appropriate organisations which, of necessity, would
have to be responsible for the success of that sector of production
which they directed. In their turn these organisations would
reciprocate with the individuals involved. This would produce
a state of affairs similar, except in name, to that which we know
and the result would be a considerable waste of time and wealth.
It is probably one of those oscillations which are rather frequent
social phenomena, but it could be one of those long-lasting
oscillations – like the one which brought about the decline of
Graeco-Latin civilisation.

993 Many people assume that all men are born equal and that
the differences between them are due only to the education which
they receive and to the social conditions in which they find themselves. These theories conflict absolutely with the facts and are
therefore untenable. This is particularly evident with regard to
intellectual differences. It is absurd to expect that an appropriate
system of education can transform everyone into a Newton. It
has always been said that poets are born. Every educator knows
that there are excellent minds which are not cut out at all for

COURSE IN POLITICAL ECONOMY

certain sciences like mathematics. If there are these differences
regarding intellectual aspects, there will also be differences
regarding moral aspects . . .

994 In reality, those inborn qualities which allow education to
develop an extremely delicate, moral conscience are found perhaps as rarely as the inborn qualities necessary for the formation
of a good mathematician, a good writer, or a good painter . . .

996 . . . To say that there are men in society who are richer in
certain qualities, is not the same as saying that theirs is a class
of men *absolutely better* than the rest of the population. The mistake is made when it is concluded that these men considered
'better' *must* govern the others.

997 The same mistake is made when one talks of a natural
'right' that certain races should have – as 'superior' races – of
dominating others; or when one talks about races and countries
where civilisation cannot develop of its own accord, and so they
must import it . . . Any animal breeder knows perfectly well that
there are no absolute, superior breeds – there are only breeds
which are superior to others in determined circumstances and
for determined aims alone. There is no sense in asking which
breed of horse is the best. It is necessary to see whether its function is racing or pulling a cart . . .

1000 . . . There is no reason for believing that the form of the
skull and the colour of the hair and eyes are evidence of racial
superiority . . . In the same way, there is no reason for believing
that the aristocracy produces a greater number of scientists than
the bourgeoisie or the common people. Anyone who has been
among workmen knows that among them can be found people
of a much greater intelligence than that of certain scientists
weighed down with academic honours.

1028 . . . In the upper classes of society, biological selection
acts less rigorously. A certain number of individuals who touch
the lowest degree of degeneration are eliminated by tuberculosis
and other illnesses, but a greater number are saved and reproduce thanks to the favourable conditions created by the wealth
that they possess. In the lower orders of society, poverty, crime
and repression of crime, destroy a large proportion of these sick
individuals, a part of whom becomes sterile, having reached the
breaking point of prostitution and alcoholism.

1029 Wealth, in itself, can be a source of corruption and decadence, but there is no need to cite this in order to explain the decadence of the aristocracy. Let us consider two groups A and B. Let us suppose in group A that the healthy, in reproducing themselves, produce a certain proportion of weaklings, and that these, in their turn, reproduce only weaklings. If these two groups are different one from the other, just because of the fact that in group A a higher proportion of weaklings reaches maturity, while in group B the higher proportion of weaklings perishes, it can be seen how, after a few generations, group A will become greatly degenerate . . .

1053 Different economic classes have different interests. Obviously an ordinary workman has not the same economic interests as a large landowner, or the possessor of a great fortune. Every class tries as much as possible to throw the weight of taxation onto the other classes. Every class tries to turn public expenditure to its own advantage. The socialists are absolutely right, therefore, in attributing great importance to the 'class struggle' and in asserting that this is the great factor which rules history. For this reason the works of Marx and Loria are worthy of attention.

1054 The class struggle assumes two forms at all times. One consists in economic competition, which, when it is free, produces the greatest ophelimity. Every class, like every individual, even if it only acts for its own advantage, is indirectly useful to others. Besides, as this competition does not destroy but produces wealth, it contributes indirectly to increasing the level of the minimum income, and in diminishing the inequality in incomes. The other form of class struggle is the one whereby every class does its utmost to seize the reins of the government, using it as an instrument to rob the other classes. The struggle which certain individuals begin, under various pretexts, in order to take over the wealth produced by others, is the motive which dominates the whole history of mankind. It can even be said that only in our own age are we beginning to find out this truth.

1066 In all ages men have attributed their ills to imaginary causes. In Ancient Rome they shouted, 'Throw the Christians to the lions!'; in the medieval cities, 'Death to the Longobards!'; now, once again it is, 'Death to the Jews!' It is no more than an irresponsible outburst, like that of a child who hits the object he has bumped into.

1068 . . . The laws of nature are far above man's prejudices and passions. They are eternal, unchangeable. They are the expression of a creative power. They represent existence as it is, as it must be, as it can be in no other way. Man can get to know these laws, but he cannot change them. The greatest things, like the smallest, are subject to them. The stars and the planets follow the laws discovered by those geniuses, Newton and Laplace, in the same way that atoms obey the laws of chemistry and living beings obey the laws of biology. The imperfection of the human spirit makes the division of the sciences necessary – distinguishing astronomy from physics and chemistry, natural sciences from social sciences – but in its essence science is one – it is none other than Truth.

NOTES

1 G. de Maria, 'Introduction' to Pareto, *Scritti teorici* (Milan 1952), p. x.
2 *Ibid.* p. xi.
3 A word invented by Pareto to signify a concept of *utility* from the subjective point of view of the particular persons concerned.
4 See Pareto, 'Lettera a Benedetto Croce', *Giornale degli economisti*, August 1900, pp. 139–62.
5 See *Le Monde économique*, 25 July 1896, pp. 99–100.
6 G. Busino, 'Introduction' to Pareto, *Scritti sociologici* (Turin 1966), pp. 27–8.

13 The new theories of economics

Even if Bousquet considered Pareto's *Cours* 'the book in which there is least to criticise in form and substance',[1] such a judgement would not have been shared by many. No sooner had Pareto finished writing the first volume of his *Cours* than the criticisms began to pour in. Although he might use the analytic method of investigation, his position was still close to that of Walras. Perhaps because of this, the English school did not like him – they were the traditional enemies of Walras' theories. To underline this fact, Pareto wrote to Pantaleoni on 15 September 1907: 'Nearly fifteen years ago Walras started his quarrel with Edgeworth. Walras treated the problem of equilibrium from a *general* aspect, Marshall and Edgeworth wanted to treat it in detail.'[2]

Criticism came not only from England, but also from socialists over his law of the income curve as it concerned the distribution of wealth (discussed above). More or less the same criticisms were made by Sorel in his review of the *Cours* in *Le Devenir social*.[3] In fact all these criticisms converged towards a more general criticism – that of determinism. To avoid this, Pareto introduced the concept of interdependence in his second volume. This volume was better received in England than the first, but did not completely placate the antagonism caused chiefly by the law of the income curve which Pareto had begun working on in 1893. But that was the year in which he believed – rightly or wrongly – that all the ills of Italy stemmed from the fact that the ruling class respected neither economic nor juridical law. In *Lettres d'Italie* he wrote: 'Unwilling to take the trouble to study political economy – as they believe they will find it condemns their actions – the governing class deny that the natural laws of production and the distribution of wealth exist.'[4]

The certain operation of those laws – both juridical and economic – which for him had been the guarantee of individual freedom, now turned against him and became the cause of his being accused of determinism. These criticisms were not silenced by his defensive conclusion in the second volume of his *Cours* on the 'eternal, unchangeable

laws of nature'. In order to escape the impasse into which these criticisms had driven him Bousquet says that Pareto wrote this essay in the
spirit of 'a consecration to a reply to the critics of his *Cours*'.[5] The two
volumes of the *Cours* – we do not know whether intentionally or not –
seem to move parallel with each other. This was also noted in the law
of the income curve on the distribution of wealth, the reading of which
thus, perhaps, became controversial. On the one hand, as Cirillo
observes, 'he was definitely aware of the limitations of his law. He
emphasised, in fact, that "certainly, when it is a question of laws
which are purely empirical, one can never be too careful".' On the
other hand, Pareto felt drawn towards a belief that 'his law was valid
for *all* people and *all* epochs'.[6] In the second volume Pareto had
already introduced an element of dynamics between the two concepts
which Cirillo notes. He moved further away from Walras who, with
his abstract vision of economics, thought that it was possible to 'draw
certain economic conclusions from metaphysical principles of jurisprudence' while still continuing to believe 'in the efficiency of experimental methods to the exclusion of others'. To make this system more
flexible he emphasised that it was arbitrary, by asserting that 'the
division into which we break up the aggregate – in studying exchange,
production and capitalisation separately – is quite arbitrary, although
it may be a useful aid to study'. One must be careful, though, that
there are no arbitrary acts inside the laws which constitute the system.
Arbitrary acts can, however, exist in the very moment of the initial
choice of system.

It is not, therefore, a matter of knowing how to read the laws of
nature, but of knowing how to discover them through artistic intuition,
Pareto being convinced that 'art has always anticipated science'. In
this concept he almost certainly began to feel the influence of Sorel.
With this concept of an arbitrary act in the initial choice, and the concept of the progression of *approximations* in mind, Pareto put forward
the premise for a further position in finding the point of equilibrium
between the laws of nature and the laws of man: myth or reason?

FROM *The Journal of Political Economy*, September 1897.
. . . As a matter of fact, art has always preceded science. When in
the course of evolution of human knowledge art and science have
drifted apart, critics have never been wanting who were ready to
assert that science was productive of no useful results. Criticisms
of this kind are largely founded on the fact that a science has not

nearly so immediate a utility as the cognate art. It is also to be said that art cannot confine itself to its teaching function; it must also demonstrate its persuasive power. Consequently art is obliged to make use of certain rhetorical devices with which science has nothing to do. As the most persuasive reasoning is not always the soundest, it happens that economic science often differs from economic art in the means of expression employed. Science considers means of expression solely from the point of view of their power to disclose the truth, whereas art must primarily consider their effectiveness as means of persuasion. From this it follows that economic science will not hesitate to use mathematics, psychology, physiology, etc.; whereas art can draw on these sciences to but a very limited extent for fear of not being understood by the majority of those whom it seeks to persuade...

Let us therefore put aside, once for all, discussions regarding the greater or lesser utility of science or its power of persuading anyone to choose for himself between alternatives, and let us direct our attention solely to the laws governing certain phenomena...

Economic questions up to this time have too often been construed to coincide with questions of law. The time has now come to separate the two, just as in its time a separation was made between chemistry and physics. What are the economic results of strikes? This is a question distinct from the other question as to whether laborers have, or do not have the right to organize strikes. Nothing is gained, from a scientific point of view, in not separating these two very different questions. It must also be well understood that in dealing with a practical case both questions must be solved. Science proceeds by analysis, whereas synthesis is required where practice is concerned.

Propositions that are exclusively scientific are of two kinds: (1) descriptive propositions, describing what has taken place – so monetary systems are described with reference to time and place; (2) hypothetical propositions, which search into what would have happened under given specific conditions – so, for instance, what would happen if paper money were issued in a country accustomed to a circulation of gold...

Many people think that the advantage arising from the use of mathematics resides in making demonstration more rigorous. This is an error. A demonstration well constructed by the method of ordinary logic is just as rigorous as one made by the application of that other kind of logic which bears the name of mathematics. The advantage of mathematics lies chiefly in this, that it permits us to treat problems far more complicated than those generally solved by ordinary logic. Most economists insist upon the mutual dependence of different economic phenomena. But a purely verbal recognition of this fact is not all that can be done or all that is required. What we want is to determine, at least approximately, the relations existing between the economic phenomena under discussion and so obtain a clear concept of their interdependence. A system of equations similar to the one used in mechanics to represent the equilibrium and the movement of bodies is afforded by this method of approximation. This representation is, no doubt, in this way approached in a rough way at best, and yet the approximation serves better than nothing. It is better to know that the earth is nearly round than to imagine that it is a flat surface.

Professor Walras' great contribution to economic discussion was his discovery of a general system of equations to express economic equilibrium. I cannot, for my part, sufficiently admire this portion of his work, but I must add that I entirely disagree with him on what he has to say in his work entitled *Études d'économie sociale*. Professor Walras thinks it possible to make certain economic deductions from metaphysical principles of jurisprudence. This opinion is worthy of respect, but I am unable to accept it. I am a believer in the efficiency of experimental methods to the exclusion of all others. For me no valid proofs exist except those that are based on facts . . . the divisions into which we break up the aggregate in studying exchange, production and capitalization are quite arbitrary, although they may be useful helps in study. In reality these three operations are simultaneous. If this is so, it becomes absolutely necessary to consider them again as a whole after having analysed them in isolation . . . This general conception of the economic aggregate finds an analogy in the conception which an astronomer has of the solar system when he has apprehended the general equations of mechanics.

. . . In the early stages of every science there is apt to be a good deal of reasoning about terms rather than of the things themselves. This method of procedure, however, is not entirely erroneous. Words are often the depositories of the experience of men, and so long as a new-born science has not succeeded in accumulating for itself a sufficient aggregate of direct experience it may find it advantageous to have recourse to the common fund of experience more or less represented by words. There comes a time, however, in the development of science at which the fund formed by direct experience becomes sufficient and at which the disadvantages attached to the vagueness of experience, such as is given in everyday words, outweigh the advantages to be derived from them. This is precisely the state of affairs in political economy. I believe this science would gain a great advantage by developing a terminology of its own, just as chemistry, physics, and anatomy have done. But in this transition period many persons judge of works which are written according to the new methods as if they had been written according to the principles which have prevailed in the past. As a consequence, criticisms which I consider of absolutely no value have been made of the terminology which I have chosen to employ in my *Cours*. For instance, it has seemed to me to be convenient to adopt Professor Walras' definition of capital; I have not, however, deduced any conclusions from it. If anyone should prefer a different definition, there would be no objection to his using it, and he would obtain the same results as I have if he reasoned exclusively about things and not about words alone . . .

. . . Science does not attempt to impose any one particular method of economic organization and it is not the business of science to do so. Science does, however, attempt to solve problems of the following kind: (1) What are the effects of a régime of free competition? (2) What are those of a régime of monopoly? (3) Those of a collectivist régime? All these questions must, of course, be treated not from a polemical point of view, but solely for the purpose of ascertaining the results which would follow upon their installation. It is especially necessary for us to discover what relation these results bear to the aggregate well being of humanity; and to do this not only a first approximation, but a second and a third, and perhaps even more, must be made, because the later approximations take account of secondary facts which are easily neglected in the earlier ones. The régimes compared may appear to yield identical results if only a first approximation be undertaken, and may differ materially in their results

when reconsidered for the purpose of a second approximation.
. . . This method of approaching the subject differs substantially from that adopted by a large class of economists, who, after giving in their adhesion to a system, put forth all their power in showing its advantages and in defending it against all attacks to which it may be exposed. I once more repeat that I am far from condemning such economists, for I regard their work as one of great utility. This being the situation, I have no desire to offer a substitute for their work, but simply to add to it a purely scientific study. All the conclusions to which deductive studies founded on the general equations of the economic equilibrium can lead us must finally be verified by a careful scrutiny of the facts, both present and past – that is to say, by statistics, by close observation, and by the evidence of history. This is the method of all the material sciences. Deductive studies in political economy must not be opposed to the inductive; these two lines of work should, on the contrary, supplement each other, and neither should be neglected.
. . . The laws of the distribution of wealth evidently depend on the nature of man and on the economic organization of society. We might derive these laws by deductive reasoning, taking as a starting point the nature of man and of the economic organization of society. Will this work sometime be completed? I cannot say; but at present it is certain that we lack sufficient data for undertaking it. At present the phenomena must be considered synthetically, and every endeavour must be made to discover if the distribution of wealth presents any uniformity at all . . . we still lack a theory that may make this law of distribution rational in the way in which the theory of universal gravitation has made Kepler's Law rational.

NOTES
1 On the theme of the difficult relationship between Pareto and English-speaking economists see further: G. Busino, 'Ricerche sulla diffusione delle dottrine della scuola di Losanna. Lettere di Vilfredo Pareto a H.M. Smith, K. Wicksell, E. Seligman, I. Fisher, E.B. Wilson, J.H. Rogers', *Cahiers Vilfredo Pareto*, no. 22–3, 1970, pp. 243–62. Also, see: G.H. Bousquet, 'Quelques remarques sur Pareto et certains défauts de son oeuvre', *Cahiers Pareto*, no. 25, 1971, p. 12.
2 Pareto, *Lettere a Maffeo Pantaleoni*.
3 See G. Sorel, *Le Devenir social*, Paris 1906, pp. 468–74. This review sparked off a relationship and a mutual influence between the two.

4 Pareto, *Lettres d'Italie*, ed. G. de Rosa (Rome 1973), p. 31.

5 See G.H. Bousquet, 'Introduction à la re-édition de *Cours*', *Cahiers Pareto*, no. 4, 1964, p. 212.

6 R. Cirillo, 'Pareto's law of income distribution revisited', *Cahiers Pareto*, no. 33, 1974, p. 79.

14 The dangers of reaction

1898 was a year of tension for Italy. The long-standing struggle between reactionaries and socialists came to a head. Famine, the extreme poverty of the lower classes, social disorder, and revelations of corruption in politics caused the wealthy classes to react from a fear of even greater social disorder. Many members of the extreme right Liberal group, among them Sidney Sonnino, with the help of King Umberto I, prepared a *coup d'état* aimed at suppressing the parliamentary regime in order to have *carte blanche* in repressing civil disorder.

In the past, Pareto had missed no opportunity of attacking in his 'Cronache' the reactionary governments which starved the peasants in the south out of vanity and their thirst for glory. As a careful student of both ancient and modern history, he observed in one of his comparisons: 'In Cicero's time a manual worker . . . needed fifteen working days to buy a hectolitre of grain. Now . . . thanks to the duty that our demi-god Crispi has granted his friends, the great landowners, a manual worker must . . . work for twenty days for the same quantity of grain.'[1]

As we know, in 1897, Pareto had ceased to write for the *Giornale degli economisti* following Pantaleoni's move to Geneva, but this did not mean that he ceased his journalistic activities, and made his opinion felt through other newspapers, especially *Il Secolo*, from which this article is taken.

He abandoned the professorial dispassionate style of his *Cours* as though cut to the quick by these new injustices, and in the theme of freedom he recaptured – if he had ever lost it – his youthful rejection of compromise. De Rosa comments: 'He wrote extremely movingly on the Frezzi case – of a workman wrongfully arrested and illegally detained, who died in prison from police brutality.'[2] After this case he again resumed with renewed passion the struggle for the independence of the magistracy and the reduction of the unlimited powers of the police. His final 'Cronaca' was a meditation on a government capable of receiving the consent of the people through persuasion – 'reformers must aim principally at changing the thoughts and beliefs of the people' – but he was also forced to admit that 'at this moment only the Socialists can change the state of our country for the better as they are the only ones, apart from the clergy, to whom the people will listen'.[3]

As can be seen, the concept of myth and faith, already present in 'The new theories of economics' as the only force capable of giving the masses strength, here becomes the instrument which a political force uses to good ends. On 6–7 May, the riots so feared by the right broke out in Milan. The army intervened under the command of Bava-Beccaris, who took extreme action, fired on the unarmed crowd and caused a massacre. The bloody suppression went on all over Italy. A state of emergency was proclaimed and *carte blanche* given to courts martial which irregularly tried civil crimes. The prisons filled up with political prisoners, while thousands of exiles crossed the frontiers.

Pareto rediscovered his passion for freedom but moments of optimism still alternated with moments of apathy. One has only to remember that on 16 May, he could write to Pantaleoni, 'You are too optimistic about Italy. The riots themselves are not indicative of a serious resistance movement against the government at all . . . There are only three parties: (1) the thieves who govern, (2) the Socialists, (3) the clerics. I do not want to follow any one of these, therefore I am going to interest myself in pure science.'[4]

Busino writes that the arrival in Switzerland of the first exiles from Italy 'awakened him from his apparent indifference'.[5] He believed that the moment had come for a Liberal awakening. In order to express his disapproval of these events even more strongly, he considered publishing a pamphlet *La Liberté économique et les événements d'Italie*, in which he had gathered the views of European Liberals like de Molinari, Guyot, Pantaleoni, de Viti de Marco and Mazzola. This struggle in which Liberals and Socialists were once more united after many years, was supported by the young Croce and Le Bon. But Pareto did not merely give moral support to the exiles and those persecuted because of their political beliefs, most of whom were Socialists. For some, like the imprisoned Turati, he could do no more than write letters of support, but to others he opened his home in Lausanne. Moneta, Ciccotti, Labriola, Lerda, were all Pareto's guests. The praise given more than once to the Socialists 'the only ones in Italy who have voted for an idea and not for money'[6] was now transformed into open admiration, while his criticism of the incapacity of the

Italian bourgeoisie became cold contempt. He wrote in *Critica sociale*, 'When the Italian bourgeoisie sought the unity of the country – which they regard simply as a machine to be exploited – and believed that they needed the people's help, they did not think about imposing a duty on grain then. Now that they have become powerful, the mask falls. They no longer need to deceive the people, they revert to force to hold the people down and enrol soldiers so that the despairing screams of the starving shall not disturb the blissful idleness of our masters.'[7] The essay on 'The dangers of reaction' matured in this climate. He saw, as he had seen as far back as 1872, that only universal respect for the law provided a stable base and stood between speculators and socialists, protectionists and revolutionaries, reactionaries and anarchists. He emphasised that, 'when the government violates the law it sows a seed which will germinate – producing a mass of anarchists and subversives'. But even as Pareto was writing, something happened which was to change his life – his uncle Domenico died and left him a large sum of money which allowed him to devote himself completely to scholarship.

FROM *Il Secolo*, 1–2 October 1898.
Among the ills inflicted on the country by the methods of the present Government is the growth of the Socialist party. This should worry all those who consider that collectivism is not the best form of social organisation. One of the main causes of this growth resides in the fact that persecution is useful to the persecuted and gains for them the sympathy and aid of many honest people. The same thing has happened in Germany where Bismarck's laws against the Socialists were the principal cause of the growth and prosperity of that party. The same thing happened in France where the Catholic party, which was weak when it was protected by the government, has been reinvigorated by Ferry's persecutions. In Italy the persecutions of the Liberals prepared the way for the changes of 1860.

The art of governing consists in not letting opponents appear as persecuted martyrs. This is managed by not going too far with repression.

Let us take an example. If, after the recent riots, only the ringleaders of the disorder had been convicted, and sentenced according to the letter of the law, their punishments would have been unanimously accepted by the consciences of the citizens.

Everyday experience shows us that looting and crimes against property are not tolerated by judges. By contrast, what causes harm to the Government are convictions for crimes of opinion . . .

Thus many would-be Liberals, who seek to respect the right of private property, are driven by the Government into the Socialist party . . . Every man is put to the test whether he must choose between bank frauds, customs duty protection and the citizen being deprived of justice when the issue involves the interests of the ruling classes, or whether to become a socialist. It is unreasonable to expect there to be no solution other than these two for a better social organisation in Italy. You who govern create so-called subversives; whoever defends the right of property, whoever seeks loyally to uphold the law in all its rigour. All these things would perhaps be acceptable if the country were given moral or material prosperity or military glory. But, in fact, the battles of Lissa, Custoza and Abba Garima have brought us little military glory, and materially and morally the country is in a sad state. The Government recognises this, and in order to repress crime is forced to resort to penal legislation such as exists in no other civilised country . . .

So, if evils exist and are recognised by all, would it not be right to ask for the help of the citizens? And why do you deny the freedom of the press and of political parties? Without these two freedoms England would have made no progress and would have found herself in that condition of wonderful prosperity in which Italy now labours . . .

Enforced silence is only useful to one's opponents – because it leads to the belief that they can propose the best remedies . . . It will be said that subversive articles can incite the ignorant populace to do wrong. This could be so. But open publication causes less harm than clandestine murmurs. Have you forgotten that Italy is the land of the Carbonari? Enforcing silence on political parties means wanting to bring about the birth of secret societies. There is only one remedy to prevent incitement to mob violence: education. This is not achieved by fine words, but by good example.

When the Government violates the law it sows a seed which will germinate, producing a mass of anarchists and subversives. Let us imagine that – for at least one generation – the law in Italy was rigidly respected, and was the same for all. Let us imagine that our people, often living in conditions worse than brute beasts, were raised to the level of human dignity. It is most probable that Italy would then lose the unenviable supremacy which it now holds for crimes of violence.

NOTES

1 See 'Cronaca', *Giornale degli economisti*, 1 January 1896.
2 G. de Rosa, 'Introduction' to Pareto, *Lettere a Maffeo Pantaleoni*, p. 10.
3 'Cronaca', *Giornale degli economisti*, 1 July 1897.
4 Pareto, *Lettere a Maffeo Pantaleoni*, p. 196.
5 G. Busino, 'Introduction' to Pareto, *La Liberté économique et les événements d'Italie* (Geneva 1966), p. XIV.
6 See *Giornale degli economisti*, March 1897.
7 'Protezionismo Italiano', *Critica sociale*, 16 February 1898.

15 The sentiment of freedom

A new reactionary *coup d'état* was attempted by King Umberto I when he summoned General Luigi Pelloux to form a government. On 4 February 1899, the latter presented a series of extraordinary measures to the House, with the aim of decreasing the legislative power of Parliament and increasing that of the Government. The restrictions on political freedom following the economic restrictions were also to affect Pareto, who was unable to publish an article attacking these laws. This was as serious and as offensive to Pareto's dignity as the police action two years earlier which had broken up a meeting at which he was speaking, and it served to increase still further his hostility towards the Government, and drove him closer to the Socialists in whose newspaper, *Avanti*, he published one of his letters. In it he emphasised how freedom was more respected in France than in Italy, and referred to the campaign of Guyot and Jaurès on behalf of the innocence of Dreyfus.

If Liberals and Socialists had united in France and triumphed over the injustice of the enemies of freedom – who, on the pretext that the state was in danger, had sought to condemn an innocent man – why could they not do the same in Italy? His enthusiasm for an alliance between Socialists and Liberals in defence of freedom did not make him forget that 'protectionism and communism are twins'. But he could not help noticing that in practice 'the offences of the Socialists against private property have been only verbal, whereas the offences committed by our pseudo-Liberal Government are a matter of *fact* – something far worse'.

As can be seen, concern for facts overrode any abstract principle. Pareto always made them his criteria: his thoughts and actions stemmed from facts, rather than from words.

FROM *Il Secolo*, 2–3 April 1899.
In Italy there are people who want to be called Liberals – in defiance of common sense and the meaning of words – while they encourage and enforce every type of action against liberty. These

people seek to make us believe that they are defending the rights of private property, where they commit direct, and permit indirect (and extremely grave), offences against it.

Recently we had a clear example of how these people conceive liberty. *Il Secolo* defends the Socialists who are unjustly persecuted and oppressed, and these so-called Liberals are shocked that the bourgeois shareholders of the newspapers should allow such a defence. *Il Secolo* condemns the ill-treatment of a poor, innocent monk, and so the Liberals shout that *Il Secolo* has become clerical. It would seem that for these gentlemen being Liberal means favouring only one's friends, even if they are wrong, and persecuting and oppressing one's adversaries, even when they are right. But if they want to change the meaning of the word, then I for one do not understand such a confusion. As long ago as 1877, I had published in *Nuova antologia* an article on the law against the abuse of the clergy, in which I defended the freedom of the clergy. So, today, I do no more than continue a work already begun a long time ago. For the same reasons, I speak for the bourgeoisie when it is the Socialists who want to strip them of everything and reduce them to slavery; and cannot support the bourgeoisie when they strip the Socialists of everything and put them in prison. It should also be noted that up to now the offences of the Socialists against private property have been mere words, whereas the offences made by our pseudo-Liberal Government are a matter of *fact* – something far worse.

. . . In an inaugural speech, Senator Negri defended private property, but he did not explain how his beautiful words can possibly be reconciled with the deeds of his friends who enrich themselves through customs protection. The writings of Bastiat, in which he shows that protectionism and communism are twins, are still waiting for a confutation from our senator.

Practise what you preach! Listen to the governing megalomaniacs, who strip the people to the bone, praising private property! Listen to those who want to impose a new slavery on the railway workers, speaking about freedom! Listen to those who want to take away the freedom of the press – given by King Charles Albert – speaking about freedom of thought! Listen to those who condemned and imprisoned our leading citizens, speaking about personal freedom! Listen to those who have broken the laws, speaking about legality!

They answer that it is expedient to act in this way; but if we accept such an excuse, every deed can be justified. How can we possibly persuade a reasonable human being that in order to maintain public order, the government had to confiscate, destroy, loot the grain, oil and soap of co-operative societies? Who could possibly consider it expedient for petty politicians to rob the treasury? How is it possible to justify the expediency of wasting millions on theatres and monuments, when people are dying of hunger? But our so-called Liberals do not even make an effort to find any reason to justify their actions. All they can do is threaten with prison anyone who does not think in the same way as they do; and they want those who complain about the intolerable burden of taxation to be punished as subversives. Even the Pope, in his encyclical *Rerum novarum* says that the government 'acts unjustly and inhumanly if it takes away more than what is right from private goods'. What wonderful Liberals you will be when, with the restrictions that your government is preparing, you confiscate the Papal encyclical, as well, and, in the name of freedom, imprison everyone who speaks the truth.

The people's conscience rejects these sophisms. Chiesi, de Andreis, Turati have been elected Deputies and, if you had wished, Don Albertario would have been elected too. What made the electors vote for these men was neither vulgar self-interest nor greed for the property of others through protectionism, and not even personal favouritism. It was a noble sentiment, both elevated and moral: the sentiment of justice and freedom.

16 Liberals and Socialists

In this article Pareto replied to the cynicism of false Conservatives who, rather than respect the law and cause it to be respected, trampled on it by means of 'special courts' forbidden by the Constitution. He also answered the hypocrisy of false Liberals who could not possibly be Liberals as – 'whoever is a Liberal must first of all demand freedom of speech'. It is important to note an observation connected with this concept which has a practical bearing on history. People, like social aggregates, political parties or governments, should be judged not by what they *say*, but by what they *do*. This consideration was prompted by the fact that the Socialists – basically republican – were the only ones, owing to the political situation, left to support the Constitution of King Charles Albert. As can be seen, both the concept of correlation between the individual will and the social will, and also the concept of equilibrium between the two wills, are implicit. But the concept of 'approximation' is also included. Just as economic science is based on approximations, so political science imposes an alliance between political forces in proximity, in the action undertaken for reaching immediate ends.

It is the history of present-day facts which must decide whether a political party is Right, Left or Centre. So, for the Italian Liberals of those days all that remained was a close alliance with the Socialists. Nobody could be scandalised by this since – just because the circumstances were what they were – such an alliance was already coming into being in many European nations. But, as will be seen, the political situation was about to undergo a sharp, rapid change. This article marked the high point of Pareto's support for the Socialists. Thereafter it was to decline rapidly.

FROM *Critica sociale*, 1 September 1899 and *La Vita internazionale*, 20 April 1900.
In an article published on 30 July, in *L'Idea liberale*,Giuseppe Massara criticised the conclusions of one of my articles published in *Critica sociale* of 1 July.

The problem must be studied carefully to know whether in certain cases – particularly in Italy – Liberals can and must be allied to Socialists. I say that they can, but Massara says they cannot. Fifty years ago, de Molinari, one of the most authoritative leaders of the Liberal economists, had already suggested that Socialists and Liberals should come to an agreement over economic matters, the most difficult thing for them to agree on. In Germany, Liberals and Socialists have already united several times on political matters. In Belgium, the same thing happened a short time ago. In France, men like Yves Guyot and Frédéric Passy fight under the same flag as Jaurès and Millerand. If such people have joined together they clearly have something in common . . . In politics, an agreement is not made on abstract principles, but on the action which seems most urgent at a certain moment. Many men in France seek to prevent the victory of militarism and arbitrary power. These men, who do not agree on other things, come as much from the Right as from the Left, but meet where they consider their work to be useful. So Gallifet and Millerand can be seen in the same cabinet.

In France there is a *threat* of militarism and arbitrary power, but here in Italy it is a reality. In France there is one Dreyfus Case, but we have *many*. I can say no more, otherwise this newspaper will be censored. If it were possible for the French government to act with the complete freedom of our rules, the Dreyfus Case would never have been reviewed. *Le Siècle*, *L'Aurore* and others would have been censored every day. People like Yves Guyot, Reinach, Jaurès would have been imprisoned in the same way that Turati, Romussi, Chiesi, Don Albertario and others have been imprisoned here. Whoever is Liberal must first of all demand freedom of speech. Whoever is Conservative must demand respect for the law. When the law is respected the accused are not brought before special courts which are forbidden by the Constitution . . .

You seek to lay upon Liberals the blame for having demanded freedom of speech, and on Conservatives for having asked for the laws to be respected. But who is with us in asking for these things? – The Socialists, who, funnily enough, have remained alone in defending the Constitution of King Charles Albert . . .

Massara says that the Socialists want 'an exclusively proletarian state which governs in the name and the interests of the proletariat'. Perhaps it is true, but such a state is already in existence in Italy, with the only difference that instead of looking after the interests of the proletariat, it looks after the interests of a part of the bourgeoisie and certain petty politicians. This is an evil which is certain and actual; the other is an evil uncertain and of the future. If Massara were attacked by two men, one putting a knife to his throat, the other at a distance telling him that one day he would shoot him, which of the two would he try to get rid of first? Up to now the Socialists in Italy have attacked private property in words only, while in reality the government has attacked it and continues to do so every day. You say that the Socialists want to build an oppressive state. But we shall not back them in this; we shall continue to support them for so long as they help us to resist the present oppression.

It is not only in Italy, but all over Europe that the strange phenomenon of the Socialists can be observed – in the fight for freedom they take the place vacated by the Liberals . . . Let us ignore theory . . . In *practice*, in Europe, the Socialists, more or less alone, resist the oppression of governments and fight against militarism and a superstitious patriotism which should not be confused with a sincere love of one's country . . .

PART TWO
Sentiments and aristocracies

17 The danger of socialism

The start of a new century – let alone that of a new millenium – has a certain fascination which influences both the men who live through it and those who study it. The changes credited to the beginning of a new century are sometimes imaginary, but this cannot be said of the start of the twentieth century. The change was partly the work of destiny and partly of man. On 29 July 1900, King Umberto I was assassinated at Monza by the anarchist, Bresci, and only a few months later, on 21 January 1901, Queen Victoria died. The death of these two monarchs whose activities and lives had been so tied to the lives of their peoples, would in itself have been sufficient to mark a change. However, these two events were secondary to another fact of primary importance for the future development of the Old World – the conquest of more power everywhere by the working classes. The Labour party was born in Great Britain, while the first Liberal governments backed by Socialists were formed almost simultaneously by Asquith and MacDonald in Great Britain, Waldeck-Rousseau in France, and Zanardelli and Turati in Italy.

Pareto's private life registered some changes, too. With his uncle's inheritance he bought a villa in Céligny, where he lived until his death. From that oasis of the peace and silence of pine woods, he seemed to observe humanity with the cool detachment of one who observes something with which he has nothing in common. But nothing apparently changed in his thinking and, always so alert to the political situation, he seemed to share the climate of mutual trust between the Liberals and Socialists of the time. In the General Election of 3–10 June, Pantaleoni was elected, with Socialist and Republican backing. Perhaps Pareto would have been elected too, if he had agreed to stand. But, as we have already said, he preferred his solitude, concentrating more and more on the study of men and events. In his letters of that year to Pantaleoni he showed his fear – as yet to be really justified – of an imminent economic crisis owing to the waste of money incurred by strikes and the arms race. This essay is a valid expression of that apprehension. For the first time he saw the Socialists – still today's allies – as the danger of tomorrow. For the first time he used not words of reproach, but expressions of contempt against the effete ruling class. The cowardly bourgeoisie, he calls them. In warning the self-proclaimed humanitarians who, through cowardice, not only prepare their own ruin but also a bloody conflict, he asserted that 'whoever becomes a lamb will always find a wolf to eat him'.

As if in a premonitory dream, he foresaw the excess of anti-freedom in socialism. He feared the return of a Middle Ages more cruel than that of the past, and confessed, 'Let us take advantage of studying these signs before the new Radical Socialist faith imposes its dogma upon us under threat of prison and perhaps even death.'

The essay contains the usual categorisation, and it comes almost as a surprise (evidence that the situation was still fluid, and a definitive judgement still impossible to formulate) when, at the end, the reader finds praise for orthodox socialists who, Pareto believed, one day 'will be the only defenders of freedom, and the salvation of our society will be due to them'. Here, too, deeds speak louder than words. There are socialists and socialists, and one must not confuse the wheat with the chaff. At bottom, there is irony, or perhaps pity, for those who believed that they could plan everything from on high and also discriminate between those who are and those who are not entitled to citizenship of this world. His heart still beat for freedom.

FROM *Journal des économistes*, May 1900.
'We were only born yesterday, and yet we already people your countryside, your towns, your fortresses, your town halls, your meeting places, even your armies, your tribes, your senate, your forum; we only leave you your temples.' Tertulian said this when speaking of the Christians, and we can say the same when speaking of the Socialists.

We are dragged towards an economic revolution which can only be compared with the one which brought down the Roman civilisation and which casts the shadow of a new Middle Ages over Europe. I believe that this revolution is inevitable – not because of the strength of the forces marching to attack society, but because of the ignorance, superficiality and negligence of the property-owning classes who will be stripped of everything they possess.

History has certainly never repeated itself in precisely the same way twice running, but it offers numerous analogies. However they are analogies which, contrasting past with present, merely give us a glimpse of what the future will be. It is only through experiment that we discover the source of our knowledge. Our age presents all those premonitory signs that foreshadow every great economic and social revolution in the past. Let us study those signs before the new Radical Socialist faith imposes itself on us under threat of prison and perhaps even death.

Never, or almost never, have aristocracies – I mean this term in its etymological sense, which means the *best* – perished at the hand of their enemies alone. Rather, it was they themselves who were the artisans of their own destruction. This has been proved by the studies made by modern critical historians of the French Revolution. It was the upper classes who were the artisans of this Revolution. It was the nobles and the bourgeoisie who sharpened the blade of the guillotine under which their heads were to fall. The arrival of Christianity in the Roman world was a very similar phenomenon ... Speaking about Christianity, Pliny the Younger noted that 'this superstition has invaded not only the cities, but also the villages and the countryside'. But in the same breath he adds 'that it will be possible to stop it and cure it'.* Today Bismarck is of the same opinion about socialism.

Up to a point the Roman aristocracy was justified in its self-confidence. The army and the ruling classes were intact. It was hard for them to believe that a few miserable wretches – possessing nothing – would dare to challenge a Roman magistrate, or to measure themselves against the Roman legions, whose victorious eagles had triumphed on the battlefield. Similarly today, some people in Germany smile when others speak of the triumph of socialism. The army is intact and devoted to the Kaiser, commanded by officers coming almost exclusively from the upper classes. How is it possible to think that the Socialists have the smallest chance of taking over power under such circumstances?

The root of all these mistakes is the same. It consists in not taking into consideration the natural evolution of doctrines, taking for granted that what exists today will exist unchanged in the years and centuries to come. Only if this supposition is accepted, is the line of reasoning of the higher Roman classes, and those who today have too much confidence in themselves,

* *Epistolae*, x, 97

right. Of course, if Christianity had not made a compromise and had remained exclusively the religion of the poor, it would never have become the official religion of the Empire. In the same way, neither Bebel's socialism in Germany, nor Jules Guesde's socialism in France will come to power. It will be another type of socialism – direct heir to those two – which, even if capable of compromise, will despoil the people like the others.

There are many brands of socialism . . . We have scientific socialists – few and without political influence, but people to be respected (some for their talent) who sincerely try to discover the truth. They often find it, but as it does not agree with the truth in Marx's books, they resort to a slight exegesis to make it agree . . . Then come the intransigent Marxists – very numerous and who could be called orthodox socialists, who have considerable practical influence . . . They recognise perfectly the importance of capital, as do economists, only they want this capital to be collective instead of private . . . At the end come the radical socialists – the most numerous, the most influential, the most dangerous of all. To tell the truth, they are socialists, but could be the followers of any other regime if they saw some advantage in it. Flattering the people today, they will flatter princes to-morrow . . . they have discovered an ingenious means of despoil-ing the people: taxes are voted by the majority, but paid by the minority. They have taken over most of the town halls in Eng-land, France and other countries. Through a *minimum wage*, they have been provided with an excellent bodyguard. Able-bodied young men receive five francs a day for doing some small job, thus damaging hard-working labourers . . . If Pliny the Younger had looked around him he would have seen a large number of people unconsciously working for the triumph of Christianity. That triumph, instead of seeming impossible to him, would have seemed certain. The worst enemies of the Roman Empire were not those who openly confessed their new faith, but far more those who paved the way for this faith: the stoics, those who followed oriental cults, those who followed a vague humanitarianism – so similar to what is dangerous in our own day. An ascetic, mystical current invaded Roman society, and one day the royal purple was worn by an ascetic – Marcus Aurelius – who was one of the causes of the ruin of the Empire, by leaving it to his sons. The Roman aristocracy which, thanks to its energy and its practical good sense, conquered the known world but came to a sad, anaemic, limp and empty end; the same fate befell the French aristocracy later on, and the same fate will soon befall our bourgeoisie...

As if it were not enough to renounce all the means of defence, the bourgeoisie also help their enemies. With their money, the 'Popular Universities' have been founded, where it is taught that their property has been acquired unjustly and should therefore be confiscated. By seeking to include this argument in the problem of freedom means betraying it. No liberal will refuse the socialists freedom to express their doctrine, to defend it, to criticise that of their opponents, to dedicate themselves actively to the propagation of their theories. All are willing to give freedom to their friends; the liberals want to give it to their enemies as well. I can discuss this problem without the slightest embarrassment because I have always defended freedom. As a defender of competition, I have never sought to give a monopoly of public education to the government, on the pretext that my opponents get some advantage out of this competition. But if freedom, tolerance and courtesy are given to one's adversaries, they should not be helped to accumulate followers. Being a supporter of competition and giving money to one's enemies are two essentially different things. Let the socialists found all the popular universities that they want – with their own money, of course – no liberal will have anything to object to about that; but I consider it absurd that my money is needed to propagate what I consider to be wrong. I intend to keep this money solely for the defence of what I believe to be the truth, be it right or wrong... There are some people who imagine that they can disarm their enemies by complacent flattery. They are wrong. The world has always belonged to the strong and will belong to them for many years to come. Men only respect those who make themselves respected. Whoever becomes a lamb will find a wolf to eat him.

If you read about a strike in socialist or radical socialist newspapers, you will always notice that the strikers are in the right... Strikers not only boast about their right to go against their employers, but also to go against the workers who want to work. They enjoy a very enviable privilege: that of executing justice by themselves... So we go back to the time of the barbarians, when the king tried and sentenced the accused...

The main fault of ethical socialism consists in imagining that it is possible to solve very complicated problems by maxims more or less intelligible, put *a priori* – ignoring the results of experiments and the sciences which co-ordinate these results.

Hygienist socialism appeals to experience, but to a restricted, one-sided experience. For example, if, after injecting red wine into unfortunate guinea-pigs, the little animals die, our hygienists jump to the conclusion that wine is harmful to man, and that the state must forbid the use of any alcoholic drink . . . The hygienists, like most socialists, do not take individual morals and customs into consideration at all. According to them everything good must be imposed by the police . . .

In the State of North Dakota, a law was introduced forbidding marriage without the permission of a doctor. Fortunately this law was not passed. A certain Dr Hegar, who proposed this law, said in a short article: 'All those people affected by any malformation, an illness, a disease of the blood, are forbidden to marry whenever there could result persistent and serious hereditary taints in their descendants.' . . . As for me, I would suggest we start by applying to this doctor the same law that he proposes. It seems to me that he is affected by a malformation of the brain, which forces him to seek to oppress his fellow men with Draconian laws. If this malfunction were to be passed on to his descendants, we should be unfortunate indeed . . .

It is surprising to see that only the orthodox socialists fight the fantastic projects of ethical socialism. The liberals have deserted the battlefield almost completely, some on account of fatigue or discouragement, others through lack of courage or energy, still more because they have a secret sympathy for ethical theories and because the strength of their prejudices is greater than their liberalism. I know that the opinion I am going to express could seem paradoxical today, even if it seems to me that the study of the facts makes it possible. Owing to the absence of any resistance from the liberals, it could be that one day the orthodox socialists will be the only defenders of freedom, and the salvation of our society will be due to them. Even now in Germany, they are the ones who defend free trade, and the freedom of science and art, threatened by the *lex Heinze*. In Italy, too, they defend freedom – they call for respect for the law and the constitution. They alone resist a government which holds elections with the help of the *camorra* and the *mafia*. I realise that someone could answer me that the Christians, too, called for freedom when they were oppressed but that as soon as they came to power they, in their turn, oppressed the pagans. Today, the orthodox socialists, oppressed, call for freedom but, tomorrow, if they are in power, will they give to us? I recognise the weight that this objection carries, so I have expressed my opinion in the form of a doubt. Hope alone remains in Pandora's box. We can only console ourselves with hypotheses, since reality is so grim.

18 An application of sociological theories

This essay appeared just one month after 'The danger of socialism' and is like a pause for reflection. Meditation reinforced the passion that Pareto felt while writing the former. Objectivity and subjectivity became stronger in his method of research. He began to analyse passions and the human instinct for creating myths. All his concepts – even if little developed – are the prelude to the more elaborated concepts which we find in *Les Systèmes socialistes* (on which he was working), in the *Manuale* and, above all, in the *Trattato*. Dialogue and controversy was no longer conducted with protectionists and Socialists or Liberals and Conservatives. The centre of his attention became man – that mixture of intuition, sentiment and reason. The ever-present dualism (between feelings and reason) began to take shape, and because of it he would later be compared to Pascal.[1] The religious fact as a primary fact was distinguished from the forms which it had gradually assumed over the centuries. In his research into the foundations of man's actions, Pareto probably analysed his own actions and discovered that, concurrently with the more or less correct course prompted by reason, every man religiously follows the direction his feelings tell him to pursue. At the basis of any social institution, as at the basis of any human action, is found the fundamental religious phenomenon which inspires not only positive religions like Paganism, Buddhism, Islam, Christianity and the rest, but also social theories like nationalism, socialism, imperialism and also fashions in scientific method, literature and art. The classification into (1) experimental, logical actions, (2) experimental, non-logical actions, (3) non-experimental, logical actions, (4) non-experimental, non-logical actions, already proposed in a lecture given in 1898 on 'Comment se pose le problème de l'économie pure', and put forward again the following year in the opening lecture of a course on sociology, was once more set out and corroborated here.[2]

The psychological, subjective, religious phenomenon does not represent the only point of orientation of the socio-individual action. It drives one towards action through emotion, but it is logic which

foresees the future, even if hypothetically, through analysis and classification. Because of it, Pareto advised his readers to be wary of new
masters who 'will not have the senile weakness of our bourgeoisie'. In
this warning he was aware that the elements both of the progressive
perfection of certain negative instruments of a new 'yoke . . . heavier
than the preceding one', and of imponderable differences, were hidden
in the cyclic reproduction of facts. This was to say that the fact of having discovered a system of repression does not guarantee that one day
it will not be used against those who have discovered it. There was no
guarantee that keeping power through military dictatorship 'can be of
use to the aristocracy of the moment'. As can be seen, Pareto's position
as a whole was close to that held in 'Proportional representation',
where he asked those who placed their hopes in force: 'Who assures
you that it will always be yours, and will never be able to pass into the
hands of your adversaries?' He still retained his faith in progress, but
feared a *negative* progress: that is, a more refined technical progress in
limiting the freedom of the individual. The optimism seen in the conclusion of 'Socialism and freedom', where he affirmed that just as 'the
human mind has been able to evolve, leaving behind dogmas, prejudices, and metaphysical principles which hindered the natural sciences
from reaching that dignity which they have now reached . . . it is now
worth doing the same in politics and social sciences' – that optimism is
now balanced by the pessimism of a possible negative progress.

FROM *Rivista italiana di sociologia*, July 1900.
The purpose of this essay is solely subjective and merely aims at
applying certain sociological theories to facts . . .
    Every sociological phenomenon has two aspects, distinct and
often completely different: the one objective, which establishes
a relationship between real things, the other subjective, which
establishes a relationship between psychic conditions. Let us
imagine that we have a concave mirror: the objects which it
reflects are deformed. What in reality is straight seems curved;
something small looks big, and vice versa. Similarly, the objective phenomena – as described by historians or contemporary
eye-witnesses – are reflected in the human consciousness. Therefore, if we want to discover the objective phenomena we must go
beyond the subjective phenomena, and deduce the former from
the latter . . .
    Maury says that: 'In Sicily, the Virgin Mary has taken pos-

session of all the shrines of Ceres and Venus, and the pagan rites have been partly converted to her worship.' * It is evident that there is a common emotion which is manifested in various forms, and that these forms are secondary in respect of that emotion. Maury adds: 'The fountain continues to receive the offerings which it once received as a divinity – this time in the name of a saint.' In this case the dominant factor is the emotion compelling men to acts of devotion towards the fountain which represents a god or a saint . . . Another is believing that the intervention of a divine being can cure one's eyes – it is secondary to pray either to Aesculapius or St Lucy. It is also secondary to invoke the Christian Devil or the pagan Hecate: the principal fact is to believe in the power of such an invocation . . .

The rising period of the religious phenomenon
A glance is enough to see that religious emotion has been growing for some time and is still doing so among civilised people. This has not only helped such living religions as Christianity, but principally has invigorated a new order of religious emotion expressed through socialism. Many leading figures, both among the socialists and their opponents, have clearly realised that socialism is a religion. Any student of history must recognise that this religious phenomenon is one of the greatest hitherto known, and can only be compared with the rise of Buddhism, Christianity, Islam, the Protestant Reformation, or the French Revolution.

Even patriotism is exalted into a form of religion. In Germany an important and authoritative magazine talks about a 'German God'; in England there is imperialism, in France, nationalism, and in the U.S.A., jingoism . . .

Ascetics, apostles, martyrs spring up ready to do anything to prevail upon a human being not to drink a glass of wine . . . There are sects (like that of the teetotallers) which stand comparison with religious orders . . . others are obsessed with hunting down immoral literature . . . These express extremely moralistic concepts in exceedingly vulgar terms. In one place, some boys were forced to sign a petition to close down brothels, but the words of the petition itself were obscene. Sometimes, as you talk to one of the more fanatical, you can see his face light up, his eyes shine –

---

* L.F.A. Maury, *La Magie et l'astrologie* (Paris 1860), p. 153.

all the signs which are typical of the male in search of a female –
at the very moment when he is interminably denouncing sexual
union, with incredible hatred for whoever enjoys making love . . .

Spiritualism, occultism and other similar superstitions have
many followers and generally increase with the growth of religious emotion. There are people now who take seriously the fan-
tasies of a hysterical woman who says that she can write in the
language spoken on Mars. Lectures have been given on this
wonderful scientific matter, to an audience of women and girls,
fascinated by mysticism . . .

Mysticism, symbolism and other vanities are making headway
in literature, art and science. If someone wants to publish a book
he can choose any religious form to sing a hymn to, but the hymn
must be there, or else the public will not buy the book, and no
publisher will print it.

Our new mystics believe that they employ reason. In reality
they seriously offend logic, and often do no more than repeat the
nonsense of the ancient mystics. For example, to prove that some
fairy story about the transmigration of a human being to Mars is
true, they pompously tell us 'Science cannot explain everything' . . .

It is useless proving that such a line of reasoning is false, as the
men who use it have not been persuaded by it – on the contrary,
they have invented it to justify *a posteriori* what they were already
persuaded about . . .

Putting to one side these secondary facts and returning to the
principal facts, it seems probable that the increase in religious
emotion will help socialism – a new religion – more than the old
religions. It has always been like this . . . and socialism will
naturally have to modify itself and borrow many things from the
opposing religions . . .

In France, the Socialists have gained power, and Millerand is
in the Waldeck-Rousseau cabinet. In England most of the
Fabians voted in favour of imperialism. In Germany there are
many Socialists who bill and coo with the Empire. The collectivist and former Lutheran pastor, Naumann, in his book *Demo-
kratie und Kaisertum* preaches openly for the Kaiser to become
head of the Socialists, and also preaches militarism, war and the
extermination of Germany's enemies – and all those, too, who
even if they are not her enemies, do not want to be Germany's

slaves. Many centuries passed from the day when Jesus preached love and peace in Galilee to the day when soldier-priests put on armour over their vestments and killed in the name of the Divine Master, but only a few years have passed since Marx, a German, cried 'Proletarians unite!' and the day when some German Socialists now cry 'Proletarians, kill yourselves!' . . .

The decay of the old aristocracy

When an aristocracy decays, two phenomena are usually observed. Firstly, it becomes milder, more humane, and less able to defend its power. Secondly, the rapacity and greed for other people's goods does not lessen; so it tends as far as possible to increase illegal possession and to usurp as much as possible of the national patrimony. On the one hand it makes the yoke heavier, while on the other, it has less strength to keep it there. The catastrophe of this aristocracy begins when both these factors are present. When one is absent, it can continue to prosper . . . The aristocracy often dies of anaemia. Even if it retains a certain passive courage, the active courage is lacking. One remains astounded on seeing how the men of the aristocracy of Imperial Rome committed suicide or let themselves be killed without defending themselves at all, if the Emperor so desired it. In the same way, we are astounded on seeing how many nobles in France died on the guillotine instead of falling on the battlefield . . .

The rise of a new aristocracy

Belief that it is the people who fight against the dominant class of the moment is an illusion. It is a new, future aristocracy who fights against it, making use of the people . . .

The new aristocracy is pliable and open to all at the beginning, but after its victory, it will behave like all the others who came before it, becoming more rigid, and more severe. Buddhism – which proclaimed the equality of men – generated the theocracy of Tibet. The religion introduced by Christ – which seemed made for the poor and humble – generated Roman theocracy. This was attacked by a new aristocracy at the time of the Protestant Reformation . . . As usual, the new aristocracy used the poor and humble. As usual, they believed the promises made to them. As usual, they were deceived – and a yoke was put on their shoulders

heavier than the preceding one. In the same way, the Revolution
of 1789, which brought about the Jacobin oligarchy, finished up
with imperial despotism . . . After its victory, the new aristocracy
will make concessions in form or word to the new weak, the new
unprepared, the proletariat, but in practice they will wear a yoke
heavier than the one before. The new masters will not have the
senile weaknesses of our bourgeoisie, at least for a certain period
of time . . .

The subjective phenomenon

The religious phenomenon is not distorted too much by the
conscience, and so the subjective phenomenon is not too far from
reality, except in its secondary aspects. Catholics, Protestants
and socialists feel – some more, some less – carried along by the
religious tide. It is true that the socialists emphasise the scientific
side of their religion, but some Protestant sects also do this . . .

For many members of the bourgeoisie the religious wave of
Christianity which drags them along seems to be a means of
fighting socialism. From the many manifestations of religious
emotion they choose – or think they choose – the one which least
opposes their interests . . .

A minority of the contemporary aristocracy once tried to trust
in freedom, reason and good sense, particularly between 1850
and 1870. Now it realises that it made a mistake, as men are ruled
by emotion, not by reason . . .

What can be used to oppose the advance of socialist religion?
The French upper classes did not have much choice. They tried
to give new strength to the old religious forms, especially the
Catholic form, to turn certain hatreds against the Socialists to
their own advantage . . . in the end it had a new religion in
nationalism . . .

The ojective phenomenon is simply the battle between the two
aristocracies . . . The divergence between the subjective phenomenon and the objective phenomenon produces many illusions.
So many imagine that they can fight socialism effectively by fighting Marx's theories, as others believe they could fight Christianity
effectively by noting the scientific errors in the Bible. There are
few educated men who do not admit these errors – but what harm
has been done to the Christian religion? None. It flourishes more
than ever. Marx's theory of value is not tenable. After various

sub-interpretations, some of the more educated Marxists admit that Marx never wanted to formulate a theory of value. All this has done very little to socialist belief. It is not Marx's book that has created the socialists: it is the socialists who have made Marx's book famous. It was not Voltaire's works which caused men's disbelief at the end of the eighteenth century – it was that disbelief that made Voltaire's writings famous . . .

An unknown element of future social modifications still remains. It is the changes which could cause long wars between civilised peoples. These wars would probably bring about a military dictatorship for some European peoples. But we do not know what the relationship would be between that dictatorship and the new aristocracy. Those who only judge by basing everything on the subjective phenomenon affirm that a military dictatorship can be of use to the present aristocracy, whereas those who base everything on the objective phenomenon will have many doubts about this hypothesis . . .

NOTES

1 See G. Busino, 'Introduction' to Pareto, *Scritti sociologici*, p. 35.
2 Now reprinted in *Cahiers Pareto*, no. 1, 1963, pp. 121–30.

19 Justice

With the assassination of King Umberto I and the defeat of the reactionary plans, the Liberals once again held a temporary balance. Their aim remained that of averting the installation of another authoritarian regime. In Italy the time seemed particularly propitious and left room for manoeuvre through the electoral, political agreements between Socialists and Liberals. Having paused for reflection, Pareto – sensitive as ever to European events, especially Italian events – threw himself into the struggle once more with surprising enthusiasm. He again put forward the pattern of a neutral Liberal state capable of impartiality in the problems of labour, where the only rule is that of the free-play of the laws of supply and demand, and where the only positive progress is that of the increase in the production of the wealth of society and of the individual. Beyond this Pareto saw only the arbitrary acts of old and new despots which could increase in intensity with the rise to power of the new aristocracies. In this essay, besides describing reality as it is, he voiced the wish that the concomitant growth of violence could be arrested. With his discovery of the rapid increase of an élite greedy for power, Pareto looked to men of goodwill to redress the situation. He observed that if today's victors were more temperate and less unjust, this would be an invitation to tomorrow's victors to be 'more moderate and less unjust'. It was as if he was in anguish over the fact that 'in Italy, the poor are oppressed by the rich; in France and in certain parts of Switzerland, the rich are oppressed by the poor'. It is therefore a matter of moderating the two injustices so that a social contract can come out of it which can guarantee a lasting social peace in which there are neither oppressed nor oppressors. What he had already said in his essay 'Whether it is worth establishing by law a minimum wage and a maximum margin of profit' about a neutral, but also tutelary state, here seems to be brought to the fore when, speaking to them as individuals, he appealed to the consciences of those who governed, saying: 'Can't you strike a happy medium and try to break that chain of oppressed and oppressors?'

FROM *La Vita internazionale*, 20 August 1900 and
5 September 1900.
... Some landowners did not agree with their labourers over the
wages for the harvest. The Government intervened and granted
to the landowners the power of employing soldiers on the work
which the labourers refused to do ... Professor Vidari defended
the right of the landowners to resist the demands of the harves-
ters without, however, discussing the real problem: the means
used for defending that right. If a washerwoman asked Professor
Vidari ten lire for washing and ironing a shirt, he would be right
to send her packing, but his having this right does not imply that
he has the right to get a policeman to wash and iron his shirt – or,
if he cannot find a washerwoman, that he should expect the
Government to do something about it.

This is one side of the problem. Now let us look at the other
side. In France, when there is a strike, the authorities regularly
help the strikers. If a citizen who has not the honour of being
'a comrade' of the minister, M. Millerand, shoots someone else,
he is tried and condemned. The gentlemen strikers, however,
can shoot the workers who want to work, beat them up, sack the
workshops, and nobody says a thing. If, by chance, they happen
to be tried, the punishment is only nominal, because either they
are reprieved or the sentence is suspended owing to the Beranger
Law ... The reasons given to excuse the workers have much less
validity than those used by Professor Vidari in justifying the
landowners ... One must appreciate that every time an indus-
trialist does not give in at once to the demands of his workers, he
'provokes them beyond all limits'. In this way everything done
against him by these glorious workers is lawful. These brave men
are easily provoked because it seems that they are very easily
irritated. If they break the windows of a house, throw stones or
threaten to loot a building, one must be very careful not to call the
police, because that action is 'always' a great provocation. The
policemen and the soliers must let themselves be stoned, too.

There is something in common between the defence of the
arrogance of landowners and that of the workmen, namely the
total lack of justice which spreads from the conflicts caused by
strikes to the relationship between the various social classes.

In Italy, the poor are oppressed by the rich. In France and in
certain parts of Switzerland, the rich are oppressed by the poor.

In Italy, owing to their megalomania and vanity, the bourgeoisie
has put heavy taxes on primary products, and so despoils the
poor. In other countries, however, owing to progressively heavier
taxes, the poor despoil the rich . . . It seems that when men cease
to be oppressed, they become the oppressors, and real justice
seems to be a point of equilibrium that is never reached . . . If I
were asked 'will those whom you defend or those whom Professor Vidari defends be the more moderate and less unjust
rulers?' I confess that it would be hard to answer . . . It can be said
that it is worth trying – even with little or no hope of success – to
put someone who has gone wrong, back on to the 'straight and
narrow'. There is a proverb which says: 'Whoever has more
sense, uses more', and it really is a pity that the Italian bourgeoisie has used so little, not simply for the sake of justice, but
also in its own interests. Why, then, instead of over-reacting,
thus encouraging others to over-react, can you not strike a happy
medium and try to break that chain of oppressed and oppressors?
. . . I dare not assert that by acting justly the ruling class would
remove all risk of being oppressed in its turn. It seems to me,
though, that this experiment should at least be tried, especially
because the road that has been followed up to now has not
brought anything good.
    . . . Now let us return to the heart of the matter. Does the fact
that the government intervenes in labour matters by directly or
indirectly fixing the workmen's wages, help society or not? To
this question there are two answers. Certain protectionists and
socialists answer that it does. The socialists go even further and
assert that it is useful for the government to regulate production
completely . . . The liberals answer that it does not help and
assert that the interference of the government is damaging and
has no utility. This is not the place to find out which of the two
schools is right – hundreds of volumes have attempted to solve
the problem. But besides these two scientific solutions, there is
another which seems to me to have nothing whatever to do with
science. There are certain individuals who reply: 'The intervention of the government helps society if it helps me. If it does
nothing for me, however, it does nothing for society.' Of course,
nobody openly admits that he thinks in this way, but everyone
cavils at covering up this line of reasoning. When the bourgeoisie
came to power at the beginning of the nineteenth century, they

said they were liberal, but then always found some pretext or other to deny the people freedom: freedom of trade – yes – but together with the protection of national industry. Freedom of work – of course – but only for capitalists; and workers must be forbidden to form trade unions, because they easily become subversive. The bourgeoisie do not consider it worthwhile for the government to intervene in order to assure a worker of a decent living wage for him and his family, whereas they consider it worthwhile to assure the capitalist of a just profit on his capital ... It seems to me that acting thus has not helped to stimulate the love of economic freedom in workers ...

On the other hand, some assert that if workers wish to leave their work without giving notice beforehand, it is wrong that the government should intervene and force them to honour their contracts. If, however, an employer dares to give workers the sack without notice beforehand, they assert that it is right for the government to intervene and make him honour the labour contract. In France, if an employer dismisses workers who belong to a trade union, he is taken to court and punished, whereas, if workmen turn a workshop upside-down and beat up or kill workers who do not want to strike, the government must not interfere. Very different from the *lasissez-faire, laissez-conduire* of the economists, this is the *laissez-faire, laissez-conduire* of criminals ... So the injustice of the one causes the injustice of the other, at least in part ... But whoever wants these contracts to disappear (and even if they cannot disappear completely, they can become less marked) tells today's winners to be more temperate, less unjust, thus trying to make tomorrow's winners more moderate and less unjust.

20 A little social physiology

In family terms 1901 was an eventful year for Pareto. It began with his move to the villa at Céligny, and then at the end of the year, his wife Alessandra Bakounine (no relation to the Russian anarchist) left him. He went to Paris in November and on his return learnt that she had run away with a servant called Ottwein. She was twelve years younger than her husband, but this is of little importance compared with the fact that she was lazy and weak-willed. As Giacalone-Monaco points out, her character was 'the result of serfdom which unwittingly worked its vengeance on the masters while at the same time serving them. It was enough to raise one's little finger for a servant to come running to do what his master could easily have done himself. With the passing of the years, the master's dormant will-power dried up altogether.'[1] Her character had not really adapted itself to Pareto's tormented, passionate nature, and only by exercising great self-control could he control his energetic bursts of emotion. The fact that she had left him damaged not only his pride, but also his privacy. From then on his life was disturbed by a series of court cases for separation and alimony for his wife. He obtained a divorce only after having acquired the citizenship of the Free City of Fiume a few months before his death. He had just time to marry Jane Régis, a woman thirty-one years his junior, whose only virtue was to remain by his side for the whole, long period of his heart disease.

As for his work as a scholar, 1901 was a fruitful year. Several essays were published besides *Les Systèmes socialistes* which will be discussed later. He had already observed that there are substantial, principal facts – and formal, secondary facts – in history. In this essay, one of the best examples of his method, he verified his intuition about the distinction between principal-general causes and secondary-incidental causes, thus confirming once more the ever-present correlation between concrete and abstract, subjective and objective, principal and secondary. If it were true that history, in the form of the history of civilisation, is the history of the alternation of the aristocracies that have created these civilisations – as he had already proclaimed in 'An

application of sociological theories' – and if it were true that the aristocracies have as much possibility of prevailing as the feelings that
inspire them, it followed that the future conflict in Europe would be
between two religions: one nationalistic and imperialistic – the other
democratic and socialist. As will be seen, what Pareto formulated in
terms of probability, took on the characteristics of a prophesy. This
essay was certainly the inspiration for his *Trattato*.

He felt that with the close of the nineteenth century an age had come
to an end – the Age of Reason which guaranteed the only justice
realisable in this world, namely liberal justice. Another age was beginning: that of the return to the wars of religion.

FROM *La Vita internazionale*, 5 September 1901.
. . . Each of us has an opinion . . . but that does not get away from
the fact that, to be really scientific, a study of phenomena must
eliminate our desires and opinions, and only concern itself with
the relationship between facts. Social facts have two types of
causes – some, principal and general, others, secondary and
incidental. Close proximity nearly always automatically causes
the observer to mistake the principal causes for the secondary
ones. So, the contemporaries of certain events make serious
mistakes, which are later rectified by their descendants, who see
those events in their true light. To avoid these mistakes, it is
necessary, as far as possible, to collate events of the same type
which have happened at different times, in different places, and
under different conditions. In this way secondary causes are
eliminated, while the primary causes comprise what those
events have in common.

The blame for the recent strikes in Italy has been attributed
exclusively to Zanardelli's cabinet and the minister, Giolitti, in
the same way that in France, the blame was attributed to the
minister, Millerand. In both cases there is truth in the accusations, but we cannot consider ministerial action the principal
cause of the strikes because in England, as in America, there have
also been extremely serious strikes . . . We must conclude by
saying that the work of these ministers is secondary and that
other and much more powerful forces determine these events.
This is not the place to find out what these forces are, because
discussion would be too long. It is enough to have brought their
existence to light.

Another general fact is that all over Europe the Liberal party is disappearing, as are the moderate parties. The extremists stand face to face: on one side socialism, the great rising religion of our age; on the other side, the old religions, nationalism and imperialism. This development first became apparent in Belgium, where the Liberal party lost power many years ago, and the Clerical party and the Radical Socialist party were left to struggle for power. In France, the moderates fell with Méline's cabinet ... In England, through the strength and genius of Gladstone, the Liberal party continued to seem alive even when it was dead. Once Gladstone was gone, the party fell to pieces ... In Germany, it melted like the snow under the rays of the sun. Now, the Reactionaries, the Catholics and the Socialists are masters of the field. In Italy, the transformism of Depretis extinguished the last spark of life in the Liberal party. And now, in Holland, the Liberal cabinet of Pierson has fallen and a coalition of Reactionaries, Clericals and Christian Socialists has taken over power. It is difficult to believe that chance is the cause of all these events which are so similar to each other. In the same way that the tide has a general cause, but assumes different forms in different ports, so the general changes in society appear in different forms in different places, and the effects of the secondary causes intersect those of the principal causes.

In England, imperialism is on the increase owing to the rivalry with Germany and the war in the Transvaal. The opposite could be said, but what is certain is the common relationship between the two things . . . In Italy, the Moderate party has only one statesman, Sonnino, who would do remarkable things if he were helped ... He may be a gallant captain, but where are his soldiers?

The Italian Socialist party is strong, vigorous and optimistic. Certain economic and social factors which not only operate in our own country, but also all over Europe, draw their original strength from this party. It is still in its youth – the epoch in which religions have a great power of assimilation. In France, Italy and other countries, young people who feel the need for an ideal turn to it, and in this the only competition for the Socialists comes from the Nationalist and Christian parties . . . It has brave leaders, untainted by scandal, who never want for devoted followers, even in moments of crisis. You have to be extremely short-sighted to believe that it draws its strength and vitality only from the help and favour of Zanardelli's cabinet. It would be truer to say that Zanardelli seeks help from this party precisely because it is strong. Until now, no sooner has there been the risk of a strike, than the employers have turned to a minister to put down the strike by using force. Now they must rely on their own resources, and this unnerves them . . . But if they pluck up courage; if they are able actively to oppose their adversaries, Zanardelli's cabinet will have worked in their favour in the end, because it will have awakened them from the apathy into which they had sunk . . .

When a social movement begins, it nearly always indulges in excess. There have been many strikes for no real reason – one or two for ridiculous reasons. Tarde has written a book on *Imitations*. Men always want to imitate what they see. Every employee dreams of striking. The exaltation will pass, but what will not pass so quickly is the backing that the Socialists receive from the peasants . . .

There are some moderates who are pleased by the schism in the Socialist party, because they hope to gain some advantage from it. I believe they are making a mistake. History teaches us that such schisms occur in every sect and every religion when the numbers of its followers have grown. When a sect has few followers, it has the advantage of being intransigent; but as the number of followers gradually increases, the advantage of being intransigent lessens, so that at a certain stage, it is advantageous for the sect to divide into two parts – one compromising, the other intransigent. I do not know if socialism in Italy has reached this stage, or whether the present schism will last. If it does not it will be replaced at some point by another schism. The same causes which produced the evolution of Bernstein in Germany and Millerand and Jaurès in France, also operate in Italy.

The social evolution in Italy can be accelerated or slowed down by the next elections of 1902 in France . . . Anyway, it is only a question of the degree of intensity in the rise of the socialist tide in Europe, which does not show any sign of diminishing at the moment.

NOTES

1 *Pareto e Sorel*, vol. 1, p. 137.

21 Socialist systems

1901 was also the year in which the first volume of *Les Systèmes socialistes* was published – the second volume would appear the following year. Conceived originally as a university course, the work was a résumé and a re-elaboration of all Pareto's earlier sociological analyses and conclusions. It was devoted more to the study of religious emotion than to socialist systems, which Pareto believed to be no more than the expression of the former. As can be seen, the theories which he held in the two preceding essays, concerning the distinction between subjective and objective, primary and secondary, find a systematic, general application here. The assumption that all men are equal is rooted in religious emotion and tends towards a dull uniformity and similarity. This same assumption becomes an article of faith under which it is believed that all must have an equal degree of freedom; all must possess identical qualities for command; all have been created good by nature. Influenced by these emotions, men act and are deluded 'regarding the motives which determine their actions', without realising that 'a great number of human actions are irrational. These actions are purely instinctive, but the actor gains pleasure from arbitrarily imagining his or her motive to be rational. In general he does not expect very much from the quality of this logic and is easily satisfied by an appearance of rationality, but he would feel uncomfortable were it entirely absent.'[1] Thus Pareto elaborated a concept already expressed in his *Cours*, where he asserted that, 'in all ages men have attributed ills to imaginary causes', and where he laid the foundations of what he was to define in his *Trattato* as residues and derivations, logical actions and non-logical actions. He sought, in a first statement, to obliterate all sentimental chimeras and Utopias. He warned those who proposed to eliminate all present evils by a return to nature with what he had already said in his *Cours*: 'Facts show that nothing is more wretched than the life of a savage, that their average life-span is very brief and that they are subject to every type of illness.' With ironic sarcasm, he once again reminded those who wanted to improve the human race through eugenics, of the miserable end of the perfectionist community of Oneida. It is enough to remember how severely he had criticised Dr Hegar in 'The danger of socialism'. He reminded the humanitarians, who, presuming an innate goodness of men, demanded pardon for the guilty, how this illusory view of justice pushes matters to the point at which criminals live in 'model prisons' which 'more than one honest workman would like to have'. He reminded those who, basing themselves on untried and therefore unproven premises of the equality of men, believe that all the ills of humanity spring from 'unequal distribution of wealth', that 'in the human species, as in all living species individuals are not born alike'. He reminded those who from feelings of pity and brotherly love, deplore the necessity for the struggle for survival, and those who talk about 'class struggle', that there is not 'only one type of struggle . . . but a multitude of struggles'. And he also reminded them how this multitude of struggles was 'the most powerful instrument of selection ever known, as much for individuals as for social organisations'. In this, Pareto added nothing new to what he had already stated. Like the concept of competition of the individual, that of the struggle for survival was also taken from the *Cours*. To his mind, it was always the individual who competed and, as Braga emphasises, his ideal man was an 'emulating man'.[2] Finer is right when he says that 'the *Cours* was written in the full flood of Pareto's liberalism',[3] but wrong when he states that 'in the *Cours* he accepted Marx's socio-economic classes and his notion of class struggle', for his position on this point had never changed over the years. In his *Cours* he stated that 'the class struggle assumes two forms at all times. One consists in economic competition which, when it is free, produces the greatest ophelimity', as 'every class like every individual, even if it only acts to its own advantage, is indirectly useful to the others . . . The other form of class struggle is the one whereby every class does its utmost to seize power and make it an instrument to despoil the other classes.' (**1054**) Clearly, both then and now, Pareto accepted a form of competition in which the opponent was not killed because in killing the opponent, not only competition ceases, but also the stimulus to produce a still greater wealth and, therefore, many luxuries, including the luxury of freedom are destroyed.[4] The same continuity can be seen in his concept of equality as it affects the differences between men. In the *Cours* he stated 'It is absurd to expect that an appropriate system of education can transform anyone into a Newton.'

The idea of the classification of the various socialist sects was not new either. 'Socialism and freedom,' 'The Introduction to Marx's *Capital*' (defined by Giacalone-Monaco as a 'first stage towards "Socialist systems" ')[5] and 'The danger of socialism,' had already dealt with this. The attack on the socialists was less bitter than in the preceding essays: had Pareto become more sympathetic towards the other systems based on faith and metaphysics? No, he had not. He continued the battle which he had always fought, not against *every* type of metaphysics, dogma, illusion, Utopia, but only against those types which had not been proved by the experimental sciences. And yet, there must be something new and different from the past if, in the preface to the 1927 edition of *I Sistemi socialisti*, Bousquet could state that Pareto 'despised humanity'.[6] The whole book is strongly tinged with a certain aristocratic, detached arrogance, but if we read the substance carefully and analyse what he writes, we see that Pareto had never despised humanity as such, then or before. He had despised petty politicians: those who, while claiming to act rationally had done no more than obey their instincts and those who treated the problems of the real world as a series of abstractions. But he certainly did not despise either scientists or those poor workmen whose sweat had enriched the speculators.

What will probably irritate the reader of *Les Systèmes socialistes* is the language, declaimed as though issuing from an impregnable tower, for Pareto was aware that he, too, was influenced by his passions. The reader could also be vexed by the atmosphere of fatalism which he breathes. Perhaps it is true that if in the *Cours* man was left a narrow margin of choice in his actions (when Pareto stated: 'the best that we can do is to keep the organisations tested by experience, seeking to improve them as much as possible'), this margin seems to grow narrower when he states: 'there can be no objection *a priori* to the reformers, but they must face several obstacles'. The first of these obstacles is that of examining whether the effects of the reforms 'will balance the effects of a new distribution considered to be better'. Now, as all the reforms proposed are determined by emotions – which are irrational – and as they are never experimentally tested, and therefore not proved, nor can their effects be scientifically verified, then at first sight it seems that nothing can be done to change the world.

Something else that might surprise us is a certain naïveté hidden behind the cold mask of indifference. How can this man who mocks humanitarians who believe that they can change the nature of criminals, this man who believes in the natural differences between men,

have faith in the foresight of men? How can he state that 'if providence could become one of the principles of individual morals in the
results of the sexual act, a great step would be made towards a possible
improvement in the species'? These questions can be answered only if
one thinks of the continual distinction Pareto made between men as
they are and as some would like them to be, and if one remembers that
Pareto had never excluded the possibility that the foresight and wisdom of the few could become that of the many. Was it not he who
supported rule by reasoned discussion? And had this position ever
been disavowed? Once over his youthful enthusiasm, he realised that
the majority of people use irrational arguments to determine their
actions. But did he exclude the possibility of the few becoming many,
and vice versa?

Examined from the latter point of view, Pareto's social theories
could give surprising results. If the whole social organisation is based
on the individual, if the concept of personal responsibility is stressed,
the result is that there are no alibis left for opportunists, flatterers and
turn-coats, who can blame no-one but themselves for their cowardice.
This discovery of his could yield results, especially in a world where
the rights of some, or certain privileged classes in turn, seem destined
to substitute the rights of everybody. In this case, too, Pareto acts as
mediator between the will of the individual and the will of society.
His work here is highly pedagogic when he puts forward the notion of
resistance to overbearingness by affirming: 'The individual A wants to
impose on his fellow men a certain system. Another individual, B, is an
'individualist'. In a way A is not wrong, as B's resistance is certainly an
individual opinion. But is not A's opinion individual, too?'

In a world which is becoming more and more organised, more and
more regulated by laws which elude control, and where any opposition
has a tendency to dissolve, in what can one have faith if not the good-
will of the free individual for re-establishing the equilibrium broken
in favour of supposed necessity? Futhermore, if this subjective aspect
is seen in relation to the structural objective aspect – as Pareto wanted
it to be – a reading of *Les Systèmes socialistes* shows it to be much
richer in suggestions than one believed at first sight. And this is so also
because individual actions always carry weight in social results.

FROM *Les Systèmes socialistes*, Lausanne, 1901.
The influence of emotion
. . . Man is not only made up of pure reason, but also of emotions

and beliefs . . . Giving reason and emotion their role in social phenomena, assigning to each a well-defined field, does not mean devaluing one or the other. The fact that when I write a scientific book I keep myself naturally and necessarily within the field of reason does not mean that I deny the existence of the field of emotion and belief. On the contrary, the reader will see that I attribute to it a breadth that many will perhaps find exaggerated. What I desire to avoid are the hackneyed dissertations in social sciences, in which reason joins in uneasy alliance with the emotions.

This is not easy. Each person has a secret enemy inside who tries to stop him from doing this, and to make him dilute logical deductions with emotion. Generally speaking, I am well aware that I am not immune from it. My emotions predispose me towards freedom, so I have had to react against them. But it could be that by doing so I have gone to the other extreme and, through fear of giving too much importance to the arguments in favour of freedom, have not given them enough. But on the other hand, it is also possible that through fear of over-reacting against some emotions with which I am not in sympathy, I have given them too much importance. In any case, although I am not completely sure whether this type of mistake exists in my writings or not, I feel it my duty to bring it to the notice of the reader.

Sources of emotions in favour of socialist systems
The instinct of sociality which exists in every social class gives rise in most men to feelings of benevolence towards their own kind. These feelings . . . are generally in favour of socialist systems. In the upper classes, in particular, they have a form different to that in the lower classes. This form is as different as the decadence of the upper classes is great.

Happy men also desire their fellow men to be happy, and this benevolence is broadened to include pets. This is reasonable and only excess is harmful as in everything. It is right for parents to love their children, and harmful to spoil them. Sentiments of benevolence often degenerate into sentimental chimera, and from here spring the Utopias, which, according to their authors, will make happiness reign on the earth. Generally, the means used to reach such an end are very simple, and consist essentially in asking for certain institutions to be abolished – institutions which exist side by side with the evils that they want to avoid, but which, instead, are considered to be the cause of these evils owing to the *post hoc, propter hoc* line of reasoning: if man is unhappy in this society, let us go back to nature where he was so happy; if misers want gold, let us get rid of gold and thus we shall have got rid of avarice; marriage has its bad side, like every other human institution, let us therefore replace it with free love. While the élite is full of strength and vigour, these illusions are accepted by a small group of writers, poets, amateurs; but, when the élite is in decline, they are accepted by most of those who make up the élite. One must not confuse the benevolence of the strong with the cowardice of the weak. It is characteristic of the strong to defend their interests and rights and to have enough control of themselves and enough benevolence for their fellow men to stop at the right moment when they begin to invade the interests and rights of others . . .

Social organisations cannot be judged from an absolute point of view – it is necessary to weigh the pros and cons
Saying that all men are subject to certain passions does not mean that all give in to them in the same way . . . No-one will confuse the rule of a Trojan with that of a Caligula. One must not let oneself be carried along by an exaggerated pessimism and totally condemn all organisations because they have faults and vices. One must simply remember that as nothing in this world is perfect – neither men nor their organisations – one must not postulate systems which are based on a non-existent perfection . . .

One should not approve of a certain organisation simply because it has good qualities, just as one should not condemn it because it has faults. Simplifying problems in this way belongs to primitive beings; for these a correct middle way does not exist; an organisation is either excellent or abominable. So, in popular plays, only sublimely honest man or frightening criminals are depicted – everything is clear-cut. All real organisations are a mixture of good and bad, and in order to compare them it is necessary to solve problems which are difficult and often complicated . . .

One is generally unfair towards the rulers of a country because one does not take into account the difficulties under which they have to act. Among these rulers there are many more men sincerely desirous of justice and disinterestedness than the opposition would have us believe. It is impossible for these honest men to go directly towards their goal – to realise what they believe to be the good of the country. They need to manoeuvre in order to include all the interests at stake. It is rightly said that politics is the art of compromise. But one's aim is not often achieved by always following tortuous ways. This explains how it is that extremely honest politicians with good intentions often finish by doing more harm than good.

It is an extremely common mistake to see only one side when judging an institution. When divorce did not exist in France, some moralists cited facts to prove that the indissolubility of marriage held grave disadvantages. From the moment that divorce has been in existence they cite facts to prove that it is an evil, and conclude that it must be abrogated.... In order to judge it is necessary to weigh the pros and cons.... These procedures obviously entail enormous difficulties, but this is the price of scientific progress.

Different ways of acquiring wealth

... The organisations which allow of private property (that is, nearly all organisations currently known) offer men two essentially different ways of acquiring wealth. One consists in producing it either directly or indirectly through work and the capital which one possesses. The other consists in obtaining the wealth produced by others. The two ways have always been used, and it would be hazardous to believe that they will soon cease to be used. But as the latter is generally condemned by moralists, one willingly shuts one's eyes to it, pretending that it is something sporadic, accidental, whereas in reality it is a general, constant phenomenon.

Social movements usually follow the line of least resistance. While the direct production of economic goods is often very hard, taking possession of those goods produced by others is very easy. This facility has greatly increased *from the moment when deprivation became possible through the law and not contrary to it.* To save, a man must have certain control over himself. Tilling a field to produce grain is hard work. Waiting in the corner of a wood to rob a passer-by is dangerous. On the other hand, going to vote is much easier and if it means that all those who are

unadaptable, incapable and idle will be able to obtain board and
lodging by it, they will hurry to do so.

From another point of view, we can observe that of the two
ways of coming into possession of other people's goods (i.e.
directly, with violence or fraud, or indirectly, thanks to the help
of public power), the second is much less damaging to social
well-being. It is a perfection of and improvement on the first, in
the same way that the breeding of domestic animals is the perfection of and improvement on the hunting of wild animals...

The class struggle

The class struggle to which Marx, especially, has drawn our
attention, is a real fact of which we find traces in every page of
history. But it does not only happen between two classes – the
'Proletarian' class and the 'Capitalist' class – it happens among
an infinity of groups which have different interests, and above all
among the élites contending for power. These groups can have
a more or less long duration and more or less permanent characteristics. Among most primitive peoples – perhaps in all of them
– sex determines two of these groups. The oppression which the
proletariat grumble about is nothing compared with what
Aboriginal women in Australia suffer. More or less real characteristics based on birth, colour, nationality, religion, race, language,
can give rise to these groups...

Even if the social organisation changes, extortion survives

In every epoch, in every place, the history of the past and the
observation of the present shows us men divided into groups,
each of which procures economic goods for itself, partly by
producing them directly, partly be despoiling other groups
which, in their turn, despoil others...

The action of these different groups – each of which tries to
get hold of the goods produced by others – would most probably
survive radical changes in social organisations, such as the
abolition of private property. But this necessarily reappears at the
moment of consumption. However perfect the wisely studied
rules for distributing the goods which must be consumed ... the
would be 'distributors' who divided the cake, give a small portion
to A and a very large portion to B...

Religious communities
In every age small societies, sects, brotherhoods have been formed inside the largest societies of completely different peoples. Religious emotion – this term is used in its broadest sense – is generally the cement of these associations, although numerous examples can be given in which self-interest and the search for pleasure are the only aims. These brotherhoods can deviate notably from the average of the type of society to which they belong, as they are dominated by an intense, religious emotion. This deviation generally consists in the exaltation of certain virtues: self-denial, scorn of wordly pleasures and wealth, the complete sacrifice of the individual to the community and society.

So we have examples of the possibility of realising an altruistic ideal on which many socialist systems are based. One cannot object that selfish emotions cannot be replaced by altruistic emotions, because we have examples in every age, in every place, of the existence of these altruistic emotions. It must be said, though, that it is only an extremely limited élite which possesses this characteristic. When a community must comprise not only this élite, but the masses as well, it is forced to change its organisation. When the number of its followers increased enormously, the primitive Christian community ceased to be communistic. Only a small élite continued the same way of life, later on founding convents and monasteries. The same evolution is found in Buddhism ...

All these different societies – like the religious ones – can be considered *in their economic aspect* as parasites on the society in which they live. In some cases this is extremely evident; in all cases these small societies would disappear if the larger society, thanks to which they live, were to be destroyed ...

The companions of St Francis were not allowed to possess anything, but as men have still not found a way of living without eating, it was necessary for someone to give them something to eat. If the people who fed them had disappeared, or if they had simply wished to imitate the good friars, the entire race would have disappeared because nobody would have produced any food...

However, there are religious orders which have dedicated themselves to doing useful work ... In most cases the monks of these monasteries dedicate themselves to work which is extremely simple, but of doubtful utility for the community. But in any case, they never produce everything they need . . .

The problem of selection

This problem exists for all new systems of social organisation. The inventors of such systems use their energy in proving that the way in which the societies that they want to reform make their choice, is wrong. The work of these reformers is easy because no society exists which approaches perfection on this point . . .

The term 'aristocratic argument' indicates the argument that the best men must govern, and that in a social organisation every place must be given to the man who is the most competent. However, these terms are not specified . . .

What is the best and most competent man like? If they reply that he is the man who is the most suitable for accomplishing a task, the proposition becomes a tautology, and it becomes the concept of a man who possesses a certain wealth, a certain birth, a certain education and who is chosen by certain procedures . . . So, with the use of deception it means admitting that a rich and noble man is more able to hold a certain position than a poor man of the people.

The 'aristocratic argument' does not solve the difficulty of how to choose men – it shifts it into the realm of the definition of terms . . .

Because men exist who are intellectually and morally better than others, it can be legitimately concluded that the former can increase their total utility by leading the latter, but we have no grounds for converting this conditional proposition into an affirmative proposition. Different factors should be observed:

(1) One can make a mistake through ignorance, but also through self-interest. Technical competence can avoid the first evil, but can do nothing against the second . . .

(2) There are different types of competence. In an industry, technical competence often not only differs from, but is also in contrast to financial competence . . .

(3) Technical competence is often linked to ability acquired through habit. All the constituted social bodies, like corporations, academies, scientific societies, political societies, have a clearly defined tendency to enclose themselves within certain

dogmas, to immobilise art or science and to refuse innovations ...
It is, therefore, extremely useful for people who are designated
incompetent because they are outside these associations, to fight
to eliminate these obstacles created by habit. Most of the great
inventors were not only born among the ranks of the 'incompetent' but were also often considered out of their minds. Man
generally manages to enjoy credit for being competent in certain
things exactly at the age when his brain becomes less receptive
to new ideas ....

(4) Understanding moral good-will is still more difficult than
understanding competence in social organisations. There are as
many ways of conceiving it as there are sects. Saying that the
best men must govern does not help us to choose, as every sect
considers its own leaders to be the best.

(5) Finally, it is often overlooked that happiness is essentially
subjective. What does it matter to a European that he has an extremely competent Chinese cook, if he does not like Chinese
food? Our modern ascetics forget a little too easily that people
cannot be forced to be happy against their will ...

... Most people who are interested in social matters place the
responsibility for certain drawbacks which depend on the nature
of men, their passions, their ignorance, on the political regime
and the law. If these people live under regime X, they are struck
by its faults, and without proper examination affirm that regime
Z does not have even one of these faults. Of course, if they lived
under regime Z, their line of reasoning would be inverted and
they would talk about regime X as being faultless ... When the
popular mass of the people lets itself be dragged along by this
emotion, revolutions break out, the most obvious effect of which
is that of substituting the power of certain politicians for that of
others ...

The argument concerning unity
... Every new reformer reflects insufficiently on the fact that if
his predecessors had been able to unify the social organisation, he
himself would not have been able to speak about his system. If
society had been crystallised into the forms desired by Plato, we
should not have had the works of Rousseau, Morelly, Fourier and
Comte – something which would not perhaps have been a sad
loss – but we would also have been deprived of the works of

Galileo, Newton, Lavoisier, Watt, Darwin and so on – something
which would not have been to our advantage. Reformers, even
when they agree on certain points, fight ferociously over other
points. In our time, insults and even blows are often exchanged
at Socialist Congresses, in the absence of sound argument.
Bruntière shares with Comte – whom he tries to imitate – the
love of unity and the hatred of disturbing individualism ...

In our time, the argument in favour of uniformity often takes
the form of an argument against 'individualism'. The individual
A wants to impose on his fellow man a certain system X. Another
individual B does not want this system and resists. It often
happens that he, too, wants to impose on A another system Y,
adding a positive action to the negative action. Hurt by B's
resistance, A declares that B is an 'individualist'. In a way he is
right, since B's resistance is certainly an individual opinion. But
is not A's opinion individual, too? ...

... The argument concerning unity presented in this way leads
us to an obvious absurdity; but we must not stop on the surface –
we must try to get to the bottom of things in order to see if there
is some grain of truth hidden under the exaggerations of the
followers of this principle. First of all, there is a subjective truth.
There is a sentiment in many animals and in man, which makes
some differences in the aspect and the way of living between a
certain individual and the generality of individuals, extremely
unpleasant. If we paint a white hen red and then put it back
among the other hens, it will be pecked to death. A dog has
enough intelligence to recognise its master in different clothes,
but cows often attack their master who has changed his suit. One
of the surest indications of civilisation is tolerance of anything
new. This tolerance distinguished Athens from the more backward cities. Primitive peoples do not tolerate anything new, or
any variation – even the most insignificant. They are like animals
in this respect. Civilised peoples admit anything new and variety
in certain things ...

In the argument for unity, there is also an objective truth which
inspired the Catholic maxim: *in necessariis unitas, in dubiis
libertas, in omnibus caritas*: in certain cases unity is almost
indispensable, in others it is extremely useful. This would
suggest that the fervent followers of uniformity are right; but it
must be added that in some things this uniformity is unimportant,

and in others it is definitely harmful. The difficulty is to know where uniformity ceases to be useful and becomes harmful. The problem is one of quantity, not quality . . .

Unity requires the help of a religious emotion
To have any influence on most men it is necessary to use emotion, as it is impossible to influence them by using reason. In this respect it could be said that religion – intended in its widest sense – is the indispensable cement of society . . .

In every social and religious organisation, there is a fight between *religio* and *superstitio*. A section of society leans towards the latter, while the wisest leaders tend to keep them in *religio*. Such a contrast between *religio* and *superstitio* is fundamental . . .

Most of man's instincts are to be found in animals, but there is one – that of asceticism – which is only found in man, and the origin of which is very difficult to discover. It is not often found among primitive peoples, especially the poorer ones; instead it develops rapidly with prosperity. In prosperity, men like self-inflicted suffering . . .

The contrast between *religio* and *superstitio* exists for the socialist *ecclesia* and causes its leaders ever-increasing concern . . . But the greatest difficulties will come on the day when socialism triumphs. They will have another cause. Among the socialists there are certainly philanthropists and people full of love for their neighbours. These will resign themselves if their *religio* does not keep all its promises . . . But there is also a large number of people for whom the collectivist doctrine, at the moment, is a form of greed, an 'individualist' desire of taking possession of what belongs to others for their own enjoyment. At present, those with this desire talk of solidarity and principles of collectivism; but under a collectivist regime they will talk of anarchist principles and suchlike. The only regime which would satisfy people like this would be one able to procure every sort of pleasure without the need for any work. The socialists and the anarchists are already in conflict and there are disagreements even among the socialists. It will be far worse when they have all the responsibility of power. They must fight on the one hand, the incompetent, the idle, the undisciplined, and on the other, the strong, the capable, the intelligent and the honest, who will be disgruntled with their share . . .

There is no reason to suppose that in the effort to establish unity, a collectivist government should be more competent and successful than any previous government. It is therefore very unlikely that it will obtain different effects, and the unity of which the socialists dream will remain a pure Utopia.

Controversy on the different meaning of the word freedom.
Men generally desire freedom and fear compulsion. The former is associated with pleasant ideas, the latter with unpleasant ones. For them to accept compulsion, it must be changed to freedom. The people who do this usually act in good faith. Their reasoning may be condemned on logical grounds, but not from a moral point of view. They try to persuade others to accept their convictions.

A well-tried if somewhat naïve method of changing the meaning of the word 'freedom', is to distinguish *real* freedom from *false* freedom. Real freedom would be doing good, false freedom would be doing bad . . .

'Ethical men' and some modern socialists have a subtler, more ingenious method of practising the deceit by which compulsion is called freedom . . . The more general meaning of the word freedom is that which indicates the absence of coercion on the part of the law or public authorities. Exceptionally, freedom can mean the effective power of being able to do certain actions . . . For example, in the Bourbon Kingdom of Naples, the citizens were not *free* to read Voltaire, because the public authorities forbade it. Some of these citizens *could have* read Voltaire, others could not have done so because they were blind or illiterate . . . The 'ethical men' seek to take advantage of this double meaning, to use as a definition of freedom a meaning that it possesses only in exceptional cases. For them, real freedom is the power which man has over things . . . They seek to proclaim that for man, freedom is a means and not an end. They are not interested in whether or not the choice is free, if the objects from which the choice must be made are lacking. They try to say that if I am left to choose between eating a trout or a chicken, without having either one or the other, this freedom is useless to me, and that if, instead, compulsion definitely offers me one of the two, I prefer compulsion to freedom.

This reasoning is not reprehensible. In fact, it has never

seriously been contested. But presented in this form, it forces us to conclude that freedom alone is not enough for human happiness, and it is necessary to add other conditions to it. Unfortunately, the aim of the 'ethical men' is completely different. They are not content with adding something to freedom, they want to replace it, and it is for this that they so often unconsciously alter the definition . . .

It must be noted that Hegelianism has dominated the thought of most of the ethical economists and some of the socialists – Marx included . . . A certain entity, called 'the state', being defined as 'The reality of the moral idea' or 'The realisation of freedom' or yet again, 'The moral idea that thinks about and knows itself' is enough to justify all the ramblings of the 'ethical men' and the academic socialists. As there are a limited number of people who have encountered 'an idea that thinks about itself' or 'a substantial will' and as nobody has ever seen this 'reality of the moral idea', it is impossible to demonstrate that any attribute is not fitting, not knowing exactly what it is.

At the end of the eighteenth century and during the first thirty years of the nineteenth century, the Democratic parties asked for freedom in its true sense – they asked for the abrogation of the restrictive laws under which the people suffered. The 'Progressive Movement' went in this direction, and the parties which supported it could refer to freedom and progress without contradicting themselves. But when all the limitations on the freedom of the people disappeared, this movement continued to fight in order to take this freedom away from others. In conclusion – then as now – the interest of a class is the only thing that matters, and it is perfectly logical that, first of all, in the name of this interest the laws restricting those classes be removed and then laws be demanded which favour them. The word 'progress' has a rather vague meaning to permit of application to either of these two processes, and neither can the word 'freedom' be applied to them. It is only because of the survival of a word that the parties at present in favour of coercion call themselves Liberals. On the other hand, there are many examples of this type of survival.

It could be believed that the change in meaning of the word 'freedom' has had the aim of justifying its survival. In some cases it is true. In general, the popular masses are not very worried about these theoretical subtleties – which remain almost exclusively the prerogative of certain members of the decaying élite. These latter – vaguely feeling like traitors to their class, whose ruin they are preparing – look avidly for sophisms and pretexts to reassure their consciences, without worrying much about the logical value of their lines of reasoning.

The religion of nature

... Good Mother Nature did her work well ... but priests and kings were the cause of all the evils of society ... Fortunately, Progress (the new god who has his place reserved in the pantheon where Nature reigns) will get rid of these monsters for us ... For the authors who idealised the past, that unknown Golden Age, instead of the future, the best thing that man could do would be to go back to nature. If this is difficult, nay, impossible, it is necessary to get as near as possible to it. On the other hand, there were certain models to take as examples, which, without reaching the ineffable perfection of the state of nature, got very near to it. In ancient times they were Sparta and Rome, and in our times, China and the savage tribes. The nonsense that the best authors have been able to spread about this is astonishing. In their eyes, the Spartans and the Romans were like heroes of a tragedy. They conceived a bizarre and inflated idea about these peoples which had no point of contact with historical reality, and they reasoned without end on this basis. As China was little and badly known, our authors could let their imaginations run riot in dreams of a China that never existed ...

Rousseau took his descriptions of savages from his imagination ... Facts show that nothing is more wretched than the life of a savage, that the average life span is very brief and that they are subject to every type of illness. But Rousseau proves, with demonstrative arguments, that a savage is very happy and extremely healthy and robust ...

The dual aim of selection: putting the right man in the right place and eliminating the weak and incompetent

... We have already spoken about the choice of men and the attempt to put the right man in the right position.

There are individuals who are not only incapable of any useful employment, but who can be positively harmful and dangerous for society and the species. It is thanks to selection that these dregs of society are eliminated and the species is preserved.

In every society two principles can be found: social defence and social assistance ... On the one hand, like every living being, society defends itself against the elements that seek to destroy or to weaken it. On the other hand, its members give each other assistance and help those in need or in danger; the strong and the fortunate willingly more or less strip themselves of what they possess in favour of the weak and the unfortunate. The first of these principles, when related to emotion, is said to be that of *justice*, the second that of *pity* or *humanity*.

A society in which either of these principles were to be taken to extremes, or in which one did not work, would survive only with great difficulty. In this case, the problem of maximum utility for society is a problem of quantity and not of quality, as has already been seen in many other cases.

Every human society has certain individuals who are unfitted for its living conditions. If the action of these individuals is not kept within fixed bounds, society itself is destroyed. There are three types of measures that can be adopted to defend against this danger which, in order of decreasing effectiveness, have the following aims: (1) to suppress the unsuitable elements; (2) to stop them from doing harm by frightening them with the consequences of their actions, by taking away all freedom of action, or by keeping them away from society either temporarily or permanently; (3) to reform them and change their nature ...

Selectionist Utopias
Direct selection, impossible in human societies, is replaced by indirect selection. There are many, but unfortunately very imperfect, ways of eliminating the inferior elements. The Utopians denounce this imperfection, and their observations often contain an element of truth. But to condemn a mechanism, it is not enough to prove that it is imperfect; it is also necessary to prove that the mechanism which must take its place is better. It is in this that the reformers' line of reasoning is faulty ...

The ancient penal laws
Otto Amman and de Lapouge think that the ancient penal laws – generally very severe – were an effective means of selection ...

However, the importance of this suppression has not yet been fully proved. We have a qualitative proof, but the quantitative proof is lacking. Even if we admit that the ancient penal laws suppressed some of the inferior elements, they also suppressed elements of superior quality – since like all mechanisms of selection, they were imperfect. Even if the elements of inferior quality which were suppressed were greater in number than those of superior quality, we do not know the proportion in respect of the total population . . . This proportion has never been considerable and the effect of selection cannot have been very important, at least, as far as we know . . .

Penal legislation has the aim of stopping unsuitable elements from doing harm, by frightening them with the consequences of their actions or by cutting them off temporarily from society. It must be confessed that of all the social mechanisms, this one is still the most imperfect. This probably arises from the fact that up to now, as the positive penal school has brought to our notice, the legislators have concentrated their attention on the crime rather than on the criminal. It must be observed that fear of punishment only has an effect on individuals who possess a certain degree of foresight. The individuals who are impulsive or completely unsuited to social life have not enough foresight to fear the penal consequences of their actions. If they cannot be reduced to impotence, there is only one way of stopping them from doing harm – eliminating them. This is becoming more and more difficult nowadays because this means going against today's sentimentalism. So all the reformers attach themselves desperately to the third means of social preservation: that is, improving the individuals of inferior quality. Every hope nourished in this direction has always been disappointed; reformers cannot quote even one fact to support their thesis, but all this does not lessen their faith in it, and, like the compulsive gambler who always hopes to win back what he has lost with a lucky bet, they constantly hope to find the universal panacea that will make all men good, honest and moral. At the beginning of the nineteenth century, our philanthropists were enthusiasts for education. They kept saying: 'Open a school and you'll close a prison.' They also gave a scientific varnish to their doctrine. They observed that most of the criminals were illiterate, without reflecting that this was obvious – as the illiterates made up the mass of the people. In a country in which nearly everyone is fair, most criminals will be fair; but no conclusion can be drawn from this fact to establish the relationship between the colour of hair and criminality.

Schools have been opened; there are countries where everybody can read and write; but the number of criminals has not decreased – on the contrary, it has increased. Our philanthropists now have other manias, as they are no longer able to pin their hopes on education. Some affirm that alcoholism is the cause of all evil. Others think it is immoral literature. Still others – the majority – blame the unequal distribution of wealth. They inflict any absurdity on us in order to avoid admitting that in the human species, as in all living species, individuals are not born alike; that they have different characters, and that certain individuals are fitted for the environment in which they live, whilst others are not...

In avoiding this mistake, one must be careful not to make the opposite error. If the exaggeration of humanitarian sentiments can be harmful to society, their lack could be even more dangerous then their exaggeration. The problem to be solved is this: first of all, is there any way of decreasing the birth-rate of the individuals who do not adapt themselves to the conditions of social life? And then, if it is impossible to decrease the birth-rate, and if the increase in these individuals becomes a danger to society, how can they be eliminated, trying to keep to a minimum the mistakes in their selection, their sufferings, and without conflicting with humanitarian sentiments which it is useful to develop?

Such is the problem presented in the cold light of reason . . . Most men revert to humanitarian sentiments and go from one extreme to the other...

If a man robs, wounds, kills another man, at first sight it would seem that humanitarian feelings should sympathise with the victim. Not at all! There are times, especially our own, in which pity and benevolence go almost exclusively to evil-doers . . . Courts are more and more indulgent; juries absolve every crime in which the sophisms of a lawyer can reveal an element of passion. Model prisons are built, and many an honest workman would like to have in his home the comforts provided for criminals. And, finally, various, frequent amnesties restore criminals to society. The latter monopolise the attentions of legislators and philanthropists to the exclusion of any thought for the protection of honest people...

It is probably a matter of one of the habitual oscillations, and this movement may one day be replaced by a movement in the opposite direction.

If something could be done to put an end to the production of individuals of inferior quality by stopping them from being born, it is clear that there would be no problem as to how to free oneself of them and stop them from doing harm. A few reformers have turned their attention to this point. If man forces himself to direct the reproduction of plants and domestic animals to his own convenience, why should he be so imprudent as to leave the reproduction of his own species to chance?

This principle has always been recognised; the difficulty lies in its practical application to human species.

Its application is not at all easy in animal husbandry, where both rigorous control and great care are necessary...

To be effectively applied to the human race, such measures would require a complete and radical change in social organisation. A small-scale attempt has been made in America by the Perfectionists of Oneida.* Members of this community were subjected, of their own free will, to a rigorous discipline and all their goods were held in common. As was to be expected, the experiment did not last long. After an existence of thirty-three years, the community was transformed into a joint stock company and made no appreciable effect on improving the race...

Where external coercive forces fail, there is nothing to be hoped for in the internal automatic forces. If providence could become one of the principles of individual morals in the results of the sexual act, a great step would be made towards a possible improvement in the species...

Evolution and ways of distributing wealth
The distribution of wealth – at least in some cases – is as imperfect as the natural selection of men...

Historical evolution, which has never been the same everywhere, has established different ways of distribution suited to the

* G. de Molinari, *La Viriculture* (Paris 1897), pp. 245–50.

different societies. Stating that any of these ways of distribution cannot be changed because it is natural, means adopting a metaphysical line of reasoning which has no value . . . So, an objection *a priori* cannot be made to the reformers. But they must surmount several obstacles . . . The new distribution will modify the principles of justice and equity accepted by men. This change will influence men's happiness and probably their productive labour. For this it is necessary to examine if these effects will counter-balance the effects of a new and supposedly better distribution.

Gide,* discussing the formula 'To each according to his work', rightly says: 'It would be right to pay each man in proportion to the sufferings he has borne, the good-will that he has shown, independently of external circumstances . . . but this is the concept that we have of Divine Justice . . . As, however, we are not God, we cannot judge on the basis of intentions, but rather on the basis of the results. It would be dangerous to try to measure the effort used in any work by the time employed. Only idleness is measured in this way.'

It must be observed that the formula: 'To each according to his merits' does not solve any of the great problems of distribution, precisely because it is so vague a term . . .

If the ideal of justice consists in rewarding suffering and effort independently of the results, it must be recognised that this ideal is incompatible with the development of production.

The followers of Saint-Simon have tried to reconcile payment by results . . . and they talk about 'every capability staying in its place' . . . It is incredible that sensible people can admire such empty, meaningless formulae. What is 'capability'? How do we know its place? . . . Where shall we put the capability of petty-politicians, liars, flatterers, hack poets . . . If an individual enjoys himself copying out the verb 'to have' ten thousand times, he does a considerable job, but what reward can he expect? If there are two men, one of whom is thirsty but who is offered something to eat, while the other is hungry and is offered something to drink, these two actions do not deserve any reward. But if the thirsty man is offered something to drink and the hungry man something to eat, even if these two actions remain what they were, they must receive the reward they deserve.

* C. Gide, *Principes d'économie politique* (Paris 1884), pp. 245-50.

The problem of social organisation cannot be solved by high-flown speeches inspired by a more or less vague ideal of justice, but only by scientific research, in order to find the way to proportion the means to the ends, and the effort and the labour to the satisfaction of each individual, so that the least effort or suffering can assure as much well-being as possible for as many people as possible.

Solidarity
Nowadays, solidarity is demanded, but nobody is agreed on the precise definition of this word . . .

In the descriptive aspect it is easy to recognise that two types of concepts are linked with the word solidarity. The first, which gives the true meaning of the word, comprises concepts which simply establish a mutual dependence between the things or beings proclaimed to have a community of interest. In this sense, it is observed that mutual dependence is the great law of nature, that the vegetable kingdom and the mineral kingdom are mutually dependent, and so too are the animal kingdom and the vegetable kingdom . . . The second specifies what mutual dependence must be, in the sense that it excludes the idea that our welfare is dependent on the destruction of beings with whom we are 'solidary', and admits dependence in the sense that our prosperity is tied to that of these beings . . .

We depend on rats for the plague, and in this sense rats and men are mutually dependent; but our interest is not in the least tied to their prosperity – on the contrary, it is tied to their destruction . . .

The right to work
The extremely fertile basis of the pseudo-juridical and pseudo-historical considerations which are applied to solve social problems has produced the theory of the right to work. The grounds for this are to be found in other rights which men once had and which have now been taken away from them . . . If these juridical claims were actually traced back to the beginnings of human society, they could take us a long way and lead us into inextricable difficulties. If the proletarian has the right to claim the land of which he says his ancestors were dispossessed several thousand years before, why could a people not claim, in the same way, the

territory which another has taken from them? Why is the use of force between different peoples more legitimate than the use of force among the same people? The descendants of the Gauls, who live in France, should try to discover and expel the descendants of the Romans, Germans and Normans, but – in their turn – the descendants of the Gauls could be turned out by the descendants of the people who once upon a time occupied Gaul. This would really cause only a grand confusion...

A scientific interpretation of the class struggle

We can deplore the necessity of the struggle for survival, we can desire with all our might that this struggle end – but this has not the least influence on the problem of whether or not it exists, and of finding out whether or not it is necessary for the improvement of the species and the selection of societies and other social organisations.

Scientific interpretation has discovered that there were not only two classes, but a large number of classes; that there was not only one type of struggle – that of direct destruction – but a multitude of struggles; and that these different forms had a different value, too, in relation to the prosperity of the species.

These different forms of struggle are ways of competing and one must not forget that this is the most powerful instrument of selection ever known – as much for individuals as for social organisations...

NOTES

1 Pareto, *I Sistemi socialisti*, trans. Celestino Arena (Turin 1951), pp. 10–11.
2 G. Braga, *Forma ed equilibrio sociale* (Bologna 1959), p. XXXII.
3 *Vilfredo Pareto: Sociological Writings*, ed. S.E. Finer (London 1966), pp. 16 and 77.
4 Pareto, 'Il crepuscolo della libertà', *Rivista d'Italia*, February 1904, p. 193.
5 *Pareto-Walras, da un carteggio inedito*, ed. T. Giacalone-Monaco (Padua 1960), p. 39.
6 See: G.H. Bousquet, 'Preface' to *I Sistemi socialisti*, p. XVIII.

22 Can the bourgeoisie rise again?

In 1902, in Italy, the Socialists abandoned the anti-protectionist battle and reached a compromise with the Zanardelli-Giolitti Government. For the traditional Liberals this meant the end of a dream and a severe defeat. For people like de Viti de Marco, Papafava, Pantaleoni and Pareto, the change of face of yesterday's allies meant isolation. For Pareto this isolation was not only moral but also material. Alone in his splendid home, tormented by his domestic troubles, his pessimism seemed to deepen as he contemplated the relation between reason and men's actions. The years 1902–5 were marked by deep bitterness and pessimism. This bitterness was also reflected in his work. His judgement of human events, both present and future, was catastrophic. In 1904 he began to contribute to *Il Regno* and engaged in controversy with other contributors such as Corradini, Papini and Prezzolini. The latter still believed in an idealistic battle capable of re-awakening the bourgeoisie, and those ideals of freedom of which it was the principal supporter. To Pareto this was outdated. Being the practical man that he was, he knew that the bourgeoisie, who were progressivists and brought new ideas when they were an élite in the ascendant, could provide no more than the sterile fruits of decadence now that they were in decline. Between the lines of bitter comment we can, however, feel an unconscious desire that these ideals, held by a few, should be made to triumph, even if the decline of the bourgeoisie could never be arrested. In spite of the passion with which he wrote, two points can be noted which he had already used in the past and would develop in more detail in the future: that by which the *energy* and *courage* of a few can prevail over the cowardice and resignation of many, and that of the validity of the legitimate defence of an individual, a group, or a class.

FROM *Il Regno*, January 1904.
[Prezzolini] reproaches me for believing that the existing bourgeoisie is in decline, and that its place will be taken by another élite rising from the common people. It seems to me,

however, that new facts confirm such an impression daily ... In Italy, the bourgeoisie has not fallen so low as in other countries ... However, even in Italy, certain events have taken place which confirm my thesis. Is there not a great difference between the activity and energy of the Socialists and that of the bourgeoisie? A few Socialists, strong and resolute, have beaten the majority in the Italian Parliament, using obstructionism. A little courage would have been enough to put these gentlemen in their place, like that of the English, who beat the obstructionism of the Irish in Parliament. Nobody found that courage – neither ministers, nor the President of the House, nor the members. Let us take another comparison. Let us see what the Socialists did for the Tsar's visit, and what the bourgeoisie are doing for the visit of Loubet. I am not talking about courtesy – from this point of view the bourgeoisie are far better than the Socialists – but this does not contradict my thesis. At the time of the French Revolution, men of gentle birth were always far more courteous and well-mannered than those who guillotined them. Without losing their good manners, the good bourgeois Italians could moderate a little that irrational love which they have for the man who represents those who want to smash and destroy them; that irrational love for the leader of the government who grants an amnesty and leaves unpunished those who set fire to food shops, rob banks and attack unarmed citizens, as they did at Armentières. We are told to take no notice of what happens in other people's houses. Look who is talking! Is not Russia someone else's house as far as the Italian Socialists are concerned? And when they insulted the Tsar, were they not taking notice of what was happening in Russia? Well, then, why should it not be legitimate for the bourgeoisie to take notice of what is happening in France? The Socialists do not like the Tsar because he represents an absolutist regime. Why should the bourgeoisie like Loubet, who represents a Radical Socialist regime which is preparing a social revolution? And yet the Socialists only needed to protest to stop the Tsar from coming to Italy, and have their enemies bow down to Loubet. Tell me, when two sides stand face to face, one ready to fight and the other – cowardly and re-signed – instead of defending itself against the enemy, encourages him, which of the two is going to be the winner? Even a poor rabbit makes some attempt to bite the person trying to kill it, while these people socialise with those who aim to destroy them.

I speak in general terms, and there are certainly exceptions – those who go bravely into battle. But will they be followed?

23 Strikers in France

Something happened in France to confirm Prezzolini's prediction of the rise of a new, courageous, enterprising bourgeoisie, and this seemed to rouse Pareto from his scepticism. The new bourgeoisie did not tolerate abuse, and answered violence with violence. This observation opened a new perspective in his entire sociological analysis of equilibrium without basically altering it. The principal thesis around which all his various sociological hypotheses revolved was that the only possible, true justice is guaranteed by the neutrality of the state and by the stuggles of the various competing powers within it. Once equilibrium is tilted in favour of one of the powers which regulate the state, and once competition disappears, society moves inexorably into decline, because with the lack of competition and slection comes the probable preservation of the worst elements. This equilibrium was first upset by capitalist speculators who used the state to their own ends. as if they were the only members of that society competent to enjoy all the rights, but having no duties. Subsequently, this rule of equilibrium was infringed by the workers who began to do as they pleased, creating and applying laws to their own advantage. By means of brute force, they changed the law.

Pareto was obliged to reconsider the role of *force* in social equilibrium. In 'The dangers of socialism' he had already emphasised the decisive contribution of force in social equilibrium when stating: 'The world has always belonged to the strong and will belong to them for a long time yet.' As an argument for awakening the bourgeoisie from its lethargy he had also similar words: 'Whoever becomes a lamb will always find a wolf to eat him.' He was obliged to admit that only a force of the intensity and strength equal to that which broke old equilibria was capable of constructing new ones. If his declarations inviting the use of force are seen in this context, they lose the wilful appearance of an invocation to use force for force's sake, and assume the form of a system of reasoning in which force has begun to take on the aspect of one of the many important elements which play a role in the life of society.

FROM *Il Regno*, 31 July 1904.

At Cluses there was a strike. Certain things happened which need to be examined ... and the following observations must be made:

(1) The school of thought which holds that freedom to strike is not a simple freedom of withholding work, but a power for seizing State lands, for using violence of every kind, for throwing stones, for breaking doors and windows of shops, for looting them and setting them on fire, causes conflict if the victims show the slightest intention of standing up for themselves. The cowardly, resigned bourgeoisie bow their shoulders to the lash, while a man and his sons belonging to the new aristocracy currently arising, fight back.

(2) Is it a crime to fight back? The courts will decide – if they are willing and able – with justice and honesty. If the Crettiez fired without first being threatened and attacked, they are murderers. But, if they were attacked, one must be cautious in saying that five men must not defend themselves with the arms they possess when they are attacked by hundreds of stone-throwing men. Besides which, they did not ask for their food factory to be burned down, and suffer the fate of many other factories. The idea that property-owners must stand by and take the stones thrown by the noble strikers while their houses and food factories are burned down, is a concept proper to a declining bourgeoisie. It is understandable, then, that those belonging to the new bourgeois élite will not stand for it. If the French bourgeoisie had many Crettiez, they would not go humbly to the slaughter, as they are doing at the moment. But, when they are destroyed and a new aristocracy has taken their place, the looters will soon be eliminated.

(3) It is worth noting that the food factory was set on fire in the presence of the police ... who cannot use arms under any circumstances, owing to the present political system in France. It is evident, in this situation, that men of violence can do just as they please...

24 Humanitarians and revolutionaries

If inciting the bourgeoisie day after day drove them towards using force, one must not forget that 'force alone is blind'. Incorporated in a system, it plays a minor or major role according to events. For this reason one must remind those who talk of Pareto as an apologist of force and who quote from the letter of 22 February 1905 to Pantaleoni, in which he wrote, 'I think that only *force*, guns, cannon, will decide who will win and who must lose',[1] that in this essay he stated that force 'must be a means and not an end'. Obviously, those who charge Pareto with paving the way for fascism, because he supported the bourgeoisie, should be asked to explain what the term bourgeoisie meant to Pareto and what it means to them.

To Pareto, the bourgeoisie was not only a class with which the proletariat clashed, it was also the class which created progress founded on the best system of selectivity known, since it was based on enterprise, initiative, courage, individual freedom and, therefore, personal responsibility. The concept of the bourgeoisie as a parasite living on the humbler classes is different. Pareto had always fought against a bourgeoisie of this sort and there is no reason to believe that he had changed his opinion. A parasitic bourgeoisie was as much an obstacle to progress as a proletarian class which had lost its spirit of emulation and put its trust in the negligent, bureaucratic actions of its leaders. It should not be forgotten that Pareto's bitterness stemmed from the fact that 'bourgeois privileges have been removed only to be replaced by popular privileges'. His disapproval arose above all from the fact that 'not even for a single second has the middle ground been held'.[2] This middle ground was important for him in that it not only paved the way for progress (also through a greater production of wealth) but also because, by encouraging the weak of that particular time, it stopped the strong winning hands down and, in their excitement in winning, destroying their opponents.

Basically, not surrendering too easily was a duty rather than a right, as those who surrender too easily contradict their precise, social, natural duty and, instead of encouraging the enemy to be more merciful, cause them to be more cruel. It was only in the light of these reflections that Pareto stated: 'Humanitarians are preparing extremely cruel massacres and destruction.' Unfortunately, this forecast was to be confirmed by reality, not only in respect of the cowardly bourgeoisie, incapable of rising up against the domineering proletariat, but also in respect of the cowardice of those who would prove incapable of opposing the Nazi domination when the time was ripe.

FROM *Il Regno*, 30 October 1904.

. . . If a reactionary party existed in Italy, I should be able to say that there are two parties with the hope of a prosperous future: this and the socialist revolutionary party. But, as the former does not exist, only the latter remains.

. . . Who does it help if you bury your head in the sand and not see the danger? . . . The socialist revolutionary party will probably win as it is the only, or almost only, party which feels no repugnance at using force – and this, from the beginning of time, is the only means of gaining and maintaining victory. While the bourgeois humanitarians faint like maiden aunts at the word blood, the revolutionaries know that everything has been produced by bloody battles.

But force alone is blind. It must be a means and not an end, and must be so for a conservative or reactionary party as it is for the socialist revolutionaries . . . However, by a strange contrast of facts, unintentionally and unconsciously, the humanitarians are preparing extremely cruel massacres and destruction.

---

1 Pareto, *Lettere a Maffeo Pantaleoni*, vol. II, p. 437.
2 Pareto, 'Il crepuscolo della libertà', *Rivista d'Italia*, February 1904.

25 Regarding happenings in Russia

Pareto's hypothesis that the age of reason was dead, and men no longer used logic but the power of demagogy, received further proof from new events. On 22 January 1905, the Imperial Guard of St Petersburg fired on demonstrators and killed some of them. They had demanded civil rights, the summoning of a representative parliament of the western type – a *Duma* – the rejection of *mir* and the system of collective agricultural economy in favour of the introduction of the principle of private property. Just seven years before, at the time of the Milan Massacre, Pareto had demonstrated his solidarity with the strikers and the politically persecuted and his antipathy towards Crispi. Now he reversed his thesis. He applauded the resolution with which the Tsarist government put an end to the uprising by force. As though satisfied by the fact that his hypothesis had had another confirmation, he emphasised: 'The events in Russia confirm that a government which is able and willing to use force, will not fall.' The events which followed show that that useless bloodshed caused a real revolution to break out throughout the country – like a dress rehearsal for the Great Revolution of 1917.

By now, Pareto was so convinced that the use of force was indispensable that he rejected the hypothesis that the right concessions might have avoided further recourse to force. Yet only five years before, he had declared in 'Justice': 'Whoever has more sense, uses more ... Whoever wants these contrasts to disappear (and even if they cannot disappear completely, they can become less marked) tells today's victors to be more temperate, less unjust, thus trying to make tomorrow's victors more moderate and less unjust.' The reader may be greatly surprised at seeing these two absolutely contrasting positions, and yet this surprise is not so great as that which hurt Pareto when he saw the same people who had suppressed economic and political freedom in Italy and France (or were in the process of doing so) fight in favour of it. In this context, this reversal of opinion seems almost an adaptation to a changing reality. As if justifying his change of opinion, a few days later he wrote: 'Socialism is tending to become

more and more bourgeois, ethical and humanitarian.'[1] In this Pareto
saw the death of a myth – the myth created by Socialist martyrs, those
Socialists who, with faith, had fought to change society for the better.
In the bourgeois socialism of the present, he found, instead, the same
characteristic of the idolatry of the absolutist Tsarist state. Socialism,
like Tsarism, fought to change radically the conditions of social
economy.

FROM *Il Regno*, 12 February 1905.
... Some years ago the followers of agricultural collectivism, like
Laveleye, emphasised the beneficial effects of the Russian *mir*,
comparing it with our *individualistic* and *liberal* societies ... How
opinions have changed. Why? It seems to me that the new élite
praises and supports collectivism as the means to the end of
taking over power ... For example, in France, Jaurès and his
companions openly supported collectivism at the beginning, thus
obtaining their first followers; but when they came to power they
no longer thought about collectivism ... and they have not
nationalised even the smallest mine, the humblest factory, the
most modest business. They shouted 'Down with capitalists!'
and they have become the capitalists' allies ... The Russian
government tends more and more to become a socialist bureaucracy, and even now – after the uprisings which it perhaps did
not want to put down, in order to make use of them later, as
Giolitti did in Italy – it turns against the liberal bourgeoisie with
all its might and tries to attract the less educated workers ... So
the western socialists and the Russian government are competing
firms who produce the same goods ...

The Russian liberals have learned almost nothing from history,
and, as the liberals of western Europe have already done, direct
their efforts to helping those who will strip them of everything
they have. For their part, our bourgeoisie have less sense than that
small fish which, when asked if he wanted to be eaten boiled or
roasted, answered that he did not want to be eaten at all. Instead,
they have chosen the way they want to be cooked, and prefer
western demagogic sauce rather than eastern bureaucratic sauce
... They cry like wounded eagles because the Russian government has killed and wounded some of its enemies, but they do
not reproach the looting, fires and woundings done by the enemies of the Russian government. They say that if the govern-

ment had made some concessions, all the trouble would have been avoided. They have forgotten how Louis XVI came to his end through making too many concessions. They hurriedly sign a petition in favour of Gorki, but they do not really know if he is innocent or guilty. But they bow down to the divine right of demagogy...

The same day that the newspapers printed the news of the petition signed by the Italian Deputies in favour of Gorki, the news also appeared that in Verona, a poor wretch who thought that he could work without the permission of the strikers, our masters, had been attacked and nearly killed by a striker. If our Deputies, weighed down by the grave worries of international demagogy, could find a little time, could they not give some protection to those poor citizens who want to work honestly?

If concerned about events abroad, should one not also bother about *other* countries – like the U.S.A., where our fellow-countrymen are persecuted, and the Tyrol, where they are insulted and attacked by the Austrians? ...

We are drawing near to the day of the supreme battle – carefully prepared by the attackers; awaited with supine resignation by the attacked – who are deaf and blind by choice.

All over Europe the new élite daily acquires importance, so that every reasonable hope of stopping its victory through persuading and convincing the majority of the citizens is disappearing.

Only force is left to decide who will be the winners and who the losers. The events in Russia confirm that the government which is able and willing to use force will not fall ...

---

1 Pareto, 'Socialismo legalitario e socialismo rivoluzionario', in *Il Divenire sociale*, 1 April 1905, now in Pareto, *Battaglie liberiste*, ed. L. Avagliano (Naples 1975), p. 465.

26 Manual of political economy

While writing *Les Systèmes socialistes*, Pareto was pondering another work which would express in the economic field the new approach which he was developing in the methodological and sociological field. This work was an elaboration of the principles already expressed in 'The new theories of economics'. The image that he had of reality was adaptable and, as Giacalone-Monaco quite rightly observed, the laws too took on a character of 'results of a particular way of elaborating facts (that is, appearances): generalising inductively – from a human, practical point of view – and therefore, temporary'.[1]

The observer seems to become one with the object observed, while the separation from the abstract methodology of Walras became more marked. 'Certainty' became the 'possibility of certainty'. In this too, Pareto seemed to be ahead of his time. Giacalone-Monaco reminds us[2] that it was several years later that the physicist Heisenberg proposed a similar principle when he stated 'that even the more precise conceptual systems *responding to all the needs of logical, mathematical exactness* are no more than attempts to find our way hesitantly in the limited field of reality.'[3]

The distinction between mathematical method and orthodox logic had already been underlined several years before, when Pareto stated: 'When we reason with orthodox logic, we can examine it as we gradually pass from one proposition to another, and if it seems to contradict the concepts that we consider true, we stop and decide whether the latter are to be modified or the former rejected. But the use of the mathematical method – more than the algebraic method and less than the geometric method – does not allow us to carry out this procedure. The intermediary propositions escape our notice. We only perceive the final proposition. According to strict logic, we can state that one proposition follows from another; but we do not know whether, along the way, we may not have wandered too far from the truth.'[4] Now he set abstract phenomena against concrete phenomena, pure economy against applied economy. But even in contrasting them he recognised that both were essential in the method of establishing knowledge. He had already stated that economy found its basis in man, and now he found that man had his basis in his emotions. His line of argument was more cautious and directed towards particulars while his old rejection of metaphysics became almost the rejection of too ambitious a system. Here is echoed what he had already stated in the Congrès International de Philosophie at Geneva in September 1904, when he said: 'I do not admit any judgement as possessing a character of manifest universality *from a scientific point of view*, as such a judgement would state something beyond the limits of time and space which surround our knowledge.'[5]

In this revaluation of subjectivity and concrete phenomena, the force of the translation of the analysis of economic equilibrium into that of psycho-sociological equilibrium is amplified. Pure political economy seems to have a reduced role as 'Whoever suggests a practical measure must take into consideration not only the economic consequences, but also the moral, religious and political consequences.' Socio-economic equilibrium becomes the mirror of subjective equilibrium. However, methodological subjectivism and economic egoism do not eliminate the necessity of also using pure economics. Pareto stated: 'When one wants to study crystallography, one begins by studying geometry; not because one believes that the crystals are perfect geometrical forms, but because the study of geometric forms furnishes indispensable elements for the study of crystals. In the same way, we begin with the study of pure economics, not because we believe that the abstract phenomena of this science are identical to the concrete phenomena, but simply because it is useful to us when studying concrete phenomena.' By doing this, he stated an apparent contradiction. He had held that science was 'essentially analytic' and practice 'essentially synthetic', suggesting that science was not arbitrary, but practice was essentially arbitrary. Now, he postulated the element of an initial arbitrary act as much in the method of seeking knowledge as in practical action, so that they assumed the symmetrical aspects of the two sides of a coin. In action as in reasoning, apart from any subsequent development, the starting point is important. According to the starting point, either an action or a theory can be constructed which remains neutral with respect to the goals which one wants to reach. It is to honour this scientific neutrality – including both theory and practice – that, as Avagliano so rightly points out, Pareto also reached in this work, 'a net position of equi-distance between an organisation based on private enterprise and on collectivism'.[6]

A few months after the publication of this work Pareto, recalling his theoretical positions before moving to Lausanne and explaining his change of opinion, wrote in a letter to Antonucci: 'Political economy, as the so-called classical economists had constituted it, was a perfect or nearly perfect science; it only remained for the principles to be put into practice. So it was necessary to imitate Cobden's Free Trade League . . . In politics, the sovereignty of the people was an axiom, freedom was the universal panacea . . . militarism and religion were the major scourges of the human race. Caesar among the ancients and Napoleon I and Napoleon III among the moderns were examples of evil-doers in my opinion . . . With the passing of the years these youthful ardours cooled down. When the left came to power in Italy and the Republic succeeded the Empire in France, I was forced to recognise that the theories did not correspond with the facts. I partly modified them and leant towards liberal-conservative ideas, a little like those of de Molinari . . . As to economics, having to teach it made me study it more closely – and I realised that many of my theories had to be modified in order to become scientific. Later, when I began to teach sociology, I underwent the same experience. I learnt above all to be distrustful of emotions so that now, if something agrees with my feelings, I only become suspicious and seek arguments against it with greater care than if it were contrary to my feelings.'[7] As can be seen from this explanation which Pareto gave of his own theoretical intellectual pilgrimage, the weight of emotion – even if relevant and, therefore, more important than in the past – is still, however, subordinated to the rigorous evaluation of reason. It is a matter of reasoning reduced to atoms, but it is not, on this account, less analytic, or less synthetic. It can be said that with this the *Trattato* is conceived, which is considered by many to be non-organic. It is, on the contrary, made up of many atomic parts, each of which has an individual value. Commenting on the French edition in 1909, translated by Bonnet, from which these extracts have been taken, de Rosa observed, 'It is clear that he is working on *Trattato di sociologica*.'[8]

FROM *Manuale di economia politica*, Milan, 1906.
Science is essentially analytic – practice is essentially synthetic

I.4 Human actions present certain uniformities and it is thanks only to this property that they can be the object of a scientific study. These uniformities also have another name – laws.

I.6 . . . If one does not admit the existence of uniformities, the knowledge of the past and the present is merely a curiosity and nothing can be deduced for the future. Reading a novel about chivalry or *The Three Musketeers* is the same as reading Thucydides' accounts. If, instead, one expects to make the slightest deduction for the future from the knowledge of the past, this means admitting – at least implicitly – that there are uniformities.

I.7 . . . But scientific laws do not have an objective existence. The imperfection of our spirit does not permit us to consider phenomena as a whole and we are obliged to study them separately. As a consequence, in place of general uniformities which are and will always remain unknown, we are obliged to consider an infinite number of particular uniformities which cross each other, superimpose themselves on each other, and contradict each other, in a thousand ways . . .

I.20 . . . There are two great classes of sciences: those like physics, chemistry, mechanics, which can base their findings on experiment, and those like meteorology, astronomy, political economy, which cannot – or, if they do, only with difficulty – and these must be content with observation . . . The sciences which can only use observation separate certain phenomena from others by abstraction; whereas the sciences which can use experiment realise this abstraction materially. However, abstraction constitutes the preliminary and indispensable condition of all research for all the sciences.

I.21 This abstraction is necessarily subjective. It is in no way objective. It is, therefore, arbitrary – at least within certain limits – because the aim that it must serve must be taken into consideration. As a consequence, a particular abstraction or a particular classification does not necessarily exclude another abstraction or another classification. They can both be useful according to the aim that a person has.

I.26 When one goes back to the concrete from the abstract, one must necessarily unite the parts which had been separated in order to study them better. Science is essentially analytic; practice is essentially synthetic. Political economy must not consider morals but whoever suggests a practical measure must take into consideration not only the economic consequences, but also the moral, religious and political consequences . . .

I.33 The origins of economic phenomena have been studied with care by many modern scholars, and this is certainly useful from an historical point of view. But it would be a mistake to believe that one could attain a knowledge of the relationships which exist among the phenomena of our society through this study. It is the same mistake which ancient philosophers made when they wanted to go back to the origins of things. In place of astronomy they studied cosmogony. Instead of finding out about the minerals, vegetables and animals which they had under their noses, they tried to find out how these things had been generated. Geology has become a science which only made progress on the day when it began studying actual problems and then going on to past phenomena, instead of doing the reverse.

I.51 Up to now we have talked about proof. Invention is something completely different. It is certain that the latter can find its origin in ideas which have nothing to do with reality and which can be absurd. Chance, bad reasoning, imaginary analogies can direct us towards true propositions. But when one wants to demonstrate these propositions, the only way to do so is by finding out whether they agree with experience directly or indirectly.

Non-logical actions and logical actions

II.1 Psychology is evidently the basis of political economy, and in general of all social sciences. Perhaps the day will come when we shall be able to deduce the laws of social science from the principles of psychology, in the same way that perhaps one day the principle of what matter consists of will give us, through deduction, all the laws of physics and chemistry. But we are still a long way from this and we need to take another route. We must begin with certain empirical principles in order to explain the phenomena of sociology like those of physics and chemistry. Later psychology, lengthening the chain of its deductions, and sociology, going back to more and more general principles, can unite and make up a deductive science, but these hopes are still too far off to be realised.

II.2 To put a little order into the infinite variety of human actions which we must study, it will be useful to classify them according to certain types . . .

II.3 Abstractly, we can distinguish: (1) non-logical actions, (2) logical actions. We say abstractly, because in real actions these two types are nearly always mixed, and an action can be non-logical for the greater part and logical for the lesser part and vice versa.

II.22 ... It is commonly thought – implicitly or explicitly – that men are directed exclusively by reason and that, as a consequence, their emotions are linked logically. But this is a false opinion and is belied by numerous facts which take us to another extreme opinion – this, too, is false – that men are directed exclusively by their emotions and not by reason. These emotions have their origin in man's nature, combined with the circumstances in which he has lived, and it is not permissible to state *a priori* that there is a logical link between them . . .

II.29 . . . Man does not want to understand that an agreeable or disagreeable sensation is a basic fact that cannot be deduced by reasoning. When a man experiences a sensation it is absurd for him to want to prove that he is experiencing a different one. If a man feels he is lucky, it is quite ridiculous to convince him that he is unlucky, or vice versa . . . An individual is the only judge of what he likes or does not like, and if for example, there is a man who does not like spinach, it is the height of the ridiculous and the absurd to try and convince him – as is done for Pythagoras' Theorem – that he likes spinach, It can be proved to him that as a result of tolerating a certain disagreeable sensation he will have an agreeable sensation – for example by eating spinach every day he will be cured of a certain illness – but he alone is the judge in knowing whether or not the compensation exists between this suffering and this pleasure; and nobody can logically prove that this compensation exists if he, to the contrary, feels that it does not exist . . .

II.42 Now let us try to find out if these sensations have an objective existence independent of the diversities of human intelligence, or if they are subordinate to these diversities of human intelligence. It is easy to see that we can only admit the latter hypothesis. Just as the emotions related to religion, morals, patriotism, etc., are expressed in ways which are literally and formally common to many men, so these men understand them differently. Plato's, Socrates' and Theophastus' 'superstitious man' had the same religion – but they certainly understood it in very different ways . . .

II.83 It is useless to try and find out if moral emotions have an individual or social origin. The man who does not live in society is abnormal and has little, or rather nothing, in common with us. On the other hand, society apart from individuals is an abstraction which corresponds to nothing real. As a consequence, all the emotions we have observed in the man who lives in society are, from a certain point of view, individual, and from another, social. Social metaphysics, which serves as a substratum to this type of research, is simply a socialist metaphysics and tends to defend certain doctrines *a priori*.

II.84 It would be more important to know how emotions are aroused, modified, and disappear nowadays, instead of trying to find out their origins. Knowing how certain emotions are aroused in primitive societies simply satisfies our curiosity and has more or less no other use. Similarly a sailor has no interest in knowing what the boundaries of the seas were in ancient geological eras, whilst his interest is to know what they are today. Unfortunately, we know very little about the natural history of the emotions of our own times.

II.94 The same idea can be expressed in different languages, and in the same language in different forms. The same discussion that some centuries ago would have taken a theological line will take a socialist line today . . .More generally, it can be emphasised that in society a phenomenon which remains basically the same, in the course of time assumes various and often very different forms. In other words, there is a permanence of the same phenomenon under different forms.

II.95 There is a particle of truth in the observation of Sorel . . . that 'Myths are necessary to expose in an exact form the conclusions of a social philosophy that does not want to deceive itself'. Every time that we want to try to understand what certain men think or have thought, we must know the language and the forms with which they express their thoughts. Grote, for example, has made it clear that we cannot understand the history of the ancient Greeks, unless we try to borrow – as far as possible – the myths that formed the intellectual milieu in which they lived. In the same way, whoever seeks successfully to manage men must speak their language and adopt the forms that they like, and, as a consequence, use the language of myths.

II.96 But Sorel's theory is incomplete, because besides these subjective phenomena, there are phenomena which are objective, and one cannot stop others from interesting themselves in them.

Difficulties in examining how certain hypothetical modifications of certain social facts act on other facts

II.97 . . . A problem of great importance remains to be studied. If one of the facts which have been seen to be related to others were to be modified, in what ways would the others change? This problem is a necessary preliminary to the solution of a second problem which consists of trying to find out the conditions which result in the greatest utility for society, a part of society, a social class, or a specific individual – when, naturally, what is meant by 'utility' is defined beforehand.

II.98 These problems arise in all man's actions and, as a consequence, in those acts which are the object of politics, too. In practice, they have more importance than all the others . . . and any other study is only of use in that it prepares a solution for them. They are the most difficult. We find them in political economy and we are able to reach solutions which are at least approximate. But, by contrast, these problems still have no solutions – not even very approximate – when it is a question of actions depending on emotions and politics. This difference chiefly explains why economic science should be advanced by comparison with the other social sciences.

II.99 In this subject the basis of all reasoning is to be found in the following problem: what effect will certain given measures have on the emotions? Not only are we not in a position to solve this problem in general and theoretically, but neither are we in possession of the practical solutions which, in the history of human knowledge, commonly precede theoretical solutions and which usually form the subject from which the latter are drawn. Even the most eminent statesmen nearly always make a mistake when they try to find these solutions. It is enough to remember the example of Bismarck. He proposed to solve the following problem: what measures would be able to weaken the emotions that sustain the Catholic and Socialist parties? He thought he had found the solution in the *Kulturkampf* and the extraordinary measures against the Socialists. Facts have demonstrated that he seriously deceived himself. The effects which followed were the exact opposite of what he had hoped. The Catholic party has dominated the Reichstag. The Socialist party has increased its influence, and every election has seen an increase in the number of its votes. The measures adopted by Bismarck have not only not

put a stop to these consequences, they have also greatly contributed to them.

II.100 The difficulties which hinder the elaboration of a theory
on this subject are partly objective and partly subjective. Among
the objective difficulties we raise the following: (1) Phenomena
are produced very slowly, and, as a consequence, do not present
the frequency necessary to constitute a theory with proof and
counter-proof. All branches of science have made extraordinary
progress, and yet in this subject the best we have are Aristotle
and Machiavelli . . . (2) Phenomena which are attached to the
emotions cannot be measured with precision, so we cannot call
on statistics – so useful in political economy. The statement that
certain emotions become weaker or stronger is always rather
arbitrary and always depends in some measure on the author who
judges events. (3) Sociological phenomena are sometimes far
rarer and more complex than those which political economy
studies. They are the result of many more causes or, more exactly,
they are in a mutual relationship with a greater number of other
phenomena. (4) As these sociological phenomena are very often
non-logical we cannot put them in a mutual relationship using
logical deductions – something which we can do in political
economy. The difficulty is accentuated even more by the fact
that men are in the habit of explaining their actions by motives
not really logical. (5) It is extremely difficult to know precisely
the feelings of others and even one's own feelings, so that the
material which should serve as a basis of the theory – in examining the question as to how certain hypothetical modifications of
certain social facts act on other facts – is always rather uncertain . . .

II.101 Now let us go on to subjective difficulties. (1) Authors
almost never look for the truth. They look for arguments to
defend their preconception of the truth and what for them is an
article of faith . . . (2) There are infinite prejudices and ideas
a priori depending on religion, morals, patriotism, etc., and they
stop us from reasoning scientifically on social problems. (3) The
objective difficulty indicated in **100** (5) is related to an analogous,
subjective difficulty: that is to say, it is very difficult for us not
to judge the actions of others through our own emotions . . .
(4) Only faith makes men react. So, for the good of society, it is
highly undesirable for the majority of men, or any large number

of them, to interest themselves scientifically in social problems. There is an antagonism between the conditions of *action* and those of *knowledge* . . . (5) The contrast between these also results from the fact that when we act we conform to certain rules of customs and morals, and it really must be so precisely because we would have neither the opportunity nor the means to go back to the origin in any particular case, and to develop a complete theory about it. On the contrary, to have a knowledge of the relationship between things – *to know* – it is necessary to put forward principles for debate . . . (6) To convince someone in scientific matters it is necessary to present the facts with as much exactitude as possible, and to put them into a logical relationship with the consequences which one wants to draw. To convince someone in a matter of emotion – and nearly all reasonings regarding society and human institutions belong to this category – it is necessary to present the facts capable of arousing these emotions, since they prompt the conclusion which one wants to draw. It is clear that these two types of reasoning are completely different . . .

General notions on economic equilibrium
   III.1 . . . We shall study the logical actions frequently repeated by men in order to procure the things which satisfy their tastes.
   III.18 . . . We see economic problems arise in reality where there is an exchange contract in which one thing is given in order to receive another; and also where there is production: where certain things are transformed into others. Now, we shall interest ourselves in these problems.
   III.19 The elements which we must combine are men's tastes on the one hand and the obstacles to satisfying them on the other. If, instead of men, we were to study ethereal beings without tastes or needs – not even feeling the material need to eat and drink – we should have no economic problem to solve. Neither should we have any economic problem to solve if, going from one extreme to the other, we were to suppose that there were no obstacles to the satisfaction of men's tastes and desires. For the man who has everything at his disposal, there is no economic problem at all. The problem occurs because tastes encounter certain obstacles and it is all the more difficult to solve since there are so many potential means of satisfying these tastes and over-

coming these obstacles. Then, the question arises: to try and find out how and why such-and-such a means is preferred by individuals. Let us examine the problem closely.

III.21 Let us consider a series of combinations of a different quantity of goods. Man can pass from one to another of these combinations, and in the end stop at one of them. It is very important to know what the final choice is, and this is reached through the theory of economic equilibrium.

III.22 Economic equilibrium can be defined in terms of different aspects which lead to the same thing. It can be said that economic equilibrium is the state maintained indefinitely if there is no change in the conditions in which it is observed . . . For example, an individual given certain circumstances and certain conditions, buys a kilogramme of bread every day. If he is obliged to buy 900 grammes one day, but the next day he has become free again, he goes back to buying a kilogramme of bread. If nothing has changed in the conditions in which he finds himself, he will continue to buy a kilogramme of bread indefinitely, and this is what is called the state of equilibrium . . .

III.90 . . . As a consequence, the general problem of equilibrium divides into three other problems which comprise: (1) discovering the equilibrium for tastes; (2) discovering the equilibrium for obstacles, or for producers; (3) finding the common point for these two equilibria and therefore forming a general point of equilibrium.

Up to now, pure economics has only given a synthetic notion of economic phenomena

III.228 Summarising . . . the most useful theories are those which consider economic equilibrium in general, and which investigate how it arises from the contra-position of tastes and obstacles. It is the mutual dependence of economic phenomena which makes the use of mathematics indispensable in order to study these phenomena. Ordinary logic can serve very well in studying the relationship between cause and effect, but it becomes impotent as soon as it is a matter of relationships of mutual dependence. In rational mechanics and pure economics these relationships need to use mathematics. The main usefulness which comes out of the theory of pure economics stems from the fact that it gives us a synthetic notion of economic equilibrium, and for the moment we have no other means of reaching this goal. But the phenomena studied by pure economics sometimes differ a little, sometimes a lot, from the concrete phenomena, and it remains for applied economics to study these differences. It would not be very rational to expect to regulate economic phenomena through the usual theories of pure economics.

IV.31 Some have believed that political economy would have acquired in its own deductions the certainty and rigour of the deductions of celestial mechanics, from the mere fact that it makes use of mathematics. But this is a serious mistake. In mechanics all the consequences of a given hypothesis are verified by facts, and the conclusion is drawn that it is more than likely that this hypothesis is sufficiently precise to explain the concrete phenomena. In political economy we cannot hope for such a result, as we know – without any doubt – that in part our hypotheses are far removed from actuality and, as a consequence, it is only within certain limits that the conclusion which we can draw could correspond to facts. The same also happens in most of the arts and concrete sciences (for example, engineering) so that theory is more often a means of research, rather than a proof, and one should never neglect to verify whether the deductions correspond to reality.

IX.1 When one wants to study crystallography, one begins by studying geometry: not because one believes that the crystals are perfect geometrical forms, but because the study of geometrical forms furnishes indispensable elements for the study of crystals. In the same way, we begin with the study of pure economics, not because we believe that the abstract phenomena of this science are identical with the concrete phenomena, but simply because it is useful to us when studying concrete phenomena.

NOTES

1 *Pareto-Walras*, p. 62.
2 *Ibid*, p. 72.
3 W. Heisenberg, *Mutamenti nelle basi della scienza* (Turin 1944), p. 106.
4 Pareto, 'Considerazioni sui principii fondamentali dell'economia politica pura', *Giornale degli economisti*, May 1892, pp. 389–420, now in Pareto, *Scritti teorici* p. 65.
5 Pareto, *L'Individuel et le social*, ed. Claparède (Geneva 1905), pp. 125–31, 137–9, now in *Cahiers Pareto*, no. 8 1965, pp. 111–35.
6 L. Avagliano, 'Introduction' to Pareto, *Battaglie liberiste*, p. 21.

7 Pareto, letter to Antonucci of 7 December 1907, now in A. Antonucci, *Alcune lettere di Vilfredo Pareto* (Rome 1938), pp. 19–23.
8 G. de Rosa, in Pareto, *Lettere a Maffeo Pantaleoni*, vol. III.

Pareto had just published his *Manuale* and was pondering an even vaster work. He began to collect a large quantity of material for it: quotations, observations, notes. His journalism, already reduced after his disappointment in 1902, was still further restricted. Throwing himself into research on another dynamic system which leaves preeminence to reason and logic without neglecting reality in all its aspects – from the mythical aspect to the religious one, the passionate aspect to the sentimental one – he published this essay which, like nearly all the essays of those years, he had conceived as part of his *Trattato*.

In the past his main aim had been to find some universal objective criteria in which the intervention of the emotions, and any other nonexperimental reality, were reduced to a minimum – or at least were confined to the initial stage of reasoning or action. One has only to recall the beginning of his *Les Systèmes socialistes* or the letter to Antonucci. He became more and more convinced that reason and faith are permanently linked. As Busino points out, he had already discovered in the period of the lecture 'Il metodo nella sociologia', delivered at the University of Bologna, that 'Those sociologies which move from certain principles *a priori* are better than the others from the point of view of social utility.'[1] In this work myth plays a primary role. He observes how all social movements which have had any impact on history have been upheld by a faith – and so their success has been guaranteed by the intensity of myth rather than by logical reasoning.

There are few novelties in *Le Mythe vertüiste*, but as a work it is important because it clarifies the *Trattato* – being conceived as part of it – and, in summarising his earlier works, it serves as a link with their successors. Fundamental aspects of his ideas remain: (1) that not only morals and religion, but also politics 'are a matter of opinion'; (2) that with regard to action, experimental science can only indicate the multiplicity of means, and it is myth and faith which help us to choose the best among them; (3) that certain *gentlemen* must be condemned not because they 'want to impose their opinions by force', but because they use a blind force, supported neither by reasoning nor by an authentic myth.

His fight remained a fight for clarity, and his main enemies were those who in the past had confused reason with a parody of reason, and those who now confused myth with a parody of myth.

FROM *Le Mythe vertüiste*, Paris, 1911.

. . . The state no longer has an orthodox doctrine of social organisation, but it possesses one on sexual feelings. An anarchist newspaper which says that 'The proletariat must rip out the guts of the bourgeoisie' can be displayed in a newspaper kiosk, while the picture of a naked woman is forbidden . . .

In the session of the House on 4 June 1910, Luzzatti said that he had ordered the police to confiscate all obscene publications that could corrupt innocent children, and quoted the words of the Gospel . . .

The sophism of 'in the interest of children' is not new and has been used throughout the ages . . . Today, there is only more of it and better. Arguments about Malthus' theory, which were allowed until yesterday, are now settled by court sentences.

The Correctional Court of the Seine on 18 December 1909, found guilty a newspaper which carried the headline, 'La génération consciente' . . . The judgement states: 'From the investigations and the proceedings, it appears that Mr X – in his newspaper, his course, and single lectures – has preached free love, equality of the sexes in the sexual act, and the elimination of the risk of pregnancy on the part of the woman owing to scientific discoveries (i.e. she does not become a mother unless she so wishes, thanks to the use of contraceptives). Such a thesis is, therefore, immoral and a permanent incitement to libertinism and corruption and presents the greatest social danger' . . . But it should be observed that, as to the utility, it is not very clear why other doctrines, like the anarchist doctrine, are allowed while only Malthus' theory is forbidden . . . Men are allowed to believe what they please about the Christian God, but they are not allowed the same freedom in sexual matters.

The minds of these followers of 'morality' are so narrow that perhaps they do not understand that Malthusian theory is substantially a problem of equilibrium between the interest of the

species and that of the individual, and that to solve it it is necessary to have that knowledge of sociology so conspicuously lacking
in those few fanatical, poor-spirited petty politicians. This is why
these people do not realise that to attempt to solve an extremely
serious scientific problem with an article of the criminal code is
ridiculous ...

The 'gentlemen' defenders of public morals are entitled to say
that their opinion is right and that every contrary opinion is
wrong ... but they must not come and tell us that only a dishonest
man can hold opinions contrary to their own.

It is essential to notice that here we are not trying to find out
which code of morals is the best, but whether there is one of
universal application or whether there are many.

If there are many codes of morals, and experimental science
does not allow the acceptance of any other hypotheses, morality
becomes indisputably a matter of opinion, just as religion and
politics are at the moment, and there is no justification for a
different treatment of any of the three ...

These 'gentlemen' start growing dangerous only when they
try to impose their opinions by force. Everyone knows that in
Rome the statue of Justice by Gugliemo della Porta has been
dressed in a copper shirt by Bernini to cover its nudity. This is
ridiculous but excusable, if one only remembers that this statue
is in St Peter's. Unfortunately, however, the moralists do not
just want to put shirts on statues, they want to destroy them as
well – or at least see to it that they are not reproduced or photo-
graphed, something which is entirely different.

Absolute prohibition of the nude figure would be understandable in those countries where prostitution is also forbidden.
But where this is allowed, it really is funny that the law should
forbid the representation of what it allows in the flesh ... All this
is inconsistent and simply leads to hypocrisy ...

All the obscene books put together have never done as much
harm to social customs as the numerous court sentences in which
the worst offenders are lightly punished, or even acquitted, if they
can excuse their misdeeds as crimes of passion or honour ...

Now let us look at the relationship between this moralistic
phenomenon and other social phenomena. Social movements are
generally rhythmic and cause successive oscillations. When a
number of these oscillations move in the same direction, they

result in a general movement of considerable size ...

In the first sixty years of the nineteenth century, the general inclination of the people was towards freedom. Then, little by little, this inclination changed direction, moving towards ever greater restrictions on freedom, and nothing can convince us that we are nearing another change ...

The economy has been hit harder than anything else. Day after day tariff protection is growing. Even free trade is now threatened in its last refuge – England . . . The ever-growing needs of the Treasury have resulted, as a consequence, in new measures which limit freedom. Everything is taxed. Everything is controlled. But the increased taxes invite fraud, and to avoid this the need arises for restrictive measures to try to stop tax-payers hiding their wealth.

Public health has served as a pretext for a great number of restrictions on freedom . . . Italy forbids the use of saccharine, thus allowing her sugar manufacturers to make colossal profits. Switzerland has discovered that the saffron which Italians put in their spaghetti is a danger to health . . . Finland forbids alcoholic drinks, but not the beer which it produces. The despotic government of the Tsar has not confirmed this law, and the Finns are still 'free' to drink wine. They would no longer have this freedom if their country were free. In the new sense of the word 'freedom', the more the things that are forbidden to man, the freer he is considered to be. So, the man in prison is the freest of all.

The moralistic movement . . . manifests itself in all its vigour . . . without bothering too much about scientific rigour. We can say that society has rhythmic periods which could be called periods of youth and senility. At present, our societies are moving towards senility. The heroic age of socialism has passed. The rebels of yesterday are the establishment of today. They no longer talk of destroying capitalism, of overturning society, of creating a new social organisation completely different from the old one . . . The old saying that when the Devil grows old he becomes a hermit is very true. This is the fate of the socialists: stout defenders of morality and decency . . . Where are the old promises? Some increase in wages, some decrease in working hours: this is the tiny mouse born of the mountain.

The moralistic movement is also helped by another cause linked with phenomena which are not rhythmic, or which perhaps have

a longer-term rhythm than the phenomena we have discussed.
Two things characterise our times: the increasing disintegration
of the family, and the decrease in patriotic feeling and military
discipline . . . So, two movements completely opposite to each
other can be observed. On the one hand, we have a growing
indulgence towards adultery . . . on the other, a growing rigour
against immoral customs. For an individual to photograph a nude
is a crime condemned by the new laws throughout the civilised
world, but for him to take the flesh-and-blood woman away from
her family and children is a mere peccadillo in which the legislators are not interested . . .

Once it was the parents who protected the morals of their
children . . . now children are taken from the authority of their
parents, who in any case, no longer see much of them, as they are
out of the house nearly all day. In modern-style families, the son
laughs at the father who still talks about the mother-country . . .
He is a pacifist . . . Science teaches him that morality is the art of
being happy and that good actions are those which are really
useful. Those who teach these things think, perhaps, about a
general utility. Therefore, do not ask him to make any sacrifices –
he will not even understand what you mean. He knows that the
duty of the state is to keep any temptation away from the individual, and that the individual does not have to resist temptation . . .

Georges Sorel* has shown us very clearly the great importance
of the myth in the life of the people. It is the ideal, manifesting
itself in the form of a myth, that excites them, leads them,
supports them, and makes them capable of great historical
actions. The people which no longer possesses either ideals or
myths vegetates and tends to disappear.

Here we have a problem: we have shown the practical absurdities, the ridiculousness of moralism, but why can we not accept
it as an ideal, a myth? Why can we not see in it one of the forces
capable of transforming society? The problem is worth examining carefully . . .

When facing great dangers, epidemics and wars, the Romans
had the habit of celebrating a *lectisternium*: that is, they offered a
banquet to the gods . . . This myth in itself was extremely
ridiculous . . . but reality is far different. The myth of *lectisternium*

---

* G. Sorel, *Réflexions sur la violence*, 3rd ed. (Paris 1912), pp. 92ff.

is only the accessory of another myth: the one which made the Romans believe that their city enjoyed divine protection. This myth, in its turn, is no other than the manifestation of an intimate emotion: that of the profound, absolute faith which the Romans had in Rome's destiny. History shows that it was the deeds inspired by this emotion that effectively made it possible for Rome to be great . . . At a certain period this sentiment only inspired sonnets by threadbare poets – thus becoming ridiculous – but it ceased to be ridiculous, and once more became sublime, when it drove the Italians to action and inspired Mazzini, Garibaldi and Cavour . . . Napoleon's little hat becomes grotesque on the head of an imbecile – but there is nothing ridiculous about it on the victor of Austerlitz . . . Embellishing his speeches to the army – where religious fanaticism reigned – with quotations from the Bible, Cromwell was a great leader. Quoting the Gospel to people whose main fault is certainly not an excess of idealism and morality, Luzzatti simply makes us laugh . . . The dissolute legislators who approve virtuist, moralistic laws; magistrates, disentangling themselves from the arms of their whores, to condemn the miserable sellers of postcards, are extremely ridiculous and even rather despicable . . .

The reality of an ideal is not to be found in the ideal itself, but in the emotion that the ideal reveals . . . Time must not be wasted in noting the contradictions, the incongruities, the absurdities of Roman mythology . . . Everywhere there have been, and there will be, similar phenomena. Everywhere – underneath the derivations lacking logical value, sometimes even absurd – will be found those emotions which are the great forces which shape and develop society.

NOTES

1 See G. Busino, 'Introduction' to Pareto, *Scritti sociologici*, p. 37.

28 The treatise on general sociology

By 1911, when *Le Mythe vertüiste* was published, Pareto already had all the material for his *Trattato* to hand. *Le Mythe vertüiste* was published separately in order to make the *Trattato* less bulky. He was now old and very ill, his illness becoming worse from 1908 to 1909, when his wife, after several years of silence, sued him for alimony, but he was unable to be present in court. Owing to his illness, he thought he would be unable to finish the book, and rather than leave it unfinished he said that he would destroy it. His tenacity and strength of will were rewarded, however, and between one crisis and the next, he expanded the work, which was ready before the war broke out. Because of the war, however, it was not published for another two years, and he confided to his friend, Carlo Placci, that this was a disappointment, as when he had written the book, 'many things which were then forecasts have now become reality'. He believed that part of the merit of his work had 'gone up in smoke' as it had lost 'the quality of prophecy'.[1]

The *Trattato* begins with a lesson on method and immediately directs its attention to those theories which pretend to be theories of theories. They are classified according to their objective aspect, subjective aspect, and utility. But he considers that only theories 'made up of the rigorously pure type, with only experimental material and a logical nexus' inspire experimental science. They are the theories in which abstractions and abstract principles – instead of assuming 'either implicitly or explicitly a value beyond experience . . . are taken exclusively from experience and are subordinate to it'. These principles seem to follow the *Cours* more than the *Manuale*, and yet as one reads on, one finds oneself facing contradictions which only after a careful examination and a meticulous re-reading, appear to be resolved. The Pareto who had abandoned any great, eternal logical construction begins to come to the fore again when the objective validity of the system proposed in the *Cours* begins to break up. The Pareto of the relativity of knowledge reappears when he affirms that 'The terms "true" and "false" are closely dependent upon chosen criteria' and when he adds that in order to judge the truth or falsity of a proposition stated by another: 'It is enough . . . for him to tell us what his criterion is.' The basic elements of scientific certainty are not eliminated, they are only methodologically broken up into atoms so that each person can put them together again according to his own criteria.

As one gradually reads on, one understands that methodological relativism becomes instrumentally structural. He continued to affirm that 'the experimental field is absolutely distinct from the non-experimental field', but he restated what he had already said at the beginning of *Les Systèmes socialistes* that, 'No man is entirely un-affected by emotion and free from all bias, all faith.' His statement that it is man's duty – at least in part – to 'stand outside his emotions, his preconceptions and his faith' is still valid. Thus, emotions make an absolutely pure, experimental science impossible, as they not only interfere at the moment of choice of his own criteria of reasoning, but also come between man and the facts. Man's duty is, however, to approximate to the ideals of pure science. To this concept of approxi-mation – already used in 'On the logic of the new school of economics' – Pareto added the concept of interpretation 'because the direct knowledge of facts is very rare'.

Slowly but surely truth takes on the aspect of probability. In clarifying this point he states, 'It is necessary to find out how, when, and how far these interpretations can be used with any degree of certainty.' So, if a purely objective, scientific theory is impossible, a theory of the interpretation of facts – especially of those of the past – becomes doubly impossible. The subjective aspect of facts had already appeared in 'An application of sociological theories' when he stated: 'The objective phenomenon is reflected in human consciousness' and also that in it 'the objects which it reflects are distorted'. Now, as historical facts do not exist outside the consciousness which observes them, the examination of past historical facts, rather than being made easier, becomes more difficult, because in studying them the decisive aspect of the passionate, emotional factor which contributes to their creation is lacking. Thus Pareto came to the conclusion that past events must be explained through present events as 'the unknown must be explained through what is known'. The events which happen about us are the only ones which can be known. As they are the proof that the actions of the men who have produced them are born of emo-tion rather than reason, it is necessary to study emotions as they exist at a particular moment.

In reality there are 'exclusively instinctive actions' which have no relation to logic, and social theories 'made up of residues and derivations'. But as 'it is exactly with the concrete reasonings corresponding to the intermediary cases that we are directly acquainted', it follows that 'the strictly logico-experimental science' is a working hypothesis more than a truth, and logical actions are no more than a Utopia towards which we go gradually and dutifully. In every logical theory there is a certain dimension of feeling present, while a certain dimension of logic is present in every derivation. The difference between logico-experimental theory and derivations is only quantitative. Reality is wholly composed of derivations more or less approximating to logico-experimental theories. Here a question arises: how is it possible to establish which derivations approximate more, and which less, to such theories? Pareto had already said that a theory is logico-experimental when it comprises 'the type that is pure, with the matter strictly experimental and the nexus logical', and when 'the abstractions and general principles which are used in it are taken exclusively from experience and are subordinate to it'. But as he knows that the instrument of verification is also tied to the interpretation of the subject, it is in order to avoid a never-ending vicious circle that he seems to base his thoughts on residues. But for Pareto, residues were not the only basis of reality, as some think, but made up this basis, and the fact that he had discovered that true history is made up of conflicts between residues, and that the history made through derivations 'has often become the history of simple nonsense' did not make him abandon the concept of correlation. When he spoke of 'mutual actions of residues and derivations', and even if he then stated that 'residues act strongly on derivations while derivations act weakly on residues', he did no more than restate what he had already said many times about the concept of correlation between subjective and objective, the individual and the social.

As usual, the problem of the number of men who base their actions on completely or almost completely logico-experimental theories is a matter of proportions and statistically calculable quantities. As a scientist, he could do no more than draw to our attention the fact that, in history, the actions which were the fruit of logico-experimental theories were few, but as a man he was a fervent supporter of such theories. As a scholar, he could only observe that, as history is a history of conflicts between residues, resolved by force, the condemnation of 'the use of force in general' belongs to 'a few dreamers'. He could not help noting that the theories which condemn the use of force in general 'either have no effect or have only the effect of weakening the resistance of those who govern'. As a scientist his work was that of discovering instruments which men would then use as they wished. His problem of conscience was no different, for example, from that of other scientists who have made discoveries like that of nitro-glycerine or atomic energy. He limited himself to saying that the men of yesterday and those of today had based their conflicts on residues and the resolution of these conflicts on force. But he was ready to take into consideration in his calculations, those heretics of today or tomorrow who are ready to base their actions on logico-experimental theories. He was convinced that nothing, not even his writings, could change men's nature, but that, if they wanted, they could change themselves. In this change, myth would show itself to be indispensable, in the same way that it has been a stimulus for the reaching of so many ideals. So, he stated that the system of scientific reasoning 'must only be used by those who have to solve a scientific problem, or partly used by those who belong to the ruling classes. On the other hand, it has its social utility for those belonging to the ruling classes who have to act – in helping them to choose one of the theologies according to the problem with which they are faced: either that which desires to keep the existing uniformities, or that which wants them to be changed.' In good, as in evil, man's destiny is still in his own hands.

FROM *Trattato di sociologia generale*, 3 vols, (Florence 1916).
Logico-experimental and non-logico-experimental sciences

7 In any given group of people, descriptive, prescriptive and other types of propositions are found, for example: 'Youth is imprudent – Do not covet thy neighbour's wife or his possessions – One must learn how to save if one does not want to end one's days in misery – Love thy neighbour as thyself.' Such propositions, combined by logical or pseudo-logical connections, and amplified with the factual narrations of various sorts, constitute theories, theologies, cosmogonies, systems of metaphysics, and so on. When all these propositions and theories are viewed from outside, they become experimental facts. We must consider and study them as such without inquiring into their intrinsic rationality, in the sense of how they are born from faith.

12 So we shall classify these theories using the same method by which we would classify insects, plants, rocks...

13 ... We may consider each theory under various aspects:

(1) *The objective aspect*: in which the theory is considered independently of who has produced it and who accepts it... To take into account all the possible combinations between the quality of the matter and the quality of the nexus, the following classes and sub-classes must be considered:

CLASS I Experimental material
    (Ia) Logical nexus
    (Ib) Non-logical nexus
CLASS II Non-experimental material
    (IIa) Logical nexus
    (IIb) Non-logical nexus.

The subclasses (Ib) and (IIb) contain logical sophistries or specious reasonings to deceive others. For our study they are often far less important than subclasses (Ia) and (IIa).

The subclass (Ia) includes all the experimental sciences; we shall call it logico-experimental. Two other varieties may be distinguished in it:

(Ia1) comprising the type that is strictly pure with the matter strictly experimental and the nexus logical. The abstractions and general principles which are used in it are derived exclusively from experience and are subordinate to experience.

(Ia2) brings us closer to Class II. Explicitly, the matter is still experimental and the nexus logical but the abstractions, the general principles, acquire (implicitly or explicitly) a value beyond the experimental...

This classification – like any other that might be made – depends on our knowledge. For example, a man who considers certain elements to be experimental which another man does not consider experimental, will put in Class I a proposition which the other would put in Class II. Whoever erroneously believes that he is using logic will classify as a logical proposition a proposition that another – seeing the mistake made by the former – will place among the non-logical propositions. Aside from this classification, that is in reality, a theory can be made up of a mixture of these types. That is to say, any actual theory can have experimental parts and non-experimental parts, logical parts and non-logical parts.

(2) *The subjective aspect*: Theories can be considered in

relation to who produces them and who accepts them, in the following way:

(a) *Reasons for which a certain man produces a certain theory.* If a man states that A is equal to B, what reasons make him do so?

(b) *Reasons for which a certain man accepts a given theory.* If a man accepts the affirmation that A is equal to B, what reasons make him do so?

Such problems extend from the individual to society at large.

(3) *The aspect of utility*: The theory must not be confused with the state of mind, the emotions it reflects. Some men produce a certain theory because they have certain sentiments. Then this theory reacts in its turn upon them, as well as upon other men to produce, strengthen or modify certain emotions.

    (I)   *The utility or harm of the emotions manifested by a theory*
        (Ia) For whoever produces it.
        (Ib) For whoever accepts it.
    (II) *The utility or harm of a given theory*
        (IIa) For whoever produces it.
        (IIb) For whoever accepts it.

These considerations also spread to society at large. We can therefore say that we shall consider propositions and theories under their *objective* aspect, their *subjective* aspect, and the aspect of their individual or social *utility*. But the meaning of such terms must not be taken from their etymological or common meaning, but exclusively from the definitions given in the text.

16 . . . The terms 'true' and 'false' are closely dependent on chosen criteria. If one wanted to give them an absolute meaning, one would go outside the logico-experimental field and into the field of metaphysics . . . One must never fight over names, so, if someone wants to give another meaning to the terms 'truth' and 'science', for our part, we shall not raise the slightest objection. For us to know if a proposition is 'true' or 'false', it is enough that he should tell us clearly what meaning he intends to give to the terms which he employs, and above all, that he should tell us what his standard is.

17 If that standard is not declared, it is useless to continue the discussion – which would lose itself in nonsense; just as it is useless for lawyers to plead their cases if there is no judge to listen to them . . .

Considerations on common language

108 . . . The words of common speech lack precision, but this is inevitable, since precision goes side by side with scientific rigour. Every argument founded on the emotions – like metaphysical reasoning – must necessarily use words which lack precision because emotions lack precision, and the word cannot be more precise than the thing which it describes. This method of reasoning relies on the lack of precision of common speech to mask faults of logic, and to *persuade*. By contrast, logico-experimental reasonings, which are founded only on objective observation, are inclined to use words merely to indicate things, and are therefore inclined to choose them in such a way as to remove all ambiguity and make them as precise as possible. Besides this, these arguments equip themselves with a special technique of language, thus avoiding the indeterminacy of common speech . . .

109 . . . Men are inclined to derive their knowledge of science from common speech for two reasons. First because they suppose that a thing must necessarily correspond to a certain word – the word is everything and sometimes assumes mysterious properties. Second because of the great ease with which everyone can then make up 'science' in this way – without any need of long, difficult, troublesome research . . . Discussing the 'principle of fire' or 'damp' is much simpler than going through all the observations of geology. Ruminating on 'natural law' is much simpler than studying the legislation of different countries in different periods. Chatting about 'value' is much less difficult than studying and understanding the laws of economic equilibrium . . .

The experimental field is absolutely distinct from the non-experimental field

142 No man is entirely unaffected by emotion and free from all bias, all faith. So if that freedom was the necessary prerequisite for a fruitful study of the social sciences, this would mean that such study was impossible. But experience demonstrates that, in a way, man can split himself into two, and, in the study of a certain subject, at least in part, can stand outside his emotions, his preconceptions and his faith, to return to them later when he has finished studying the subject. Pasteur, for example, was a fervent Catholic outside his laboratory, but inside he used exclusively the experimental method. We can also recall Newton, who when writing to comment on the Apocalypse, certainly used methods rather different from those used when writing his *Principia*.

143 Such splitting of a person is much simpler in the natural sciences than in the social sciences. It is much easier to study ants using the sceptical indifference of experimental science, and much more difficult to study men using the same system. But the fact that one must force oneself to do it remains – thus reducing to a minimum the influence of emotions, preconceptions and faith. Only in this way can progress in the social sciences be achieved, and all hope of such progress would otherwise be in vain.

Logical actions and non-logical actions

150 There are actions that use means appropriate to ends and which logically link means to ends. There are others in which this characteristic is absent. These two classes of actions differ markedly according to whether they are considered under the objective or the subjective aspect. Under the latter, nearly all human actions are included in Class I. For Greek sailors, for example, sacrifices to both Poseidon and rowing with oars were equally logical means of navigation. . . . It is useful to give names to these classes of actions. We shall give the name of *logical actions* to those actions which logically link the actions to the end, not only with regard to the subject who performs these actions, but also with regard to those who have a wider knowledge, that is, those actions which are both subjectively and objectively logical. The other actions will be called *non-logical* – which does not mean 'illogical', at all . . .

151 It is useful to give a synoptic table of this classification:

GENERA AND SPECIES	HAVE ACTIONS A LOGICAL END?	
	Objectively	Subjectively

CLASS I LOGICAL ACTIONS – the objective end is identical to the subjective end		
	Yes	Yes

CLASS II NON-LOGICAL ACTIONS – the objective end differs from
the subjective end

Genus		
Genus 1	No	No
Genus 2	No	Yes
Genus 3	Yes	No
Genus 4	Yes	Yes

SPECIES OF GENERA 3 AND 4

3a 4a The objective end would be accepted by the subject, if he knew it.

3b 4b The objective end would be rejected by the subject, if he knew it.

The end which is spoken about here is a direct end, without taking the indirect end into consideration. The objective end is a real one located within the field of observation and experiment; not an imaginary end located outside that field, which would, instead, be a subjective end.

304 . . . The cult of 'reason', 'truth', 'progress' and other entities, like all cults, is part of non-logical actions. It was born, grew and continues to prosper to oppose other cults in the same way that oriental cults sprang up in Graeco-Roman society to oppose the polytheist cult...

305 The induction made so far has shown us that, in some particular cases, a tendency exists to eliminate the consideration of non-logical actions, even when these non-logical actions impress themselves on the minds of whoever begins to reason about human societies, and have great importance.

Interpretations

546 Exactly because the first-hand knowledge of facts is very rare, interpretations are indispensable. Whoever would like to do without them completely would have to do without history and sociology. But it is necessary to find out how, when, and how far these interpretations can be used with a degree of certainty. The search must be made through experience like all research in experimental science.

The unknown must be explained through what is known

548 In general the unknown must be explained in terms of what is known, and so the past must be explained by the present rather than the present by the past – as many began to do at the beginning of sociology, and as many continue to do.

571 The possibility of making direct verifications, in the sense of being able to make new observations, is also a reason for explaining past events through present events – since these can more easily be observed.

Residues

887 . . . For the study of the conditions of social equilibrium which we are at present conducting, 'origins' are of little use, while the instincts and emotions which correspond to residues are of great use.

888 Let us begin by classifying residues, and then derivations. Let us not forget that in social phenomena, besides emotions which are manifested through residues, there are also appetites, inclinations, and so on. Here we shall only concern ourselves with elements connected with residues. In these elements many, and often very many, simple residues are found – as, for example, in the case of rocks, there are many simple elements which can be separated by chemical analysis. There are also concrete phenomena in which one residue prevails over the others, and they can therefore approximately represent this residue. The classification that we shall now make is of an objective type, but we shall sometimes have to add a subjective consideration.

CLASSIFICATION OF RESIDUES

CLASS I INSTINCT FOR COMBINATIONS 889–990

889 It is made up of the residues corresponding to this instinct which is powerful in the human species and has probably been and still is, an important factor in civilisation . . . In his laboratory a scientist combines things following certain rules, certain points of view, certain hypotheses – reasonable for the most part, but sometimes at random – he mostly performs logical actions. An ignorant man combines things led principally by fantastic, puerile, absurd analogies . . .

a *Generic Combinations* **892–909**
892 . . . Thousands and thousands of people who buy lottery tickets select a number on the basis of things seen in dreams . . .

b *Combinations of similars or opposites* **910–943**
910 The similarity or dissimilarity between things, even if imaginary and fantastic, is a powerful reason for making combinations. It is enough to think about the association of ideas. Non-logical rationalisation often occurs through an association of ideas.

   b1 *Generic similars or opposites* **913–921**
   b2 *Unusual things and exceptional events* **922–927**
   922 . . . In southern Italy, many people carry a miniature bull's horn attached to their watch chain to ward off the evil eye.
   923 The rarity of the object . . . can also be imaginary, and the rarity of many talismen and relics is often imaginary.
   b3 *Objects and occurrences inspiring awe and terror* **928–931**
   931 This residue is also found in magical operations which take place at child-sacrifice . . .
   b4 *A happy state associated with good things; unhappy state associated with bad* **932–936**
   932 When a certain state A is considered to be happy, one is inclined to link up to it everything which is considered good . . .
   b5 *Assimilation: physical consumption of substances to produce effects similar or rarely opposite to the character of whoever assimilates them* **937–943**
   937 Men often believe that by assimilating certain things they participate in the quality of those things. Sometimes these phenomena can be confused with a mysterious communion between Man and his totem, or his god . . .

c *Mysterious workings of certain things; mysterious effects of certain actions* **944–965**
944 This residue is found in many magical practices . . . it corresponds with a feeling that things and actions are invested with a hidden, indefinite, often inexplicable power.
   c1 *Mysterious operations in general* **947–957**
   947 . . . On 2 May 1910, a certain Muff was executed at Lucerne for arson and murder. The newspapers told how, on

his way to the block, he carried a tiny piece of the cross, which
Mme Erica von Handel-Mazzetti had sent him together with
some words of consolation. It is impossible logically to relate
this relic to the judgement which God would have had to pass
on this man . . .

c2 *Mysterious linking of names and things* **958–965**
958 A name is bound to an object for no experimental
reason . . .
960 A very good example of this are the so-called perfect
numbers . . . What precisely the word 'perfect' means is not
known, in the same way that we do not know what 'right',
'good', 'true', 'beautiful' mean . . . It would be a waste of time
to list all the nonsense of the Pythagoreans here . . . not to
mention the many Holy Trinities . . .

d *The need for combining residues* **966–971**

e *The need for logical development* **972–975**
972 . . . In substance, men seek to reason, and the need of logic
is satisfied both by a strict and a pseudo-logic . . . The various
theologies, metaphysics, ramblings on cosmogony and cosmo-
logy and other similar things illustrate the importance of this
need.

f *Faith in the efficacy of combinations* **976–990**
976 Observation through experiment is insufficient to make us
believe that A is necessarily linked with B, since logico-
experimental science can only deduce from experiment the
lesser or greater probability of A being linked to B. The
character of this necessity is sustained by a non-experimental act
of faith.

CLASS II GROUP PERSISTENCE OF AGGREGATES **991–1088**
991 Certain combinations make up an aggregate of parts closely
linked in the form of a single body which, in this way, acquires
a personality similar to that of other real beings.

a *Persistence of relations of a man with other men and other
places* **1015–1051**
1015 . . . Feelings of love which man has towards his family,
property, country, mother tongue, religion, companions, are of
this type. Man sometimes conceals this residue behind derivations and logical explanations of these feelings.

a1 *Relations with family and kindred groups* **1016–1040**

1016 When the young of animals . . . are self sufficient, they leave their parents and no longer recognise them. Instead, in human young, perhaps because they need their parents or those who substitute them for a much longer period of time, notable and sometimes powerful residues spring up.

a2 *Relations with places* **1041–1042**

1041 One's native land is spoken about. This is the place where one spends one's childhood . . .

1042 Looking at things superficially one could believe that modern patriotism is territorial, as modern nations take the name of the territory which they occupy. But, on looking more closely at things one realizes that the feeling of patriotism rises from a complex of feelings of a race which considers it has tongue, religion, traditions, history etc. in common . . .

a3 *Relationships of social class* **1043–1051**

1043 Living in a given collectivity impresses certain conceptions on one's mind, certain ways of thinking and acting certain prejudices, certain beliefs which later remain and acquire a pseudo-objective existence . . .

b *Persistence of relations between the living and the dead* **1052–1055**

1052 The accumulation of relations of a man with other men remains in abstraction even after his death . . .

1055 Thinking carefully about this one realises that the concept of survival after death is more than a prolonging of another very powerful concept in us, that is the concept of individuality over the years. In reality the corporal part and the psychic part of a man change. An old man is not the same as he was as a boy, neither materially nor morally, and yet we admit that there remains in him an individuality. This individuality is called soul by those who go beyond the experimental field and yet who can give no clear explanation of what happens to this soul when it ends up in lunatics or the senile. Nor can they explain when this soul enters the body of the unborn child – whether it is at the moment when the male seed enters the female uterus or at the moment when the first cries of the new-born baby are heard . . .

c *Persistence of relations between the dead and the things belonging to them in life* **1056–1064**

1056 . . . From this comes the very common custom of burying with the corpse objects which belonged to the dead man and killing his wives, slaves and animals.

d *Persistence of abstractions* **1065–1067**

1065 When an agglomeration of relations is constituted . . . a corresponding abstraction is born, which can persist and then a new subjective being is created.

e *Persistence of uniformities* **1068**

1068 An important example of the persistence of abstractions is found when a general character is given to a particular uniformity or a single fact. A fact is observed and it is expressed in an abstract way and this abstraction persists and becomes a general rule. This is the way that people who are not used to reasoning scientifically reason daily.

f *Feelings transformed into objective reality* **1069**

1069 . . . The introspection of the metaphysicist, the inner experience of the Christian and other similar operations transform feelings into objective reality.

g *Personifications* **1070–1085**

1070 This happens when a name is given to an abstraction, a uniformity, a sentiment, thus transforming them into objective individuals . . . even touching on anthropomorphism.

h *The need for new abstractions* **1086–1088**

1086 When certain abstractions are no longer used one feels the need for new abstractions . . . In the educated classes, learned, subtle, abstruse mythologies take the place of popular mythologies . . . Those who stop adoring saints' relics pass on to adoring solidarity, those who abandon the theology of the Roman Catholic Church turn to modernist theology as it is more scientific.

CLASS III THE NEED TO MANIFEST FEELINGS THROUGH ACTIONS **1089–1112**

1089 Strong feelings are usually accompanied by certain actions which may not be in direct relation to these feelings, but which satisfy the need to act. For example we can observe these phenomena in animals when a cat opens and closes its mouth when it sees a bird, a dog becomes excited and wags its tail at the sight of its master, and so on.

a *The need to act through combinations* **1092–1093**
1092 . . . The need to act is overpowering and imagination works to find a way of satisfying it. This residue is foremost, while the residues of Class I, that is combinations, are secondary . . .

b *The need to act through religious exaltation* **1094–1112**
1094 The calm, considered need to act can grow more intense and reach exaltation, enthusiasm and delirium . . .

CLASS IV RESIDUES OF SOCIABILITY **1113–1206**
1113 . . . All domestic animals, with the exception of the cat, live in a community when they are free. But, as a society is impossible without discipline, sociability and discipline have certain points in common.

a *Particular societies* **1114**
1114 The need for particular associations can be observed in most peoples. There are different types, having as an aim entertainment, religion, politics, literature . . .

b *The need for uniformity* **1115–1132**
1115 If a hen is painted red the others attack it immediately. In savage tribes the need for uniformity is far greater than in civilised peoples.
    b1 *Voluntary* **1117–1125**
    1117 For example imitations . . .
    b2 *Enforced* **1126–1129**
    1126 Man not only imitates others in order to become uniform with them, but he also wants others to do the same . . . by persuasion, more often by public opinion and even more by force . . .
    b3 *Neophobia* **1130–1132**
    1130 This is the feeling which stops innovations which would disrupt uniformity. It is very strong in savage peoples, but also among civilised peoples where it is only overcome by the instinct of combinations.

c *Pity and cruelty* 1133–1144

  c1 *Self-pity extended to others* 1133–1141

  1138 . . . This does not arise from logical reasoning, but from a mixture of feelings . . . Here is approximately the reasoning which corresponds to such sensations: 'If I am unhappy, it is the fault of *society*. If another is unhappy, it must also be the fault of *society*. We are companions in our misfortune and I feel the same indulgence for my companion as I feel for myself . . . '

  c2 *Instinctive repugnance to suffering* 1142–1143

  1142 . . . This feeling has given rise to the proverb 'a soft-hearted doctor makes the wound gangrenous'. Such a feeling can often be observed in weak, cowardly people, and those lacking in energy. But it happens that when they manage to overcome this feeling they become extremely cruel. This explains why women are more sympathetic but also more cruel than men.

  c3 *Reasoned repugnance to useless suffering* 1144

  1144 Such a feeling is found in strong, energetic beings who are capable of stopping themselves at the precise point that they consider it is useful for them to do so . . .

d *Self-sacrifice for the good of others* 1145–1152

  d1 *Risking one's life* 1148

  1148 . . . When domestic animals – even if they are of different species – live together, they defend one another . . . In men it is impossible to distinguish this feeling from the one which makes us desire public approval.

  d2 *Sharing one's property with others* 1149–1152

e *Residues of sociability in respect of feelings of hierarchy* 1153–1162

1153 These feelings of both those who command and those who obey can be observed in animals and are very widespread in human societies . . . Hierarchy is transformed but continues to exist just the same, even in the societies which apparently proclaim popular equality . . .

  e1 *Feelings of superiors* 1155

  1155 These are feelings of protection and benevolence to which are often added feelings of domination and pride which can co-exist with feelings of apparent humility, e.g. in religious orders or ascetics. In good faith one can be proud of being humbler than the others.

e2 *Feelings of inferiors* 1156–1159

1156 . . . One accepts the authority of those people who really have, or imagine they have, some superiority or other. So, the bow of the young man to the old man is that of the inexperienced to the experienced.

e3 *Need of group approbation* 1160–1162

f *Residues of sociability in respect of asceticism* 1163–1206

1163 A special type of feeling can be observed in men which has no corresponding feeling in animals, and which makes Man bring suffering onto himself in opposition to the instinct which makes him seek the agreeable . . .

CLASS V INTEGRITY OF THE INDIVIDUAL AND HIS BELONG-INGS **1207–1323**

a *Feelings contrary to alteration in social equilibrium* 1208–1219

1208 This happens when an individual suffers even when he is not harmed by this alteration, and even if he sometimes gains some advantage from it . . .

b *Feelings of equality in inferiors* 1220–1228

1220 These are frequently a defence of the integrity of the individual belonging to a lower class and a means of helping him rise to a higher class . . .

c *Restoration of the integrity of an individual by means of operations on the individual who has suffered an offence to his integrity* 1229–1311

c1 *Real subjects* 124–1295

1240 . . . In men the feeling of integrity is among the most powerful and has its roots in the instinct of conservation of life . . .

1241 What we call remorse is a manifestation of the conception of the alteration of integrity. Whoever is used to observing certain rules feels at a disadvantage when he does not observe them, and he feels that his personality is diminished. To escape this pitiful state he seeks and practises some means of cancelling this stain, and of re-establishing this pristine integrity . . .

1246 In order to re-establish one's integrity one can use material means exclusively just as if a material stain were to be removed . . . Water removes material stains, and it is supposed that it can also remove moral stains.

c2 *Imaginary or abstract subjects*

1269 . . . The persistence of an abstraction (IId) gives it a personality whose integrity can be attacked. Each individual who feels this abstraction deeply also feels deeply the offence given to the integrity of this abstraction . . .

1297 So, it is possible to understand the punishments given to those who offend the dominant religion or the customs of many peoples.

d *Restoration of the integrity of an individual by means of operations on the person or object which has attacked his integrity* **1312–1323**

1312 There is a feeling which makes animals or men, who have been attacked, pay back the harm received. Until this happens the man whose integrity has been attacked feels at a disadvantage . . . Examples of these feelings are those which lead to a duel or a vendetta.

d1 *Real offender* **1313–1319**

d2 *Imaginary or abstract offender* **1320–1323**

1320 This residue appears clearly when men get angry with their idol, some saint, spirit or god . . .

CLASS VI SEXUAL RESIDUES **1324–1396**

1324 Even if the simple sexual appetite operates strongly in the human race, we must not lose time over it here. Above all, we must study the sexual residue in reasonings and theories . . .

1325 Graeco-Latin antiquity considered the sexual act as the satisfaction of a need like eating, drinking, dressing . . . For our extremely virtuous men all free love is illicit . . . In his *Digesta*, Ulpian tells us that in many places the brothels were run by honest people. Later, for reasons unknown, towards the end of the Roman Empire the consideration of the sexual act imposed itself on men's minds and assumed religious forms which were often manifested with a sacred horror. It is really extraordinary that today this consideration of the sexual act with sacred horror is the last religion to be backed by the state among certain

civilised peoples. Without fear of being punished, one can curse
God and the saints, preach civil war, massacre and theft, but
obscene books or illustrations cannot be published . . .

1332 The sexual residue can exist in very innocent and chaste
relationships and it is an obvious mistake to suppose that where
that residue is, there is also necessarily a relationship of physical
love . . .

1333 This depends on the individuals. There are some who are
more easily drawn towards acts of physical love by chaste talk
and writings, and there are others who are more easily drawn
towards these same acts by obscene talk and writings . . .

1335 We can add that sexual religion has its dogma, its belie-
vers, its heretics, its atheists, like all the other religions . . .

Derivations

1401. . . . Concrete theories about social matters are made up of
residues and derivations. Residues are the manifestation of
emotions. Derivations include logical reasonings, sophisms and
manifestations of emotions. They are manifestations of the need
of man to reason. If this need could be satisfied just by logico-
experimental reasonings, there would be no derivations, and in
their place would be logico-experimental theories. But man's
need to reason is satisfied in many other ways; by pseudo-
experimental reasonings, by words which stimulate emotions,
by vain, inconclusive talks. In this way derivations are born. They
are not to be found at the two extremes, i.e. in exclusively instinctive actions and in the strictly logical-experimental sciences,
but in the intermediary cases.

1402. It is precisely with the concrete reasonings corresponding to these intermediary cases that we are directly acquainted.
Here we have made an analysis, separating a nearly constant part,
(a), from a mostly variable part, (b), to which we have given the
names of residues and derivations, and we have seen that for
social equilibrium the more important part is that of the residues.
So we have moved contrary to popular opinion which, dominated
by the concept of logical actions, is inclined to turn this relationship upside-down, and give greater importance to derivations.
Whoever encounters a derivation believes that he is accepting or
rejecting it for logico-experimental considerations, and does not
realise that usually he is moved to act by emotion, and that the

agreement or conflict between two derivations expresses the agreement or conflict between residues. In the study of social phenomena some stop at derivations without going on to residues. Thus the history of social institutions has become the history of derivations, and has often become the history of simple nonsense. It was believed that the history of religion was to be achieved through the history of theologies, the history of morals through moral theories, the history of political institutions through the history of political theories. In addition to this, as metaphysics had provided all these theories with absolute elements from which it was believed that equally absolute conclusions could be derived through pure logic, the history of such theories became the history of those derivations of certain ideal types (existing in the mind of the author) which could be observed in reality. Several men of our time have known intuitively that in this way one lost touch with reality, and in order to get back to it they replaced these kinds of reasoning with research on 'origins', without realising that in this way they often substituted one kind of metaphysics for another. They have explained the better known through the lesser known, and facts subject to direct observation through imagination which, as they refer to times long since past, cannot be proved; they then add principles which are beyond experimentation like that of a simple evolution.

1419 CLASSIFICATION OF DERIVATIONS

CLASS I ASSERTION 1420–1433
1420 This class includes simple narrations, affirmations of fact, and assertions in agreement with feelings, not expressed as such, but in an absolute, axiomatic, doctrinal way ...

a *Of experimental facts or imaginary facts* 1421–1427
1421 An assertion can be subordinate to experience. In this case it is an assertion of logico-experimental science – it is not a derivation. But, if the assertion exists independently of experience, then it is a derivation.

b *Of feelings* 1428–1432
1428 An assertion can be an indirect way of expressing certain feelings. But those who have feelings believe this to be an 'explanation' of them ...

c *Mixture of feelings and facts* **1433–1434**
1433 Ia and Ic are separated in theory but nearly always mixed in practice.

CLASS II AUTHORITY **1434–1463**
1434 Here we speak about persuasion . . . In this class we have several derivations . . . that serve in deriving the residues of the persistence of aggregates . . .

a *Of one man or more* **1435–1446**
1435 . . . There are types of derivation in which the competence of the individual is not experimental but can be deduced from false clues or can also be completely imaginary . . .

b *Of tradition, usages and customs* **1447–1457**
1447 This authority can be verbal, written, anonymous, of a real or legendary person. In such derivations the residues of persistence of aggregates have an important role, by means of which 'the wisdom of our ancestors' regarding the past, or 'the party traditions' for the present acquire their own and independent existence . . .

c *Of divine beings, personifications* **1458–1463**

CLASS III AGREEMENT WITH FEELINGS OR PRINCIPLES **1464–1562**

a *With feelings* **1465–1476**
1465 Of a small or large number of people . . .

b *With individual interests* **1477–1487**
1477 If one wants to induce a certain individual to do a certain thing A, who could not do it spontaneously, there are various ways of doing so and only a part of them belongs to derivations.
1479 The following cases belong to derivations: when one affirms that by doing A, it would be useful to a certain individual – even if it is not true . . . when doing or not doing A is forced on the individual by an external power through a sanction in the case that this afore-said individual will feel remorse or displeasure at having, or not having A . . . The aim of these derivations lies in the affirmation that individual interest and collective interest are identical.

c *With collective interests* **1498–1500**

1498 This is found when the interest is not real and so the individual does not carry out the logical action to reach it . . . A certain number of petty politicians want something for themselves and ask for it for an improvement for the proletariat and the working class. Certain industrialists want to obtain favours from the government for their factories and say that it is for the good of industry in general and the working class . . .

d *With juridical entities* **1501–1509**

1501 The man who lives in a civilised society acquires familiarity with moral or juridical relationships which give form to his life and which impregnate his mind, and end up by becoming part of his intellect. Later on, owing to the persistence of aggregates, for the inclination to give an absolute character to what is relative, he extends them beyond the confines within which they can be valid . . . In such a way, conceptions of absolute morals and an absolute right arise. Still later, he supposes that this relationship which was born and grew with society already existed before society, and gave rise to society. So, theories of a 'pact', a 'social contract', 'solidarity', 'social debt' and other similar things spring up . . .

e *With metaphysical entities* **1510–1542**

1510 In these derivations an agreement is sought with certain unities which have nothing to do with the experimental field.

f *With supernatural entities* **1533–1542**

1542 . . . Leaving aside experience, even under a logical aspect one cannot reconcile the conception of an omniscient God with that by which Man can judge His work. So, it is considered that the ignorant and inexperienced are absolutely incapable of understanding what a scientist does in his laboratory . . . It can therefore be seen how vain the pretence is of the man who has little knowledge, but wants to judge the work of someone who possesses a more widespread knowledge. As an indispensable premise, similar judgements on personifications dictate that the personification be made mentally in the image of whoever creates it.

CLASS IV VERBAL PROOF **1543–1686**

1543 This class is made up of verbal derivations obtained with the use of terms of an indefinite, dubious, equivocal sense which do not correspond to reality . . . These logical sophisms usually only deceive whoever is disposed to being deceived. In other words, theirs is no deceit, but the author of the reasoning and those who accept it understand each other for a mutual agreement of feelings to which they also add the guise of a logical sophism.

a *Indefinite terms indicating real things; indefinite things corresponding to terms* **1549–1551**

b *Terms indicating things and giving rise to incidental feelings, or incidental feelings determining choice of terms* **1552–1555**

c *Terms with several meanings, and various things by a single term* **1556–1613**

d *Metaphors, allegories, analogies* **1614–1685**

e *Vague indefinite terms corresponding to nothing concrete* **1686**

1686 This is the extreme limit of verbal derivations which end up seeming a simple music of words . . .

Residues in relation to the concrete beings to which they belong

1691 In order to recognise and classify residues we have considered them independently of the intensity of emotions which are manifested through them and independently of the number of people who possess them. By making abstractions we have separated them from the beings to which they belong. Now it is necessary to consider all these circumstances.

First of all let us discuss intensity. We must distinguish between the intensity which belongs to residues and that which residues acquire from the general inclination of the individual to be more or less vigorous: that is, someone who has a deep feeling of patriotism, but is a coward, will fight for his country with much less vigour than the man who feels patriotism less strongly, but is brave. Someone who has a strong business instinct but is lazy, will put through far fewer business deals than someone who has the same instinct to a lesser degree, but is active. It can therefore be said that certain circumstances which we call vigour – and its opposite, weakness – can lift up or lower the general level of certain residues.

Distribution and change of residues in the different strata of a society

1723 Residues are neither equally distributed nor of equal intensity in the various strata of an average society . . .

1727 . . . On the whole, it must be admitted that emotions vary according to type of work. From this point of view, the theory of economic materialism could be considered similar to the theory of residues – if it is observed that the residues depend on the economic situation; and this is certainly true. But the mistake lies in wanting to separate the economic situation from those other social phenomena with which it is interdependent, and also in replacing the many analogous relations which function simultaneously, by a single relation of cause and effect.

Mutual actions of residues and derivations

1735 Residues may act on: (a) other residues, (b) derivations. Similarly derivations can act on: (c) residues, (d) derivations. Here we only consider such effects intrinsically, without studying the relationship they have with the utility of the individual or society.

We have already spoken about the way in which residues act on derivations, and we have demonstrated, contrary to common opinion, that residues exert a powerful influence on derivations, while derivations have a feeble influence on residues . . .

Propagation of residues

2003 If certain residues become modified in certain members of a community, this modification can spread through direct imitation. It is very difficult to distinguish this kind of modification from the other – of indirect diffusion – which takes place because, beforehand, certain circumstances have first produced a modification of residues among certain people, and then, little by little, have also changed them in others. However, it is easily seen that this latter case is much more frequent than the former, because the modifications of the residues can be seen to combine with the modifications of economic, political and other circumstances.

Propagation of derivations

2004 In the propagation of derivations there are also analogous cases, and as the residues are the principal circumstances which determine derivations, the following three cases can occur: (1) propagation through imitation or other direct ways, (2) propagation owing to the modifications of residues corresponding to derivations, (3) propagation owing to other circumstances which operate in society.

The upper and lower classes in general

2047 A society can be divided into at least two strata: an upper stratum for those who govern, and a lower stratum for those who are governed. This is so evident that even a casual observer can see it. The circulation of individuals between these two strata is also evident. Even Plato observed this circulation and wanted to regulate it artificially. Many others have talked about 'new men' and *parvenus*, and a great number of literary studies have been written about this problem . . .

The use of force in society

2170 Societies generally exist because the residues of Class IV – that of sociality – are alive and powerful in the majority of their components. But in human societies, there are individuals in whom such sentiments in part fade, and can even disappear. Two very important and apparently opposite effects take their origin from this: one which threatens to dissolve society, and the other which procures civil progress. In substance, the movement is one, but can follow different ways.

2171 It is evident that if in every individual the need for uniformity (IV b) was so powerful that none of them would differ in any respect from the existing uniformity of the society in which he lived – then there would be no internal motives for it to dissolve. But neither would this society have internal motives to change either towards an increase or a decrease in the welfare of the individuals, or in its own welfare. At the other extreme, if the need for uniformity were totally lacking, society would not exist: every individual would be on his own like the great cats, birds of prey and other animals. Surviving societies, and those which change, are those which are at an intermediate stage between these two extremes.

2174. The problem of whether or not one must use force, or whether or not it is useful to use force in society has no meaning; as force is used both by those who want to keep certain uniformities and by those who want to transgress them, and the violence used by the former is contrary to the violence of the latter . . .

2175 To solve the question of the use of force, it is not enough to solve the other question of the general utility of certain organisations. It is also necessary to weigh up all the advantages and disadvantages, both direct and indirect. This way of reasoning brings us to a solution in a scientific form, but it can be – and effectively it often is – different from the solution which leads towards an increase in the welfare of society. Therefore, it must only be used by those who have only to solve a scientific problem, or partly used by those who belong to the ruling classes. On the other hand, it has its social utility for those belonging to the ruling classes – who have to act – in helping them to choose one of the theologies according to the problem with which they are faced: either that which desires to keep the existing uniformities, or that which wants them to be changed.

2183 ... Every government uses force and claims that it bases it on reason. In fact, whether or not there is universal suffrage, it is always an oligarchy which governs, and which knows how to give its own expression of the 'will of the people': from the law which gave *imperium* to Roman emperors down to the votes of the majority of an assembly, however elected; from the plebiscite that gave the Empire to Napoleon III, to universal suffrage that is wisely led, bought and manipulated by our 'speculators'. What is this new goal called 'Universal Suffrage'? It is no better defined, no less mysterious, no less beyond reality than many other divinities. Clear contradictions are not lacking in its theology, just as they are not lacking in other theologies. The faithful followers of 'Universal Suffrage' do not allow themselves to be led by their god – it is they who lead it. Even if those who are in the minority proclaim the sanctity of the majority, they squash it with obstructionism. Even if they burn incense to the god 'Reason', in certain cases they are not ashamed of calling in the help of artfulness, fraud and corruption.

2185 The theories which approve the use of force by those who are governed agree with the theories which condemn the use of force by the public authority. Few dreamers condemn the use of force in general. But these theories either have no effect, or have only the effect of weakening the resistance of those who govern, leaving the field free to the violence of those who are governed ... It is enough to limit ourselves to considering the phenomenon under the latter aspect.

2202 ... If one observes that governments which do not know how to use (or cannot use) force fall, one also observes that no government lasts by using force alone...

Various types of capitalist

2233 ... The people who have an essentially variable income depending on their artfulness in finding sources of income can be put in category S. In this category, apart from exceptions, there are entrepreneurs, those who own shares in industrial and commercial companies ... the owners of real estate in the city where there is building speculation, Stock Exchange speculators, and bankers who make money with loans to industries and commercial concerns through state financing. We add to these all the people who depend on these industries and commercial concerns and derive profit from it: lawyers, engineers, petty politicians, factory workers and office workers. In short, it includes all the people who directly or indirectly make use of speculation and, with *savoir faire*, make their incomes grow, ably taking advantage of circumstances.

2234 We shall put the people who have fixed (or more or less fixed) income, and who therefore depend to no great extent on astuteness, in category R. In this category are the people who have simply saved money ... those living on incomes ... with fixed interest rates ... All the people who neither directly nor indirectly make use of speculation...

2235 ... In the first category, S for speculators, the residues of Class I predominate. In the second category, R for those who live off *revenue*, the residues of Class II predominate ... The two categories have work of different utility in society. Category S is mainly responsible for change, for economic and social progress. Category R, on the contrary, is a powerful element of stability which in many cases eliminates the dangers of the adventurous shifting of category S. A society remains immobile and crystallised if the individuals of category R are uppermost. On the other hand, a society is lacking in stability if the individuals of category S are uppermost, and the equilibrium can be destroyed by the slightest accident from within or without...

Consent and force

2245 If consent were unanimous, the use of force would not be necessary; but this extreme has never been reached. Another extreme is that of a despot who stays in power by means of his armed forces against the hostile population, and this is a phenomenon of which there have been concrete cases . . .

2249 Making use of existing emotions in a society in order to reach a certain goal is in itself neither useful nor harmful to society. What is useful or harmful depends on the results achieved. . . . If the ruling class aims at a result which is to its advantage without considering the governed, it cannot be said that the latter are necessarily harmed. There are a great many cases in which the ruling classes, working exclusively for their own good, work unwittingly for the good of those who are governed . . .

2251 All through history consent and force have shown themselves to be means of governing. Even in the time of the *Iliad* and the *Odyssey* they made the power of Greek kings secure as they did that of the Roman emperors . . . and even in the time of the barbarian kings, medieval republics and the divine right of kings, right up to modern, democratic regimes, there has always been this mixture of force and consent.

2252 Just as the derivations are more variable than the residues which they manifest, the forms through which the use of force and consent are manifested are much more variable than the emotions and interests from which they originate, and the various relative proportions of these emotions and interests. There is a similarity between derivations and forms of government, and both act on social equilibrium much less than the emotions and interests from which they spring. This has been understood by many scholars who, perhaps exaggeratedly, have stated that it does not matter *what* form of government there is.

The equilibrium of nations

2454 . . . In countries where the residues in Class II are powerful, and are kept stimulated by a sagacious government capable of making use of them, the population willingly accepts the mechanism of war. Where, instead, these residues are feeble, or weakened by a government whose only concern is with certain material interests without thought of the future, the population refuses the burden of national defence. If we study history carefully, we realise that nations which have gone down in defeat and ruin have been warned to return to prudent policies. Very few governments were so improvident as not to listen to this warning. The power to make such nations consider defence was there, but it acted more or less effectively according to its intensity, which depended mainly on the intensity of the residues of Class II . . . The Roman people defeated the Greeks and the Carthaginians mainly because the feelings of group-persistence that are known as love for one's country and other similar sentiments which sustain it, were more intensely felt in Rome than in Greece or Carthage; her rulers had an abundance of residues of Class I, so that proper advantage could be taken of the residues in the masses.

The equilibrium of the various social strata

2477 . . . Now let us study the equilibrium of the various social strata: that is, we shall study the examples of the circulation of the élite. We shall begin with a study of how the ruling class can defend itself by eliminating the people able to overthrow it. The means of eliminating these individuals are as follows:

2478 1 *Death* is the surest way, but also the most harmful for the ruling élite. No race of men or animals can bear such destruction and decimation of its best elements for long. This means has been greatly used, especially among the ruling families in the East. Whoever came to the throne killed his nearest relations who could have aspired to power. It was also widely used by the Venetian aristocracy in eliminating the citizens who wanted to change the organisation of the state, and those who had become too famous because of their wealth, courage, virtue or genius.

2479 2 *Persecution: imprisonment, financial ruin, removal from public office.* These are not very efficient means, since they create martyrs who are often far more dangerous than if they had been left alone . . . persecution tends to exalt the qualities of energy and character in the subjected class . . .

2481 3 *Exile and ostracism* are quite efficient. In modern times exile is perhaps the only punishment for political crimes which procures more advantages than disadvantages for those who employ it to defend power. Athenian ostracism brought neither profit nor loss . . .

2482 4 *An invitation to every individual who could possibly be dangerous to the ruling class to become part of it . . .*

2483 This device has been used by many peoples in many periods. Today it is the only means which the demagogic plutocracy uses to keep power. It harms the élite both because it exalts the character which the élite already has and because, through corruption, its inseparable companion, it greatly weakens man's character and opens the way to those able and willing to use violence to overthrow the power of the ruling class.

NOTES

1 See Pareto, Letter to Carlo Placci of 26 October 1914, now in *Vilfredo Pareto, dal carteggio con Carlo Placci*, ed. T. Giacalone-Monaco (Padua 1975).

29 Conflict between races, religions, and nations

Some, like Finer, have claimed that with the *Trattato* Pareto's intellectual pilgrimage came to an end, and that his subsequent works were no more than applications of those sociological laws discovered in it.[1] Others, like Fiorot, have more correctly spoken of these subsequent works as a verification of these laws.[2] As Pareto often said, it is really a matter of a much more complex relationship in which painstakingly classified forecasts are proved, or not proved, by later verifications. Pareto would have been ready to apply only rules or conclusions which were certain or definite.

However, Pareto, being so sensitive to events and so emotionally involved in them, regarded no concept as definite, and we shall see that up to the end he was to modify judgements and concepts from day to day. When he wrote this article, Europe had been a battlefield for only a few days. On 28 July 1914 Austria declared war on Serbia. On 30 July the Tsar ordered general mobilisation. On 31 July, Germany declared war on Russia, and on 2 August, on France. On 4 August, the English Liberal, Asquith, declared war on Austria and Germany. Carried away by these warlike passions, not only financial groups, but also the Socialists all over Europe declared themselves for war. Socialist pacificism seemed to have died with Jaurès – the last dreamer of social fraternity – assassinated in Paris on 31 July by a nationalist. Spirits were inflamed. Having declared the war to be just and holy, the governments had the unconditional support of all their citizens in pursuing it.

For Pareto, accustomed and resigned to the duplicity of man, this was one of the many occasions – perhaps the one he had waited longest for, though not desired – which demonstrated that his forecasts were confirmed and verified. In the confusion of emotions and ideologies generated by war, he analysed the situation according to one of his old working hypotheses. The scheme is this: (1) there are élites on the upsurge – in this case the German and Slavonic peoples – full of vitality and exalted by a strong myth; (2) élites on the crest of the wave, but ready to fall – the Anglo-Saxon peoples – who have lost their force for expansion, and whose myth is now only that of conservation; (3) élites in decay – the Latin races – in whom myth and faith have vanished and who are ready, passively, to accept anything.

The myth of the first group had its model in aristocratic militarism, while the myth of the second group had its model in social democracy. From these premises, it followed that the war was the result of these two religious expressions of strong, human emotions.

In the essay, Pareto took a particularly harsh line against those who had represented history as a conflict of interests. He acutely observed, 'If it was only the interests of the various states that were at stake, a long-lasting treaty would easily be possible, because interests are not irreconcilable, but as there are the other two causes of war, there is no hope that a long-lasting peace can be reached – if one of the two sides in war is not completely beaten first.' Unfortunately, in this case too, his hypothesis was to be proved right, and certainly despite his wishes.

FROM *Il Giornale d'Italia*, 25 September 1914.

. . . Like all social phenomena, the present events spring from many and varied causes, but not all of equal importance. If we put the forces that support this great conflict of nations in order of intensity, we can see that there are three which are more important than the others. They are: (1) the rivalry between Germanism and Slavism; (2) the rivalry between aristocratic militarism and social democracy; (3) the particular interests of the various states. Let us examine them in order.

I have no wish to solve the problem of racial origins, and when I speak of Slavs, Germans, Anglo-Saxons, Latins, I want only to indicate the communities which are normally called by these names – without trying to explore their composition. Having said this, it is easy to recognise that the Slavs and the Germans are experiencing a period of massive expansion at the moment. The Anglo-Saxons once experienced it, too, but are now somewhat in retreat and on the defensive. The Latins lost it long ago. The Spaniards, French and Italians do not feel any inclination to converge upon a common centre as do the Slavs and the Germans, and do not even try to help each other like the countries of the British Empire. Their literature contains not even the slightest echo of Ancient Rome; or of the pride of birth which is shown by the Germans, Slavs and Anglo-Saxons. German writers hark back to Arminius, and proclaim that as their ancestors once destroyed the Roman Empire, so it is now their task to destroy the decadent Latins. In Italy, nobody is spurred on by a similar emotion to recall the revenge for Varus taken by the legions of Tiberius; nor do they remember Marius' victories over the barbarians or the many Germans he took captive to Rome. I say this, not to make a rhetorical point, but merely to indicate these expressions of inclination and emotion. I do not want to determine whether or not these manifestations of Pan-Germanism are laudable, or whether it is reasonable to decline to imitate them – I am only seeking an indication of emotion . . . The Germans, consciously or unconsciously, aim at hegemony in Europe, and want to make of Berlin what Ancient Rome once was, while the tendency of the Slavs is to agglomerate and build an empire on the German pattern. The Anglo-Saxons seek to keep the British Empire intact. The British aim would have been easily realised if Germany had imitated Rome, who did not attack all her enemies at the same time. Instead, the clash between the Germans and the Slavs was fatal and inevitable, even if it was secondary causes that made this war break out . . . England has shown herself to be wiser than Ancient Greece, who let Rome destroy Carthage without thinking that she would be the next to be attacked and beaten. Perhaps if there had been another Bismarck, he would have foreseen the English intervention and would have tried to avoid it.

Let us look at the other principal cause of the war. We are so involved in the events themselves that we miss the fact that a great change is taking place in the world, namely the spreading of a social democratic faith, which has all the marks of a religion . . . Almost all of Western Europe has this social democratic faith. Germany and Austria have remained faithful to aristocratic militarism, so there is a genuine war of religion between these two and Western Europe. This, too, was inevitable sooner or later. Within their own borders, the peoples of Western Europe have all defeated the conservative party, which supports the German model. So, now Germany must be beaten . . . Russia is estranged, in part, as much from the religious current of social democracy in Western Europe as from the religious current of aristocratic militarism in Germany. She leans towards the former because she lacks any sort of aristocratic and military caste. So, she was driven into conflict, not by a religious faith, but by reasons similar to those that made England enter the war: that is, she thought that she could not let Germany eat the artichoke leaf by leaf. Wars of religion often produce similar alliances: Christian princes have been the allies of Muslims; some Catholic princes burned Protestants within their own kingdoms whilst defending them abroad ... If Western Europe has the social democratic faith, its organisation is principally plutocratic ... Plutocracy did not seek war, but unconsciously prepared for it ...

Finally, the particular interests of the various countries should be discussed ... This can be the aim in the conflict of certain countries like Italy ... Existing emotions cannot be changed, but they can be used to advantage. If it was only the interests of the various countries which were at stake, a long-lasting peace treaty would easily be possible, because interests are not irreconcilable, but as there are the other two causes of war, there is no hope of establishing a long-lasting peace, unless one of the two sides in war is completely defeated first. So, it is possible that the war will be long, and now it can be seen what a grave mistake those made who argued that nowadays wars would be impossible owing to the very great strength of weapons of destruction. Those who believe that this war cannot last because of financial difficulties make a mistake, too. Modern countries have immense economic reserves ... In a century when expenditure on luxury has increased enormously ... people can return to what they were a century ago, even to suffering, but without any serious danger of economic destruction, because even a century ago, people lived and prospered ...

NOTES

1 *Vilfredo Pareto, Sociological Writings*, ed. S. E. Finer.
2 D. Fiorot, *Pareto* (Milan 1969), p. 365ff.

30 War and its principal sociological factors

The war was still in its beginnings, but it already had demonstrated a sophisticated ferocity of the most terrible kind. Every day the belligerent powers – as if trying to justify the escalation of cruelty and the systematic abuse of every right, every agreement, every custom – deployed fresh propagandist arguments to prove the guilt of their enemies. In these hypocritical skirmishes, the democracies of the Triple Entente seemed to have come off best. But demagogy aside, what was the real reason for this war and its atrocities? Once more, Pareto thought the facts seemed to confirm that the conflict was one of *religions*: to determine which of them shall gain world supremacy; rather than a defence of interests or a conviction of being in the right. He observed, 'The weak and cowardly, even if enemies, can live side by side without fighting. It is different for the strong and the brave.' The justifications given for this war were justifications *a posteriori*, as it was 'sentiments of benevolence or malevolence' and 'sentiments of rivalry and enmity' which alone had caused it.

He, himself, seemed to put all his faith in myth when, having stated that only emotions and myths can give man victory (as if having no confidence in reason), he said: 'Trying to find the deep forces which act under various guises can be harmful both to faith and to the work that it does.' And yet, this statement is not so serious if one remembers that the one thing Pareto counted on was clarity, and if one remembers that everyone – or almost everyone – had chosen, openly or secretly, the path of fanaticism and violence.

FROM *Scientia, revue internationale de synthèse scientifique* March 1915, now in *Fatti e teorie* (Florence 1920).
. . . Polybius writes (III, 6) 'When writing about Hannibal, some historians, in seeking to give the causes of the war which broke out between the Romans and the Carthaginians, postulate the siege of Saguntum by the Carthaginians as being the first cause, and the fact that the Carthaginians crossed the River Ebro – in defiance of treaty – as the second. I think that this was the *begin-*

ning of the war, but do not agree that it was the *cause* . . . The men who state this do not distinguish how the beginning differs from the cause and the pretext.' Two thousand years have passed since this Greek historian made these remarks, but his observations can still influence today our judgement of the war in Europe. Can it be, perhaps, that – after so much progress in the fields of science and history – men are still unable to distinguish the beginning from the cause and the pretext? Or do they fail to make such distinctions for reasons other than ignorance? If we try to discover these causes we shall easily find them in emotions, inclinations and interests . . . This general rule is valid for the present war in Europe. For example, Austria's enemies say that the cause of the war was Austria's ultimatum to Serbia. Her friends reply that the ultimatum was the consequence of Serbia's hostility towards Austria. The former observe that Serbia's hostility was caused by Austria's bad behaviour towards her. The latter reply that this behaviour was just resistance to Serbia's overbearingness. One can go on arguing like this for ever – stopping only when one side or the other is instigated by sentiments of benevolence or malevolence . . . Similarly it would be a mistake to believe that the present war is a direct consequence of economic rivalry. Instead, it is an *indirect* consequence of such economic rivalry, due to the influence this rivalry has had on our emotions. When it happens that peoples who wish to extend their dominions meet, the conflict between them becomes – if not inevitable – at least, very probable, and secondary causes or pretexts are always at hand to ignite this conflict . . . The weak and cowardly, even if enemies, can live side by side without fighting. It is different for the strong and the brave. So it was inevitable that sooner or later, on one pretext or another, war would break out between the Germans, the Russians and the English . . .

Among the circumstances for which rivalry between peoples is maintained and feelings of enmity are strengthened, it is necessary to mention the differences of religion and political institutions, but these facts were the direct cause of war only in a few cases – and in far fewer cases than a superficial observation suggests. Often, such facts were the form by which feelings of rivalry and enmity were expressed. Usually, they are only *indirect* causes: that is, they act on emotions and, through them, on war and peace . . . If we try to classify the political inclinations of the peoples who are at this moment at war, the differences between the Central Powers and those of France and the British Empire are immediately clear. The political inclinations of the former are defined as 'militarist' both by the enemies and friends of Germany. The political inclinations of the latter are called 'democratic' by the friends of France and England. The peoples of these last two countries say that they are fighting for the triumph of the democratic institutions which they call 'free'. Anyway, such a contrast is universally acknowledged . . . An apparent exception is Russia. It seems strange that her government, defined as despotic, can have certain things in common with democratic governments. In reality, Russia is governed by a bureaucracy which is very similar to the democratic bureaucracies, while very different from the military and aristocratic bureaucracy of Germany and Austria. In Russia, the aristocracy stems from the power of the sovereign, while in Germany the power of the sovereign stems from the aristocracy. Such a difference is fundamental. The organisation of the western peoples, called 'democratic', is really a democratic plutocracy which now tends towards a demagogic plutocracy.

Lloyd George was able to destroy the age-old power of the House of Lords with the help of his banking friends, by generously giving old-age pensions, at the exclusive expense of the state, and other such presents at the expense of the tax-payers. In France, too, this is usual . . . In Prussia no government dreams of weakening the power of the House of Nobles by asking the help of the plutocrats . . . In Germany, the government imposes its will on the plutocrats, while in France and England it is the plutocrats who impose their will on the government . . . In general, all over Europe, the triumphant party of the democratic plutocracy is made up of men, who, through intermediary stages, go from one extreme of blind faith to the other extreme of scepticism. The former gives strength to the party, the latter gives that *savoir faire* which can lead to victory. If a break comes between them, the strength of the party can lessen and disappear. Today, such a schism does not exist, but it could come in the future . . .

All men are inclined to give abstract, mythical, theological forms to their emotions. Whoever seeks to sway the masses must project himself in this way, because this is the only language they understand. The Romans were convinced that the gods protected their cities. Contemporary Germans have the same conviction about their *Kultur*; the democrats have it about holy Progress, very holy Democracy and divine Universal Suffrage . . . The faith of the democrats is less ardent, especially among the ruling classes perhaps owing to the scepticism of the plutocrats and the folly of the humanitarians; perhaps because many democratic leaders are induced, more than anything else, to preoccupy themselves with satisfying the greed of their followers. This makes for less strength, but also for less cruelty. Perhaps the triumph of the democrats will end up by costing the losers more money, less blood. The Germans show that they are not worried by international law. Many, inspired by sentiments similar to those held by those who approved of the Holy Inquisition – which took no notice of the rules of penal procedure of those times – approve of them. But it must be noticed that the democrats who so severely reproach the Germans for these transgressions, are not ashamed of making analogous transgressions within their own countries. Considered in terms of strict logic, it is not easy to understand why, if the strength of universal suffrage can 'create' the domestic law of the state, similarly the strength of armies cannot 'create' international law. If strength creates law in conflict within a country, why should it not create it in external conflicts?

Trying to find the deep forces which act under various guises can be harmful both to faith and to the work that it does, but it is useful to experimental science, which provides a forecast – even if limited – of future events: which are determined, at least in part, by these forces, which remain even if they change their outside appearance . . . Those who believe that war is determined by the declaration of war suppose that an act which can be done or withheld without great difficulty is the cause of events which arise from other powerful causes. For the most part, these causes are independent of the uncertain chances of the human will. Most people are inclined to place the 'responsibility' for the war on whoever declares it. Today, because of this, every state tries to get the enemy to declare war. But when neither of them manages to get the other to do so, it ends up by war breaking out without a declaration, and then they only recognise 'that the state of war exists between such and such countries'. Saying that the war between France and Germany of 1870 was caused by the famous Ems Telegram, could easily have been replaced by another pretext . . . That the present war was caused by Austria's ultimatum to Serbia, prepared behind the scenes like a melodrama through the perverse ambition of Germany, means returning to fairy-tale history . . .

It makes one laugh when they say that we shall have an idyllic peace when we have re-established the European equilibrium – which was upset, according to some, by the immoderate German ambition; according to others by the intervention of Russian greed; according to still others by the haughtiness of the English in dominating the seas; or by the desire for revenge of the French. But – since when has this beautiful, desired, praise-worthy, European equilibrium even existed? Since when has a lasting peace, which could become perpetual, been seen in Europe? Since when have victors who arm themselves ever more heavily to maintain their power not been seen? Or losers who arm themselves for their revenge? Or neutral countries who arm themselves to keep their independence? Surely, those who dream of a future completely different to the past willingly shut their eyes to experience, and fly off into the nebulous regions of their imagination. Exactly fifty years ago they tried to persuade us that war had become impossible . . . All that chatter has brought us to the present war, which is the most widespread, the most expensive, the most tremendous of all the wars which have ever taken place. Unfortunately, the tracts which are being written on the idyll of a future peace will have no better luck. They may be useful consolation to those who suffer – they are certainly not probable forecasts of the future . . .

31 The supposed principle of nationality

De Rosa tells us that on 6 July 1917 Pareto received 'the first solemn recognition . . . of the universal importance of his scientific work'.[1] In Lausanne he celebrated the jubilee of his professorship, but apart from this brief parenthesis, his life was more and more lonely and overshadowed by the serious illness from which he suffered. He had always been a predominantly European thinker and writer, because, as we have seen, so often his work was a distillation and refinement of the intellectual experiments of the old Europe – from Hegel to Marx, Hume to Kant, Pascal to Voltaire. Now that the world was at war and economic and social problems, once national, had become world problems, Pareto widened his horizons still further. He was not concerned with the victories of armies. He did not write one word on the Italian victory over the Austro-Hungarian fleet on 10 June, and not even on that of the River Piave on 23 June. Consistent with what he had already stated, the real conflict was not that between nations, or in the sevice of interests, but between emotions and religions of which the armies were the instruments.

In one of his now rare letters to Pantaleoni on 2 May 1918, he sadly confided: 'I believe – and every-day experience confirms it more strongly to me – that men are moved by emotions and interests – very few by reasoning.' He reminded those who proposed to resolve the existing conflict by using the principle of nationality, or of universal suffrage, how, for at least two million years, men had invoked these two principles in vain, and how they had been 'of no use in the solving of potential conflicts'. He concluded bitterly that in order to solve the conflict 'It is necessary to find other principles or let force get on with its work.' Resorting to force alone, already rejected both in *Le Mythe vertüiste* and the *Trattato*, now appears as a fact of necessity in a world where – as he had stated in 'War and its principal sociological factors' – 'those who dream of a future completely different to the past willingly close their eyes to experience and fly off into the nebulous regions of their imagination.'

FROM *Rivista d'Italia*, 31 July 1918, now in *Fatti e teorie*.
. . . The characteristics of a *nation* can be found in the race, in the religion, in the language, in the historical traditions. The Athenians were proud of being autochthonous* and so they were convinced that they were purer than the other Hellenic races . . . In the modern ethnic groups of Europe and America, the races are so mixed that this characteristic cannot be used. An example which can prove this, has been given us by the long, useless discussions on the settlements of these races in the Balkans. Even the characteristic of religion gives us little or nothing. In the past it could be used, but today, the more united and compact nations have different religious sects: that is, Italy and France have Catholics, Protestants, Jews, Free Thinkers and so on. Something more is obtained from the language, but it is only in appearance, because rulers impose unity. What help can the language give us, for example, in solving the problems of Alsace-Lorraine or Ireland? The historical traditions are mobile like the waves of the sea and can be interpreted as desired . . . We have not been able to define *nation* precisely, not even with the Ollivier Formula which defines it as 'the association of men, called a people'. The difficulty is old – very old. In 387 BC, the King of Persia imposed on the Greeks the Peace of Antalcidas. The King of Persia kept the Greek cities of Asia Minor for himself, granted certain islands to Athens, and established that 'the other Greek cities, small and large, must be independent'.** The Persians did not say what this really meant. It was discussed at the congress held at Sparta, where all the cities had to swear to uphold the peace. The Thebans interpreted the independence of the cities in the sense that the Bœotian League was to remain intact, considering themselves representatives of it. The Spartans, however, wanted every city of Bœotia to be separately represented and the League to be dissolved. As usual, nothing was concluded by reasoning and the difference was settled by force. Threatened by war, the people of Thebes gave in, and every city of Bœotia took the oath separately. Sixteen years later . . . the difference over the interpretation of independence sprang up again. Thebes wanted to take the oath representing Bœotia, and

* Aboriginal inhabitants.
** Xenophon, *Hellen*, v.I, 31.

once more Sparta refused. Once more force gave the answer which reasoning could not give. This time force favoured Thebes who broke the power of Sparta at Leuctra. It is worth noting that Sparta thought that it was lawful for her to take the oath representing her allies, while she thought that it was not lawful for Thebes . . . Today, too, there are those who say that others must grant the autonomy which they themselves are not prepared to give.

Even supposing that these difficulties of interpretation have been overcome, other important difficulties remain. The first thing is that we must know how the will – admitting that it exists – of that organisation that we have called 'the people', is expressed. Fortunately a modern dogma saves us at this point. This dogma is both evident and mysterious like that of the Holy Trinity: that is, the dogma of universal suffrage. We accept it, of course, in order to prevent our difficulties from becoming greater by discussing it. Under what conditions does universal suffrage take place? At Brest-Litovsk, the Russians rightly told the Germans to 'withdraw your troops from the countries which vote, as the presence of these troops removes the freedom of the polls'. The Germans replied – not without reason – 'If we withdraw, we leave a gap and such a gap will immediately be filled by your gangs of anarchists, which pillage, murder and terrorise – things which hardly favour the freedom of the polls' . . . Can – and must – universal suffrage always express the will of the people or can it change occasionally? The principle of nationality does not give us any explanation on this point. Neither does it give us any explanation on the other problem: 'When one speaks about the totality of a people, of which majority must it be made up?' Let us imagine that England lets Ireland solve the problem of self-government by means of universal suffrage. In this case would Ulster have to vote together with the rest of the island or could it express its majority and its will separately? The American Civil War caused conflict between two parts of a unity. Excellent reasons can be found to prove that one of the two sides had the 'right' to impose its will on the other. But it is certain that such reasons cannot be deduced from the principle of nationality or from that equivalent – the freedom of the people – not even with prodigious sophisms or marvellous interpretations. Thus, these two principles are of no use in the solving of potential conflicts.

It is necessary to find other principles, or let force get on with its work.

NOTES

1 G. de Rosa in Pareto, *Lettere a Maffeo Pantaleoni*, vol. III, p. 184

32 Hopes and disappointments

The balance between reason and force began to assume secondary instead of primary importance, while the balance between foxes and lions which was secondary, seemed to become primary. On the one hand there were demagogic plutocracies which, by manipulating emotions under the cover of pretended democracy, managed to guide the masses. On the other hand, there were military aristocracies which achieved the same end by using force. Pareto was divided between supporting the victory obtained through out-and-out (but sanguinary) force and that obtained through deceitful (but not sanguinary) manipulation. Sometimes he had praised force, but at other times he had claimed, 'To convince someone in a matter of the emotions – and nearly all theorising on society and human institutions falls into this category – he must be presented with facts to awaken these emotions, as it is they that prompt the conclusion one seeks to draw.' He observed that the demagogic plutocracy had now won. But, ever attentive to the problems of equilibrium, he believed that it had not won decisively, since bolshevism – which had inherited many of the characteristics of military plutocracy – had now begun to oppose it. This new enemy, a new élite full of religious, mythological, warlike energy, was a far more formidable enemy than its predecessor. He reminded the petty politicians, so absorbed in their intrigues, that 'The beast which has been awakened will not be tamed, like Cerberus, by throwing it some sops; and neither will it succumb to the siren-song of Lloyd George and Wilson.'

He seemed to regret the defeat of military plutocracy in Europe. But perhaps he had been driven to this reaction by the fact that the new enemies of European civilisation were much more warlike. In order to maintain the existing level of civilisation and to survive, Europe had to some extent to adopt the arms of the enemy. The enemy was as confident of victory as it was swift to act because it put its trust in force and did not respect the fundamental freedom of man: 'it pays not the slightest heed to the goddess, the majority'.

FROM *Rivista d'Italia,* 31 March 1919, now in *Fatti e teorie.*

. . . The hopes which are placed in the outcome of the present world war can be divided into two classes according to their origin: those born of the promises made in good faith, and those born of the promises imposed by necessity and with little chance of being kept . . . In every age, leaders have inspired their followers by promising them that they would share in the division of the spoils . . .

Military plutocracy dominated the Central Powers. Among the Allies, demagogic plutocracy prevailed. This explains the different types of promises and the various difficulties in keeping them. The promises of the military plutocracy were mainly political and they could certainly have been kept in the case of victory. The promises of the demagogic plutocracy are mainly of the social order type, and keeping them is contingent upon procuring the powerful resources to do so. Had Germany been victorious, she would have sought to take away France's colonies. Evidently, this would have been possible, and this she would have done, just as the now victorious French got Alsace-Lorraine back. In his speeches, Lloyd George declared his aim of improving the wages, consumption, health and dignity of the poorer English classes. If the other Allied governments seek the same objectives it remains to be seen if they have the means to achieve them. However, it seems most unlikely that this will come about, since such an improvement in the general living standards needs enormous expenditure and economic wealth, and it is a mystery where it will all come from. There is a contradiction between theory and practice here. A somewhat puerile and hackneyed theory affirms that the poor can be made better off by taking from the rich. This would be true if the disproportion between the rich and the poor was not so great . . . Another absurd theory is swallowed eagerly by the people. It states that state intervention could do much to increase production . . . But the state has been unable to distribute goods efficiently. Every day in the city, thousands of men and women can be seen wasting their time waiting in queues to buy those goods which, before the *beneficial* intervention of the state, they were able to obtain in a few minutes . . . This is a strange way of increasing production, when time meant for work is wasted thus . . . Goods rot on the docks and cannot be found in the places where they should be. Cattle transported by rail die

of hunger. Industries produce what is not useful for consumption
and neglect the production of what is necessary. Farmers no
longer produce those foodstuffs of which the government fixes
the prices or requisitions. Often this has had the effect of making
certain goods disappear from the market. Anyone with money to
spend can always find something to buy, but must pay extra as a
bonus for the risks which the seller runs. The poor have other
consolations which make them forget their anger. At the time of
the Plague of Milan the alleged plague-spreaders were very useful
for distracting attention from the main problem. Today the
hoarders can be blamed. The public does not worry about splitting hairs, and makes no distinction as to whether the hoarder
forces up the prices of the goods he buys, or whether he causes
them to fall, or acts in such a way that they do fall when he sells.
The public is completely oblivious of those special cases where
hoarding is impossible as, for example, with milk. And yet many
cities are without milk . . . For these reasons and others easily
guessed at, it seems clear that those who think it will be possible
to obtain from the expected reductions in armaments what is
necessary to support the heavy expenditure called for by the
promised social reforms, will be disappointed . . .

Demagogic plutocracy has won. It has destroyed the bureaucratic and military plutocracies . . . Today, it has only one formidable enemy which is rising up against it – bolshevism . . .
This holds part of Russia subject, and like a drop of oil, spreads
towards other countries where it acts – even indirectly – upon
different political movements. Sorel's observation is acute and
profound when he thinks that in Germany 'The transformation of
social democracy into trade unionism would be more dangerous
for capitalism than the presence of Russian Soviets, because it
would be accompanied by a social philosophy as powerful as
Marxism has been: the German people have exceptional metaphysical qualities caused by the attachment to religion, mythology, and the poetry of nature . . .'*

We cannot say definitely whether the Bolsheviks, the Sparta-
cists and others who will rise under other names, will inflict on
our plutocrats and petty politicians set-backs similar to those
which Metternich and his friends received from the revolu-

* G. Sorel, *Il Tempo*, 19 February 1919.

tionaries of their time. But it is certain that the phenomenon born with the actual revolutionaries is not to be neglected . . . The beast which has been awakened will not be tamed like Cerberus by throwing it some sops, and neither will it succumb to the siren-song of Lloyd George and Wilson, taken up in chorus by the humanitarians. This beast will become more ferocious as the cowardice of its enemies gradually increases. A movement towards a crisis has already begun, and even if our civilisation should be sacrificed, it should be remembered that the world has already seen the alternation of the Middle Ages and the Renaissance several times . . .

The new revolutionaries repudiate some of the ideologies of past revolutionaries. They do not pay the slightest heed to the goddess – the majority – and deny its divinity. It could happen that, just as the sale of papal indulgences favoured the birth of Protestantism, so the use and abuse that the plutocrats have made of the dogma of majority rule has played a part in shaping these modern revolutionary heresies. It is very true that it is the last straw that breaks the camel's back. Ours are the revolutionary heresies of the present religion which condemns the use of force to maintain the government as being abominable . . .* A still confused climate of opinion is gradually emerging which tends to upset the relationships between social classes and to try to put those of low social standing on high, and vice versa. Some economic and social relationships are already beginning to change. Through their various trade unions and their alliance with the plutocrats, workers have a much greater power over the government than the bourgeoisie have. With the increase in wages and the decrease in working hours, many workers are financially better off than the bourgeoisie and than many teachers, professors, scientists and magistrates. It is true that such a supremacy has been gained by the help of the plutocrats, and nobody knows what will happen if this alliance is dissolved, and whether the working class will then become stronger or weaker . . . It is very difficult to know where the present movement will end, but there is no doubt that great changes and grave social disturbances must be foreseen. So it does not seem likely that the hopes for peace and social prosperity can be realised in the near or not too distant future.

* *Trattato* 2201, 2170.

33 Utopias

The war was over, but an armistice rather than a real peace followed it. Nobody knew how long the armistice would last – not only because of factors which caused the war, but also because of others added to them. Previously, Pareto had waxed ironic on the principle of self-determination. Now, with his usual bitterness, but complete awareness, he pointed out once more how his prophecies had been fulfilled, and how this principle, instead of guaranteeing peace for the future, had only been able to rouse new separatist passions and conflicts. There were still 'the Irish question, the Egyptian question, the Turkish question, the Russian question' on the point of exploding; and, for Italy, there was also the problem of the city of Fiume – Italian in language and customs, and yet denied to Italy by those who supported the principle of nationality. Acute observer of the passions, Pareto realised that the problem of Fiume could rouse those feelings of patriotism and nationalism until now semi-dormant in all Italians, by convincing them that they had been cheated of victory and that the bloodshed in the war had been useless. It must not be forgotten that when D'Annunzio and his volunteers – in the flush of enthusiasm and against the advice of the central government – created the State of Fiume by force, and Pantaleoni assumed the post of Minister of Finance (something which indicated the fresh approach to the ideal of nationalism, activism and voluntarism – not only to Pantaleoni, but also to many intellectuals) this would be the dawning of the long fascist day. But nationalisms and provincialisms were not the only elements of disturbance and instability in the existing, precarious balance. It was made still more unstable by the heterogeneity of the victorious powers. Pareto was also sceptical about the League of Nations; accustomed to drawing parallels between the present and the past, he saw here a sort of Holy Alliance – but much more precarious and insecure than the original, and above all, more grotesque because, instead of presenting itself as it really was, 'a form of imperialism of the victorious countries', it presented itself in the humanitarian guise of an organisation that sought 'to bring about a better understanding between countries'. In the effort it made to surpass itself in promising things which it could never possibly fulfill, and in rousing passions which it was not strong enough to control, demagogic plutocracy represented a grave danger to world peace.

Once, protectionists and socialists ruined their country's finances by their inability to achieve the happy medium between 'the *right* to steal certain amounts from those who save' and 'knowing what amounts can be taken from them without damaging or ruining production'. Now the victorious states, with the same demagogy, made the same mistake on a world scale when they confused 'the problem of knowing what sum they have the *right* to take from the defeated enemy with the problem of knowing what sum the latter is able to pay in reparation'.

As will be seen, these worries of Pareto's were shown to be well-founded, and the intransigence of the victorious powers would fan the flame of the German spirit of revenge and the Italian frustration which the victors would have neither the strength nor the power to control. In the interpretation of these facts Pareto once more uses the concept of equilibrium between what one wants and what one can have. Human justice is only able to move between these two extremes. Many years before in his essay 'Justice' he had said: 'So the injustice of some brings about the injustice of others, at least in part . . . but whoever wants these contrasts (even if they cannot disappear completely, they can become milder) tells today's victors to be more temperate, less unjust, thus trying to make tomorrow's victors more moderate and less unjust.' As can be seen, his main course – even in the storm of events – had not really changed much with the passing of the years.

FROM *Il Resto del carlino*, 12 February 1920.
Economic, social and political instability greatly increases the troubles of modern life and is caused, in part, by the organisation called the League of Nations. There are certain people who want to impose this organisation on the world in order to bring about a better understanding between countries but, instead, it is only a form of imperialism of the victorious countries. I do not want to discuss the nature of the League of Nations here: I shall limit myself to making a few observations to demonstrate how, little by little, the Utopias which are to be found in it are coming to the surface. Among these is the idea of giving a lasting peace to the nations. Much has already been written about the various hopes

raised by the supposed principle of self-determination which, according to Wilson, should have put an end to the extremely serious international conflicts. Its failure was foreseen from the beginning, and this was confirmed daily by events. Instead of solving existing conflicts, the principle of self-determination causes them to break out again. So, in the U.S.A. the Republican party rejects Wilson's Covenant of the League of Nations. A covenant like Wilson's is of no use either for solving the Fiume question for Italy, or the Irish question, or the Egyptian question, or the Turkish question, or the Russian question, or any other question . . .

Yves Guyot, capable leader of the Economic Liberty party in Europe and a worthy successor of Cobden, has written a trilogy, the first volume of which deals with the causes and consequences of war. The other two volumes deal with the guarantees for peace. In the first volume there is an analysis of the lessons of the past. In the second, there is a critical examination which sets out to prove that the League of Nations is 'the resurrection of an old myth, comparable to the Holy Alliance'. He writes: 'I have studied objectively the negative results obtained by the Holy Alliance. But is there a greater consensus between the Allies of today than there was then between the Emperor of Russia, the King of Prussia, the Emperor of Austria, the ministers of England and King Louis XVIII?' The answer is 'no' and so the impossibility of the League of Nations bringing peace to the world is evident. By 1915, in the volume on the causes and consequences of war, the author was writing: 'The Germans seem deliberately to encourage and to deserve a deep hatred. Hatred is a facet of war which is useful while the war is on . . . but as neither individuals nor peoples live on hatred, whoever is fed on it, is devoured.'

This is truer than ever at the moment, and it is certainly not with feelings of hatred that grave economic and social problems can be solved. It is not by shouting 'Death' to one man or another that production is increased, and it is not by moral prejudices that consumption is diminished. These moral prejudices can have an effect on a few cretinous members of the bourgeoisie, but not on the rest of the populations made up of those who know how to conquer and enjoy the wealth of the weak.

The financial difficulties of the victorious countries arise from the fact of their having confused the problem of knowing what sum they have the right to take away from the defeated enemy, with the problem of knowing what sum the enemy is able to pay in reparation. The same thing happens when demagogic pluto-cracy confuses the right to steal certain amounts from those who save, without knowing what amounts can be taken from them without damaging or ruining production. The owner of the hen which laid the golden egg certainly had the right to kill her. But did he reap any benefit by doing so? Perhaps bourgeois cowardice will set no limit to the demand of the wage-earners and the sharks who are their bosses. But is there not a limit imposed by the conditions of production? Every decrease in working hours, every wage increase today is only the excuse for a fresh demand, but can we always go on ahead like this? . . .

Many believe that they can find an exclusively economic and financial prescription to heal economic and financial illnesses, but it is a vain hope. These illnesses depend mostly on social and political organisation and they cannot be studied independently of that organisation. A minister once said, 'If you make good policies, I can make good the economic situation.' Such a remark is true for all countries and all ages.

34 The collapse of central authority

The post-war period saw not only a complete alteration in the map of Europe, but also a change in the internal balance of many of the nations until then considered among the most stable. At the end of 1918, with the fall of the Hapsburg Empire, independent governments were formed in Yugoslavia, Czechoslovakia and Hungary. With the break-up of the Tsarist Empire, the Republics of Lithuania, Esthonia, Latvia, Finland and Poland rose again, the last named having been partitioned in 1795 with the bulk of the country going to Russia. It now emerged as a self-governing state, formed from some provinces which had previously belonged to Russia and others which had belonged to Germany. With the passing of the German provinces to Poland, Germany proper was divided from Eastern Prussia, and by putting the city of Danzig under international control, a nationalistic resentment was created in the Germans like that felt by the Italians over Fiume. But in Germany the Nationalists were not the only group in ferment. The Socialist movement which had been loyal to the Kaiser during the war once more discovered its revolutionary character under the shock of events in Russia. On 7–8 November, the Socialist, Kurt Eisner, proclaimed the Socialist Republic of Bavaria, while in Berlin the Kaiser abdicated and the Social Democrat, Friedrich Ebert, proclaimed the Republic of which he was to become the first President. In Italy, too, social ferment clashed with national frustrations, and both contributed to the creation of an explosive atmosphere. Worn out physically and morally, the soldiers returned from the war and could find no work. Their dissatisfaction at being out of work was increased and amplified by their complex frustrations at the uselessness of what they had suffered. The suspicions of the Great Powers prevented annexation to Italy of the city of Fiume, even after a plebiscite. As we have seen, this was to allow D'Annunzio and his volunteers to take over Fiume, and install a provisional government with the explicit aim of uniting it with Italy. This would be yet another cause of tension, as it was to place the central government – and in particular the Prime Minister, Francesco Saverio Nitti – in the position of having to use force against its own seditious fellow-nationalists in order to make them respect the international treaty which made Fiume a free city. Socialist maximalism exploded simultaneously with the outburst of nationalism. Factories were occupied and strongly revolutionary programmes published, but in the meantime precious time was being wasted, industrial production was stopped, officers were insulted and spat at in the streets – their only crime being to have fought in the war. Soldiers, guilty of having obeyed their superiors, were jeered at. Shops were looted in the name of the illegitimacy of property. All this created – particularly among the middle classes – an uneasiness which Pareto once more tried to interpret accurately. He realised that the demagogy on the principle of self-determination had broken up countries into little pieces and that the demagogy against the right of property had increased the number of speculators, thus damaging the middle classes, the stability of the state, and central authority.

He noted that 'the present World War, which has thrown entire populations into battle, has seriously shaken central authority as much in the defeated as in the victorious countries'. From Italy to England, France to Germany, Russia to Austria, Europe was shaken by a tragic institutional crisis. Once again, Pareto compared the past and the present without deluding himself. Twenty years before in 'The danger of socialism' he had foreseen 'an economic revolution which can only be compared with the one which destroyed the Roman civilisation and spread the shadow of the Middle Ages over Europe'. Now, he realised that it had turned out to be a prophecy. As if abandoning his bitterness over the developments of the present, he restated his belief in the continuity of history. He retained a hope for a better future. He was basically convinced that history is the product of a continuous cyclical alternation of decay and rebirth. In spite of the chaos, he stated 'it is difficult for a civilised people to survive without laws', and foresaw that 'the present state can, therefore, only be transitory'. It only remained to be seen who would be victorious in the struggle and establish new laws capable of ensuring social equilibrium and, therefore, progress.

This essay, too, is closely tied to the emotions of the time, but presents few structural innovations in Pareto's concepts. Equilibrium, the cyclic reproduction of events can be found here, too. Here, as always, practice precedes theory: 'The state of fact precedes the ideal and legal state.'

FROM *Rivista di Milano*, 5 June 1920, now in *Trasformazioni della democrazia*, Milan 1921.

There are two contradictory forces in society. One, which can be called centripetal, tends towards the concentration of central authority. The other, which can be called centrifugal, tends towards the dispersion of central authority . . . The point of equilibrium between these two forces moves first to one side, then to the other, not in a regular identical way, but varying, according to the period; such oscillations are expressed by many different phenomena . . .

In the period of the shifting of the point of balance towards the centrifugal force, central authority (it does not matter whether monarchic, oligarchic, popular, plebeian) gradually fades away. What is defined as its authority tends to become an empty name and collapses, littering the country with its ruins. The power of some individuals and some groups – which in theory should still be subordinate to central authority, but in practice acquire independence – increases. As a consequence, those who do not belong to them – the weak – no longer being protected by central sovereignty, look elsewhere for protection and justice. They put their trust in a powerful man; they join with other weak elements, either publicly or secretly; they become part of a corporation, community, syndicate. This shifting of the point of balance produces opposite effects. As protection slowly evolves, it changes to subjection . . . When the circumstances tend to favour this latter development, the original central government or a new central government, by short-term and sudden violence or by long-term erosion, overthrows the dominant oligarchy and restores central authority . . . International conflicts can act in shifting the point of balance equally towards the centripetal force as towards the centrifugal force. Defeat in war can be a contributing cause in toppling central power and thus favouring the centrifugal movement. Victory can have opposite effects, but this does not always occur. The present World War which has thrown whole nations into battle, has as seriously shaken central power in the defeated as in the victorious countries . . . At the beginning of the nineteenth century in England, there was a shift in the point of balance towards the centripetal force. Then, parliament really was sovereign . . . Today, little more than a century later, its power has partly disappeared and crumbled,

the trade unions have inherited it and treat the government as
their equals . . . On 10 February 1920, Lloyd George told the
Commons: 'The difficulties which are encountered in the building of cheap houses originate in the shortage of labour and the
behaviour of the trade unions who do not allow 350,000 demobi-
lised workmen, who would be able to do this work, to be employed.' So these workmen must have the permission of the
trade unions in order to work . . . Until recently the opposite
occurred, and it was thought that parliament, and not private
associations, had to see to it that private interests did not prevail
over general interests. These are strange consequences. In Italy,
to prevent cattle being destroyed there is a decree which lays
down that meat shall not be eaten on Fridays and Saturdays. If
anyone eats a beef steak on these two days, he is punished, but
if a member of a trade union consumes a whole ox, he goes
unpunished. When the government decreed these hypocritical
restrictions, farm labourers in Italy were on strike. Under the
paternal, benevolent eye of the police, the strikers prevented
water and food being given to the cattle. They even beat up the
cattle-owner if he tried to do so . . .

The ability to extricate oneself from the justice of the central
authority is a sure sign that it is crumbling. The fact that one is
obliged to subject oneself to the justice of the central authority
is a sure sign of its revival. Even here the state of fact precedes
the ideal and legal state through which the state of fact is gradually transformed. We are now watching one of these transforma-
tions. The 'immunity' of trade unions has not yet reached a precise form like that of the Church under the Carolingians, but it is
slowly taking shape . . .

From the present rise and progress of anarchic organisation
there is a consequence to which nobody pays much attention at
the moment, although it is already manifesting itself in various
events. If this movement goes any further, the number and
seriousness of the conflicts between the various trade unions will
increase. There will be conflicts not only between the workers'
trade unions and the rest of the population, but also between the
various trade unions of each category . . . As central authority
grows weaker and weaker, the manifestations of rivalry of its
enemies get stronger and stronger, and private wars break out . . .
At Padua, on 18 April 1920, fighting broke out between 5,000

Reds and 5,000 Whites in the Signoria Piazza, and quite a battle resulted, with fifteen wounded. Central authority was nowhere to be seen to keep order. It watched the private war benignly, as the feudal kings once looked on at the wars of their barons . . . Is this legal according to the law in force? But who bothers about it? Certainly not the workers who already apply a law which will be put into force. Certainly not the central government which only thinks about not disturbing the beast which can devour it. Were the usurpations of the barons legal at the birth of feudalism? But who bothered about it? Certainly not the barons, who replaced law with force, and not the feudal king, who was powerless to make the barons obey him . . .

It is difficult for a civilised people to survive without laws. They can be written, regulated by use, or fixed in another way, but they must exist. The present state can, therefore, only be transitory.

35 Fascism

The description of equilibrium by centripetal and centrifugal forces favoured the latter. Pareto had already written that 'it is difficult for a civilised people to live without laws'. He was waiting for someone able to re-establish order and redress the broken equilibrium. He had also written: 'The present state can, therefore, only be transitory.' It seemed that he was being proved right by events. All the revolutionary movements which had broken out in Europe, brought on by the wave of enthusiasm aroused by the Bolshevik victory in Russia, began to subside. The week of bloodshed in Berlin from 6–11 January 1919, had seen the execution of the leaders of the Spartacist League, Rosa Luxemburg and Karl Liebknecht. The Communist *coup* by Béla Kun in Hungary had no better success, and at the end of 1919, Admiral Horthy installed an authoritarian government. In Italy, by 1921 the Fascist party had formed itself out of a heterogeneous group made up of out-of-work war veterans, nationalists, people used to living with war who were happy to make trouble and fight and who had battled with the Reds for command of the streets. They were now strengthened by the support of the bourgeoisie and assumed the guise of supporters of law and order.

Until then Pareto had never really taken fascism seriously, considering it to be one of the elements contributing to the collapse of central authority. On 2 May 1921, in a letter to his friend, Pantaleoni, he wrote: 'In *Trasformazioni della democrazia* you will find considerations on the collapse of central authority which are now largely confirmed by fascism.'[1] In the same letter he began to wonder whether fascism, once past the 'romantic' stage, would 'transform itself into an historically important phenomenon', and therefore tend towards the centripetal movement. But the changing situation and the new face of fascism caused him to reflect further. He was not interested in fascism for what it was in theory, but for what it did or could do to the disturbed social balance. He stated that fascism was not a transitory fact, but a structural fact, and that 'even if the doctrine dies, the Fascists will remain and be one of the elements of social equilibrium, even if under some other name'. This statement, too, marks a turning-point in the way in which he had considered fascism. It is enough to remember that in another letter to Pantaleoni, on 20 June 1921, he expressed a concept shared by all the Liberals of that time, according to which it was believed that Giolitti would give free rein to fascism in order, then, to 'intervene at the right time'.

FROM *La Ronda* January 1922.

. . . Firstly, it is necessary to study what the principal character-istics of the phenomenon called fascism are . . . All concrete phenomena of society are visible as a mixture of various elements continually changing both in themselves and in their proportion within the whole. The latter can only be investigated if, in all this fluidity, there remain some points which are less mobile, almost static. Who knows what democracy means? What and how many 'Liberal' parties there are? How many 'Conservative' parties? How many 'Socialist' parties?

The same thing happens when various elements are found under the name of religion . . . Let us see then, if there are rela-tively static parts of fascism. At first sight, there are two . . . The first consists in the use of illegal violence . . . The second, now on the decline, comprises a myth of which the core is nationalism with all its attendant emotions . . . The immediate problem is to discover if fascism is predominantly something original or if it is the manifestation of much more general phenomena. Un-doubtedly, the second is the main characteristic. In the history of civilised nations, the use of illegal violence seems to be of every-day occurrence, even among the more pacific peoples, and ex-tends from the individual violence of the criminal . . . to the collective violence of wars – both civil and foreign – so, it can be said that man's conflicts take place all the time, now inside, now outside certain laws of right or custom.

A rather imprecise, but powerful emotion exists in man, called justice . . . Thus, it is very important to establish: 'Who started this conflict?' . . . Did the socialists use violence before the fascists, or vice versa? You can give what answer you like, depending where you stop your inquiry, and you can go gradually back as far as Cain and Abel. This would be a splendid and even more agreeable literary exercise that that of studying which comes first – the chicken or the egg. In reality between socialists and fascists there is a chain of action and reaction which exists independently of socialism and fascism . . . To the strict logician the fascist faith is far inferior to the socialist faith, the more so because it is still in an embryonic state . . . The socialists have a more solid body of doctrine than the fascists who need to adopt a more precise form of doctrine if they are to endure for any length of time. But in that case, even if the doctrine disappears, the fascists will remain and be one of the elements of social equilibrium, even if under some other name.

There are two sorts of courage: physical and moral. The phenomenon of fascism shows that our bourgeoisie have plenty of the first, just like the classes which in the past were the élite. Moral courage is rather lacking . . . Physical courage alone does not determine political or social change, it becomes important when it helps moral courage and intellectual force . . .

The bourgeoisie acclaimed Napoleon I, then the Restoration, then Napoleon III. It was like a flock of sheep with no initiative of its own, but ever ready to follow some intrepid leader. In Italy, it supported D'Annunzio when words alone sufficed. It deserted him when deeds were needed as well . . . Now, it accepts the leadership of fascism because it is advantageous. Perhaps it gives secret financial support, but it would never openly lift a finger to defend it from its enemies . . . From what we have said it seems that we can conclude that fascism is probably the expression of a numerous class of analogous facts essentially transitory, which can have an intrinsically temporary importance, but which remain secondary and subordinate to the great factors of social evolution of which they can sometimes be the expression. In this case they acquire importance for the study and forecasting of social phenomena.

NOTES

1 Pareto, *Lettere a Maffeo Pantaleoni*, vol. III, p. 279.

36 Today and a century ago

Pareto's life was slowly but inexorably drawing to a close. His heart attacks became more frequent. Just after one of these, on 27 February 1922, he wrote to Pantaleoni, stoical in the knowledge of his imminent death, 'I think about those who will be left when I am gone, not about myself. I now have a short time to live. I have had many warnings. Some nights ago I was on the point of death; it was as though I was dead. This time I got over it, but next time I shan't be so lucky. It needs a lot of optimism to give me twelve months to live.'[1] He was right here, too, as de Rosa tells us that he lived for another eighteen months.[2] During these last months his greatest effort was concentrated upon gazing into the future rather than studying the present. With the aid of his past experience he tried to project himself in imagination into a future which illness and old-age would not allow him to experience in reality.

Meticulous as ever, in this essay he also recapitulated the essence of previously expressed ideas, so as to clarify the original ideas which he introduced. The concept of the repetition of historical phenomena recurs, as does the observation that it is easier to steal wealth from others than produce it by one's own labour – both ideas which he had developed in *Les Systèmes socialistes*. Once more he was apprehensive about the failure to establish a post-war balance. However, he prophetically foretold that demagogic plutocracy would decay still further into a demagogy of consumption. To introduce this concept he stated: 'If the Allies . . . remain in this situation in which consumption exceeds production, they will find themselves facing an insoluble problem.'

The problem of consuming in excess of production is insoluble, and Europe is feeling the full effects of it more than fifty years after Pareto's death.

FROM *Il Secolo*, 25 March 1922.
Two meetings of European statesmen, one at Verona in 1822 and the other a century later at Genoa in 1922, are in part different,

but in part similar. At the Congress of Verona the governments present were absolutist, while at the Conference of Genoa they were popularly elected. Even the aims were different: that of the former was principally political, that of the latter economic. The difference between the social forces which operate is analogous ... The intention is similar – that of regulating the state of the nations. Both presumed that they had sufficient power to carry out this enormous task. At least for some powers, faith in the strength of the existing treaties is the same, and they expect them to be as intransigent as they are difficult to uphold. The mystic faith of Tsar Alexander in the pact of the Holy Alliance is similar to the mystic faith of our contemporaries in Wilson's Fourteen Points and in the League of Nations which seems a democratic transformation of the Holy Alliance of 1815. The future will show whether the results of the two congresses are the same or different. After the defeat of Napoleon and the Revolution, the Allies of 1815 no longer had an external enemy to fear. They had taken the wise precaution of attracting to them a France which was weakened, but not pauperised. The internal difficulties remained, as the Allies had not seen or had not wanted to see the irresistible tide of democratic feeling ... Now, they tell Germany: 'If you kick the Emperor out and institute a democratic government, we shall admit you to our society.' Germany has done all this, but still remains isolated, because they say that her conversion is not sincere, and they say nothing about when it will be considered so ...

If the Allies . . . remain in this situation in which savings are wasted and consumption exceeds production, they will find themselves facing insoluble problems. The present position of society is unstable ... Russia will not produce what is expected of her. Once her government has exhausted its stock of gold and jewels, it will have very little left for international exchange. It is pointless to stand and stare at her natural resources – they are worthless unless realised through exploitation. But how can this be done under the present regime? . . . Slowly but surely, the social structure of Russia is moving towards the type of state which could be called Red Tsarism, and it will then be forced to seek that wealth that it cannot obtain through economic work in war and conquest. Nobody can say how this will happen. A Russian movement can be foreseen similar to the one which, in the past, caused the Nordic peoples to invade the fertile lands of the countries further south.

Germany will not pay all that is demanded of her . . . Without German reparations, with the American Debt to settle, and not reducing expenditure, following the depreciation of savings and the hunt for capital, both the public and private economies of several countries will be crippled. They will get further and further away from a well-balanced position and nearer to those violent movements which usually untie – or rather cut – the knots of similar, intricate situations.

The Congress of Verona initiated the beginning of the end of the Holy Alliance; the Conference of Genoa could mark the beginning of a distant end of the existing post-war equilibrium.

NOTES

1 Pareto, *Lettere a Maffeo Pantaleoni*, vol. III, pp. 304–5.
2 *Ibid*, p. 264.

37 Russia

The old Europe was in decay, as if sliding down a slope, resigned to its fate, 'and no human force is in sight which can stop this natural course of events'. The war was a world war only in words. In reality, the Europeans paid the highest price regarding loss of life and material ruin. However, the old style of governing went on quite happily. As always, petty politicians said one thing but wanted something different, and they exaggerated the danger of Russian power supported by German strength, for reasons of domestic policy.

Here too, Pareto tried to distinguish the more real and immediate danger from those which were imaginary or remote. There is something clairvoyant in his stating: 'There can be no doubt that the reawakening of the Orient, not only of Japan and China, but also of India and of Islam, is about to become an important factor in the world balance of power.' His foresight becomes all the more remarkable when he set 'the Russo-German alliance' in 'the near future', and Russo-European economic co-operation ('Europe cannot live economically without Russia') in 'the distant future'. Once more faithful to the principle that deeds not words matter, he observed the phenomenon of bolshevism dispassionately; he was waiting for the Bolsheviks to act before passing judgement. Social balance became increasingly important for him, since, if it was preserved it would bring about an increase in industrial production, social well-being and respect for the rights of the weakest, but, if broken, bankruptcy and moral decadence would ensue.

Pareto considered that the important thing was to re-establish the effective organisation of the state upset by centrifugal forces. This could be achieved as much by forces declaring themselves to be Bolsheviks as by others calling themselves Fascists. But he was convinced that neither Bolsheviks nor Fascists would survive unless they won the fight against those centrifugal forces by which the equilibrium with the centripetal forces had been disrupted. Thus, he stated: 'A nation not only needs for its industrial production to have natural resources, labour and capital, but also social and economic

organisations able to make these elements work efficiently – give these
organisations any name you like . . . If bolshevism survives, it will end
up by transforming itself in this way.'

FROM *Il Secolo*, 13 June 1922.
About thirty years ago the fear of the 'Yellow Peril' was the
fashion. It was said that China and Japan were about to advance
towards the economic and perhaps also military conquest of
Europe and other regions. Much was written to stress the vast
size of the yellow races, their modest standard of living which
ensured the low prices of manufactured goods, the political
sense of Japan, the reawakening of China after a sleep of centuries. Then gradually these fears abated and were replaced by
others . . . The 'Russian Peril' is like the phases of the moon:
first it appears, then it disappears, then it reappears. On St
Helena, Napoleon thought that Europe would have become
'Cossack' within a decade. The height of Russian power was
under Alexander I with the Holy Alliance. Then came the
Crimean War, followed by the Russo-Turkish War; then the
Russo-Japanese war; and finally the revolution itself. All these
have shown how little real strength there was in that giant. But,
look how that fear – like the moon – returns with the threat of the
power of the Bolsheviks, heirs (and soon, perhaps, rivals too) of
the Tsar. It is said that Europe cannot live economically without
Russia, and that the Russo-German Alliance is militarily a great
danger for western civilisation. There is a mixture of truth and
falsehood in all of this. The first statement refers to the near
future, the latter to a distant future. There can be no doubt that
the reawakening of the Orient, not only of Japan and China, but
also of India and Islam, is about to become an important factor
in the balance of world power, and no human force is in sight
which can stop this natural course of events. Similarly, it is very
probable that Russia and Germany will end up by coming to an
agreement – even if after various ups and downs – because their
common interests are very powerful. United, these two peoples
are really very formidable . . . Today, for reasons of domestic
policy, some statesmen exaggerate the danger of Russian power
supported by German strength, but in reality this does not seem
to be so very great – at least for many years to come – unless one
of the great western powers joins them. This raises the question:

'Is it probable that one of these states will join them or not?' . . .
The governments which now ask Russia to accept the 'principle
of private property' have respected and respect this principle
only when it suits them. In fact, it is sometimes more a case of
verbal distinction than fundamental difference . . . A nation not
only needs for its industrial production to have natural resources,
labour and capital, but also social and economic organisations
able to make these elements work efficiently – give these organisations any name you like . . . If bolshevism survives, it will end
up by transforming itself in this way, but this will not happen
without a serious clash between the resistance of fanatical belief
and the stimulus of sound politics. The Bolshevik government
will have to strengthen its will and this will not be easy . . . If it
does manage to do this there is the danger that this nation will
rise to a dominant position economically, militarily and politically.

38 The phenomenon of fascism

In the elections of May 1921, fascism obtained its first *legal* success, managing to get thirty members elected to Parliament. A few months later, it formed itself into a party. Socialist maximalism, however, having helped to destroy the old legality, was unable to form a new one. On 31 July 1922 the proclamation of another general strike gave Mussolini the chance of declaring his party the Party of Order. He gave an understanding that if the government left the streets open to demonstrators, the Fascists would think about restoring order. On 24 October 1922, the National Fascist Congress at Naples formally recognised an agreement between the upper and middle bourgeoisie, the army, the land-owners, most of the Royal Family and nearly all the Liberal intelligentsia.

Among the old Liberal ruling class only Amendola immediately declared that he was against fascism: he was beaten to death, thus paying the price of his dissent with his life, like another young Liberal, Gobetti, who met the same fate at the same time. All the other Liberals, from Croce to de Nicola, only found their anti-Fascist vocation much later on – when nothing could be done about fascism. On 28 October 1922, fascism carried out its final act on the road to legality. It aimed to govern the country, and threatened those who resisted it with the march on Rome to restore 'national pacification' and 'social order'. The weak king, perhaps encouraged by the trust placed in fascism, charged Mussolini with the formation of a new government. So the first Mussolini cabinet was formed which, designed to reassure everyone and only to frighten the Reds, offered every appearance of a right-wing coalition. Besides moderate Fascists, it also included Nationalists, Liberals like Salandra, two representatives of the Popular Catholic Party and General Armando Diaz and Admiral Paolo Thaon de Revel, two representatives of the armed forces which had defeated the Central Powers in war, but had been humiliated by the 'unjust' peace. In his maiden speech as Prime Minister, Mussolini showed himself at his most conciliatory. As if to demonstrate the goodwill of a man above factions he stated: 'I could have made this grey, deaf room into a bivouac of maniples[1] of soldiers.'

In this new climate, Pareto examined the phenomenon of fascism. He had already said: 'It is difficult for a civilised people to survive without laws.' Now he repeated: 'Order is absolutely necessary for civilised people . . . because of this, a new regime had to rise, formed either of Fascists or their enemies.' He had also said that if bolshevism wanted to last it should be careful to create 'a social and economic organisation able to make these elements work efficiently'. He had given his warning: 'The Bolshevik government will have to strengthen its will and this will not be easy . . . If it does manage to do this there is the danger that this nation will rise to a dominant position economically, militarily and politically.' The Fascists had won in Italy just as the Bolsheviks had won in Russia. But they had won because, in 'strengthening their will instead of wasting money without bothering about the future', all their efforts had been concentrated on the 'seizure of central authority'.

On 17 June 1921, he had written to Pantaleoni defining Mussolini as a 'Jack of all trades and master of none'.[2] Now his changed view of fascism included Mussolini himself, whom he defined as 'a politician of the first rank'. In spite of this, his support of fascism was not unconditional, instead he warned: 'Sooner or later we must abandon temporary expedients and solve our grave constitutional problems.'

FROM *La Natione*, 25 March 1923.

Like most social phenomena, the study of fascism presents difficulties which arise from the very complexity of such phenomena. There are also special difficulties like the one – the most important – in which the name serves to indicate two completely different things. At first sight fascism seems very different if we consider it before and after the 'March on Rome'. In an article in *Gierarchia* its 'Duce' has heavily underlined this difference, speaking about a 'second Fascist period'.

In the first period, fascism was a spontaneous reaction – a bit anarchistic – by a part of the population against 'Red Tyranny' to which the government had given every licence, leaving the private citizens to protect themselves. In that first phase fascism was not concerned with theories, and many of its supporters state that fascism is action and ideology . . . One of the main aims of every government is the protection of people and property. If this aim is neglected, forces able to make good this lack of protec-

tion rise out of the population . . . Order is absolutely necessary
for civilised people. Sooner or later, an old or a new government
will once more resume the task momentarily left to private
initiative. It was possible to foresee, therefore, that the fascism
of the first period would not last long, and that it would give way
to a new organisation . . . able to re-establish the authority of the
government and public order. This is what happened . . . Civil
servants no longer obeyed the cabinet, the state was completely
powerless, and because of this a new regime had to rise, formed
either of Fascists or their enemies. The former managed to do so.
Why?

The immediate difference between these two is easy to see. The
latter wanted quick results to satisfy their greed, and to gain
material advantages. They fought to possess the things and positions useful to them, without really bothering about the future
. . . Their gaining control of the town councils was just the
opportunity to misappropriate the taxes (which were increased
still more) and to waste money . . . The contrast with the
Fascists is great. There are black sheep in any flock, and there
are those among the Fascists who are interested in lining their
own pockets, but these are extremely rare cases. The vast
majority pursued a more or less mythical ideal: the exaltation of
national sentiment and the power of the state as a reaction to the
democratic, pseudo-liberal, pacifist, humanitarian ideology. In
most of the Fascists this ideal very probably assumed the form
of ill-defined emotion which drove them to action, but they were
directed skilfully and firmly by their leaders – one could say by
their chief – towards a lofty goal of great importance: the conquest of central authority. At the moment when they were about
to obtain it, some tried to stop them by offering them ministries.
Mussolini refused. He wanted all or nothing. He obtained all.
Here is another application of one of the laws already studied in
the *Trattato*, which says that collectivity wins where the leaders
have a strong instinct of combination and where the masses have
powerful, idealistic feelings . . .

Another difference between the Fascists and their enemies
comes out in relation to economic and financial conditions. Every
problem produced by these conditions has two possible solutions:
one aims at ensuring maximum economic welfare, the other at
the maximum satisfaction of certain emotions and certain par-

ticular interests. Weak governments – which count more than anything else on the greed and particular prejudices of their dependents – are inclined to use the second solution. Only powerful governments which rely on strength and intense, idealistic emotions are in the position to adopt the first solution rigorously. While society is rich and prosperous, the first solution can even be neglected; but when wealth is exhausted and crises arise, persistence in sacrificing economic welfare to interests and prejudices can lead to the worst catastrophes . . . At the moment the whole of Europe is in such difficulties, and its ruling classes cannot find solutions for the worrying problems that exist. In Italy, fascism is trying to find a solution . . . The future will show us whether a new era has begun with fascism, or whether there will be a return to the old errors which are taking us towards an anarchy like that of the Middle Ages.

After the war, nearly everywhere – and especially in Italy – popular feeling shows a curious anomaly. The conditions of the mass of the working class have certainly improved considerably – take, for example the eight-hour working day and the sometimes appreciable increases in wages. On the other hand the conditions of the lower middle-classes, and above all the conditions of the so-called 'intellectuals', have worsened generally. In certain particular cases it can be observed that they have reverted to a state of poverty. Thus, it seems that the former should bless war and the latter should curse it, but just the opposite occurs. The explanation of this is not difficult to find. The working-class masses accept the advantages brought by the war as something which is their due, and make new demands, ask for fresh advantages. Their shallow minds think that these advantages are obtainable if they appropriate the property of the other classes . . . In Italy, fascism has come to correct, in part, a logical mistake in the sentiments of the social classes. It has had the capacity to activate the religion of nationalism: the defence of the state and social renewal. The essence of the 'Fascist Revolution' lies in this.

Incidental causes are added to general causes. One of the most important of these certainly is the fact that fascism has found a politician of the highest rank in its leader . . . In foreign policy, Mussolini is eminent for his firm moderation. It was feared that he would reverse everything, but he has been able to distinguish the impossible from the possible, and as a consequence has been able to develop policies and take measures which adhere closely to the demands of reality. In domestic policy, it would be premature to make a definite judgement. It can only be said that the beginnings are good and promise a happy future. But we are sailing in troubled waters. Sooner or later we must abandon temporary expedients and solve the grave constitutional problems . . .

NOTES

1 Maniple: a subdivision of a Roman legion.
2 Pareto, *Lettere a Maffeo Pantaleoni*, vol. III, p. 285.

39 The war goes on

This is one of Pareto's shortest essays, but one which gives rise to many reflections. The factual methodology is the same as ever, but the multiple hypotheses are reduced to the single hypothesis of 'the inevitable necessity of things'. It seems to go back to his *Cours* and the 'eternal unchangeable' laws of nature. There is, however, a psychological change. Previously, the scientific rules not only helped in an understanding of the world, but also to humanise it both subjectively and objectively; now, the extent of the influence of man's actions seems less, although it has not disappeared completely. However Pareto's inclination towards pessimism was not altogether without reason. It is not that he rejects his suggestion 'to remember that the world had already seen the alternation of Middle Ages and the Renaissance several times', but rather that the deeper the foundations of the present Middle Ages, the more distant, and the more difficult to reach, will be the future renaissance. Europe's state of decay was discouraging, as were the bickerings of petty politicians which unfortunately reflected the bickerings of their peoples. Their state of degradation was such that they strove to achieve mutually irreconcilable aims – such as to keep Germany poor and yet able to pay the heavy war reparations; they were unable to understand why a peace treaty is incapable of changing the customs and standard of living of a people overnight.

In observing how the use of demagogy became more widespread and how petty politicians, without looking to the future, played upon some passions more than others in order to become popular immediately, Pareto drew the conclusion that perhaps the worst had not yet come to Europe, and the day would perhaps dawn when 'everything will be turned upside down'. Afraid of this he prayed that these events 'can come with changes neither too violent nor destructive of too many lives and too much wealth'. Unfortunately, future events would surpass his most pessimistic forecasts.

FROM *Il Secolo*, 20 April 1923.

Europe suffers, and compassionate doctors tell us that she needs to be 'rebuilt'. Then knowledgeable politicians congregate and, with the wisdom and help of experts, study and deliberate and, using many statistics, deliver a great number of speeches. However, the chatter tends to die away, and then comes the disappointment, followed by oblivion . . . The fault does not lie in what the proposals say, but in what the proposals do not say . . . No expert – not even a scientific genius – can say what Germany will have to pay tomorrow, because that depends on circumstances which only a prophet can know. The overall situation contains contradictory elements. For example, among those who want Germany to pay more are people who fear above all else that Germany should prosper, and in this find the strength to take her revenge. However, it is evident that Germany will be able to repay much if she prospers, and little or nothing if she is ruined.

Sooner or later a new Treaty of Versailles will be drawn up and imposed on the defeated victors. But could this new treaty be any better observed than the old one? And if past experience is repeated, what will be gained by those who again force themselves into an impasse? Similar considerations are valid for Germany too. There, too, people close their eyes to the reality of things, passions are flattered, interests are favoured – especially those of demagogic plutocracy – and they refuse to resign themselves to the inevitable necessity of things . . .

Serious errors are behind the illusions created by believing in the efficacy of conferences and treaties, for insufficient attention is paid to the fact that the achievement of any government is mainly the result of the forces present in the country concerned. So, if these forces do not change, the achievement of the government cannot easily change. For this reason our governments are often unconsciously obstinate in seeking to solve the insoluble: the extreme importance of consuming less and producing more; to be able to change the character and mentality of a people made up of many millions of individuals by the mere articles of an enforced treaty . . . In such a way cul-de-sacs are entered, and the day will dawn when, in order to find a way out, everything will be turned upside-down and the governing classes and their sentiments and interests will be created afresh. Perhaps similar events are still a long way off for Europe, but they do not seem impossible. The hope remains that they can come with changes which are neither too violent nor destructive of too many human lives and too much wealth.

40 Freedom

'The more general meaning of the word freedom is that which indicates the absence of coercion on the part of the law or public authorities. Exceptionally, freedom can mean the effective power of being able to do certain actions.' Pareto wrote this in *Les Systèmes socialistes*, polemically attacking ethical thinkers and those who thought that 'freedom is a means and not an end'. In this essay he seems to turn this position upside-down. Freedom, so far from being an end, becomes an empty word to which 'everyone gives what meaning he wants'. It seems that Pareto considered freedom as no more than a masked dictatorship. Accordingly he stated: 'Italian unification was brought about by a bourgeois dictatorship'. As we shall see, he was to repeat the same concept in his last work when he claimed, with regard to England, that 'up to now, her government has been substantially the dictatorship of one or other of the two historic parties'. Ceasing to distinguish between democracy and dictatorship, he now condemned Marxism, not because it destroys freedom, but because it is inefficient. He said: 'The dictatorship of the proletariat must not be rejected because it is a dictatorship . . . but rather for its poor showing.' Here, too, the changes are not so great as they seem at first sight. This poor showing is judged poor only in terms of the wealth and the welfare of society.

His method of judgement had always been linked to the use of 'quantitative considerations in place of qualitative notions'. Once he had held the view that maximum production resulted from the relationship and equilibrium between the individual and society. Now that totalitarianism seemed to be in fashion, his concept of equilibrium became that of equilibrium between two different dictatorships; that of the proletariat – which destroys wealth and wipes out private enterprise – and that of the Fascists – which, through the initial conciliatory aspect, promises a greater production of wealth by means of private enterprise. Pareto realised that if the Bolshevik government made a bad showing owing to an excess of centripetal forces, Europe made the same bad showing owing to an excess of centrifugal forces. Perhaps he hoped that if European fascism took command it would be possible to re-create an equilibrium which would lead to the disappearance of both Fascist dictatorship and Communist dictatorship. This theory carries more weight if one considers what he wrote to Pantaleoni on 27 May 1921: 'Think carefully: in the end it could be the case that the Fascist interlude could serve socialism by freeing it from the Communists.'[1]

For this he was convinced that fascism had the task of re-establishing European equilibrium and, with a touch of nationalism, he stated: 'Italy, already the mother of many forms of civilisation, could have an important role in generating a new one.' In this role as a counterweight to bolshevism, the first thing fascism had to do was to preserve all the different individual liberties: but inside the law. In support of this thesis, Pareto said: 'The enemies of fascism are right to ask fascism to let them know which things are allowed and which are not.' In the past Pareto had often warned against the mistake of confusing one's hopes with the reality of facts. Now he seemed to have forgotten his own teaching. His hopes of a fascism which would bring about new forms of civilisation, were to be belied by events. In this desire to see the centripetal forces restored, he did not foresee that the Middle Ages he feared so much would come precisely from the total victory of the centripetal forces over the centrifugal forces, and from respect for law no matter what the law is – even a law imposing racial extermination. But perhaps in this case too, these future horrors were to be caused by another break in the equilibrium which Pareto had always considered so important.

FROM *Gerarchia*, July 1923.

The term 'freedom' is one of the most ill-defined, among the already very loosely defined terms, which common language uses when dealing with the problems of social organisation. It is used so much because everyone gives it whatever meaning he wants ... In Cavour's time, the party which called itself Liberal wanted the freedom to use wealth as one pleased to be respected. Then this party limited this freedom so much that they allowed the occupation of lands and factories and also the boundless demagogic tyranny of the years 1919 and 1920, of which the Prime Minister has now given us an extremely good and truthful reminder ... The fools of 1919–20 were opposed by other fools who made punitive expeditions and then the 'March on Rome'.

The Liberals certainly did not oppose the 1919–20 fools – the others did that. The former are ready to reappear if the conditions of those two years return. Why must the action of the former be called *liberal* and that of the latter *anti-liberal*? We do not know. The first aids the rise of the proletariat, while the latter impedes it. But this takes us . . . into the field of social utility. So, whereas in 1920–21 'freedom' forbade Fascist resistance to Red tyranny, now Fascist tyranny is expected to allow the factious opposition of the Reds . . . At this point it is necessary to replace qualitative notions by quantitative considerations. It is useless to try to discover whether or not it is right for freedom of thought to exist; instead, for example, it is necessary to examine within what limits it brings more good than harm.

In nearly every age, and among all people it is acknowledged that exceptional circumstances demand exceptional restraints on freedom . . . Passing from the general to the particular we must study whether fascism is spending too much time in the dictatorial phase; whether it should remain in this phase, or whether it should imitate Kerensky and prepare the way for another Lenin; and whether the prohibitions and obligations of fascism produce more ill then good. The followers of the experimental method can solve such a problem not with sentimental declamations on freedom, but with data taken from facts . . . 'The dictatorship of the proletariat' must not be rejected because it is a dictatorship . . . but rather for the bad showing that it has made . . .

Italian reunification was brought about by a bourgeois dictatorship which was good, not because it was a dictatorship, but because . . . it had good effects . . . The Fascist regime is not good merely because it is dictatorial – it could be extremely bad with the wrong dictator – but because the results up to now have been good, as has been proved by the improvement in the present state of the country by comparison with conditions during the 1919–20 period of the Red tyranny. What will the future bring? Only events can give a definite answer, but we cannot exclude the likelihood of being able to make a favourable forecast if present trends continue.

There are, however, formidable dangers which must be overcome. Some have already been removed by the wisdom of the leaders, like that of foreign ventures . . . others remain . . . A grave danger would be that resulting from the long absence of constitutional reforms . . . The enemies of fascism are right to ask Fascists to let them know what is allowed and what is not, but they are wrong to expect this to be done in the brief period of bitter conflict. In this period one can only say that what does not endanger the Fascists is lawful, and what does is unlawful . . . Fascism is not an exclusively Italian phenomenon – it is only the expression of an emotion which is more intense in Italy, but which exists to some extent everywhere, and the more it increases the bigger the troubles of parliamentarianism and the crimes of demagogic plutocracy will be . . . Italy, already the mother of many forms of civilisation, could have an important role to play in generating a new one.

NOTES

1 Pareto, *Lettere a Maffeo Pantaleoni*, vol. iii, p. 284.

41 A few points concerning a future constitutional re-organisation

This article – planned before his death and published one month later – is a puzzle to those who study Pareto. Just as the word fascism was once an honorific but is now a pejorative – so it is now thought to be an insult to Pareto to call him a Fascist. Tremendous efforts are made to emphasise how even in the last few months of his life, Pareto remained faithful to a liberal society. In fact, he still said that: 'Parliament is extremely useful – with extensive freedom of the press and the use of referenda being indispensable.' But if read in the context of the article itself and what he had said in the preceding article, this claim assumes a different aspect. For several months past Pareto had been applauding the earliest acts of the new Fascist government. In fact, after December 1922 his perplexities over fascism became things of the past. Although Giacalone-Monaco quotes from a postcard sent to him on 1 June 1922, in which Pareto said: 'I may be wrong, but I cannot see a deep abiding strength in fascism', in order to prove that Pareto had never been a Fascist, Pareto's final attitude proves him wrong. Slighted by his countrymen, Pareto began to succumb to the flattery of fascism, and, at the end of 1922, accepted Mussolini's personal invitation to join the League of Nations Disarmament Commission. Busino may think differently, but the letter in reply to the invitation is quite explicit. Pareto wrote to Mussolini: 'I accept, not without hesitation . . . Not that this hesitation springs from the fear of being unable wholeheartedly to realise Your Excellency's ideas on this subject – perhaps I am over-presumptuous in believing that I know their principal lines – as I am firmly convinced that I would willingly support them, but rather from doubt that my strength will be sufficient to perform the task efficiently.'[1] In fact, Pareto was never able to take up this position because of serious illness. However, in a letter to Sensini on 9 March 1923, he declared himself 'grateful and much obliged for the kindness shown me'.[2] Only a few months later, he showed that he had lost his enthusiasm, and wrote to Naville on 9 May 1923, 'It seems to me that for the moment this institution is marking time and, in order to justify its existence, is spending its time on trivialities. I have resigned as member of the Disarmament Commission, mainly owing to my poor health, but also because it is a waste of time to go round in circles.'[3] So, it might be said that if he accepted, it was only for the great pleasure that he would have taken in performing that task, the thought of which made him forget his serious state of health which, some years before, had prevented him appearing in court, and thus allowed his wife to win the case for alimony. He nurtured illusions that fascism could re-establish an equilibrium between speculators and *rentiers*, besides countering the danger of bolshevism and thus allowing the middle classes to survive. Had he lived a few years longer many of these illusions would have disappeared.

Pareto deluded himself that fascism would accept advice. After the invitation to be a member of the League of Nations Disarmament Commission, Mussolini had nominated him Senator – together with Pantaleoni – just a few months before his death. But the flattery given to intellectuals by the fascism of that time was only a means towards the complete seizure of power. Pareto was not to live to see it, nor would he be there when *all* the political enemies of the regime were so cynically eliminated. His adhesion was only to a fascism completely different from that which developed in the years to come. So de Rosa is right when he says that 'if he had lived a few more years he would have expressed completely negative judgements on fascism'.[4]

Thus it is unfair to judge Pareto's position by attributing to him responsibility for a type of fascism which was yet to come; rather he should be judged on the basis of his work taken as a whole. Dissecting Pareto's work and selecting only certain writings is, as Meisel says: 'equivalent to saying that the blossom of a flower is the only important thing, and that all the rest – the leaves, the stem, the soil which feeds the roots – are a mere mistake'.[5]

FROM *Il Giornale economico*, 25 September 1923.
Using Machiavelli's *The Prince* as a model, I shall put forward some proposals taken from historical experience and applicable to the events of today . . . Sooner or later the present dictatorship will come to constitutional reform. It would be advantageous if it were to come as soon as possible, and respect as closely as possible the existing forms, renewing their content, after the example of Ancient Rome and England. Strength and consent – as the *Trattato* demonstrates – are the foundations of government. For

this reason, one is bound to praise the two fundamental measures taken by fascism – the formation of the national militia, and the formation of a government consisting of representatives of all the main currents of existing opinion in the country, and not of parliamentary gangs. One must be careful to remain in this stream, hard though it is – yet careful to guard against the infiltration of hostile elements in the militia; careful, too, to judge dispassionately the current opinion; careful not to surrender to those who seek to use the government to impose their own views on others. In particular, it is an excellent idea to respect Catholicism, but it would be very bad to seek to impose – even indirectly – either this or any other religion. Experience shows that governments which do this only reap trouble without any advantage. One must imitate Ancient Rome – not occupy oneself with theology and ideology, but interest oneself in action.

However one views parliament at this point, it is better to retain it. The problem to be solved is that of finding a way of obtaining the maximum benefit and the minimum disadvantage. The solution cannot be found by seeking the best electoral system. The democratic ideology of the people's government leads to the belief that 'the best government is the people's government. But as millions of citizens cannot govern directly it becomes necessary to look for someone to represent them, and if a system could be devised for this, there would be a perfect government.' On the contrary, the people's government is not very effective and is less effective than the government of its representatives. In Switzerland, a remedy was sought in the referendum. As for England, up to now her government has been substantially the dictatorship of one or other of the two historical parties. Now, this organisation is changing and we do not know what fruit it will bear. I am not trying to say that the electoral system is of no importance, but that the problem of the power which must be assigned to parliament is more important. Prince Louis Napoleon gave his country universal suffrage which is considered to be a democratic measure, but to balance this he greatly restricted the power of parliament. We already possess this 'well-deserved' suffrage, which has had the 'benefit' of proportional representation tacked on to it. It now remains for the antidote to be found. The present parliament is well suited to fascism – it cannot do any harm, and that is quite enough ... What are you grumbling about? You will replace the impotence of parliament with the competence of a good council of state, a good council of producers which remembers the consumers ... Parliament should express views, interests and even prejudices – the important thing is that they should be general ... If you hope for a parliament that will draw its power for a large majority of one party over the rest – you hope for your ruin. Who guarantees that the elections will give you a majority party favourable to you? And, if the Bolsheviks were to win, what then? ... Remember that, in the supreme interest of the state, Bismarck was able to resist the Prussian parliament. One cannot govern only by the consent of the majority - however large – because it is necessary to keep the dissidents in check. Neither can one govern for long by strength alone – one has to ascertain the will of the majority. Because of this, parliament is extremely useful, and wide freedom of the press and the use of referenda indispensable. In France, the Second Empire made the terrible mistake of taking the freedom of the press almost completely away. And what has its removal done for Russian tsarism? Be careful then, not to succumb to the temptation of limiting it too much ... Let people write what they like, but be inexorable in repressing subversive acts...

There are great currents of opinion which never disappear, even if they only appear every now and again on the surface, such as the currents of faith, scepticism, idealism, materialism, positive religion, free thought. Whoever thinks that he can eliminate them is deceiving himself. Under the democratic ideology flowed the Fascist current, which is now spreading over the surface. Now, under it, flows the stream of its opponents. Take care that it does not surface. Take care not to strengthen it by trying to stop it completely. The worst enemies of a social organisation are those who try to drive it to extremes...

The only aim must be that of freeing oneself from the democratic ideologies of the sovereignty of the majority. Let this sovereignty retain its shadow – it flatters powerful emotions – but let the substance pass to an élite for the objective good.

NOTES

1 Pareto's reply was later published in *Giornale d'Italia*, 3 Jan 1923. See also G. Busino, 'Vilfredo Pareto e la società delle nazioni' *Giornale degli economisti e annali d'economia*, Sept–Oct 1962, pp. 661–6, now in 'Materiaux pour servir a l'étude de la pensée politique et sociale de Vilfredo Pareto', *Cahiers Pareto*, no. 7–8, 1965, p. 131.

2 *Corrispondenza di Vilfredo Pareto*, ed. Guido Sensini (Padua 1948), p. 139.

3 Letter to Naville edited by G. Busino & S. Stelling Michaud, in *Cahiers Pareto*, no. 6, 1965, p. 236.

4 Pareto, *Lettere a Maffeo Pantaleoni*, vol. III, p. 264.

5 J.H. Meisel, 'Introduction' to *Pareto and Mosca* (New Jersey 1965), p. 25.

PART THREE
Conclusion

I   Pareto and his contemporaries

Pareto's works may be full of surprises – at once fascinating and disconcerting – but that of his contemporaries can also be said to possess the same characteristics. Unqualified admirers or implacable enemies, they have read what they wanted into his work and, as their mood takes them, have called him rationalist or irrationalist, liberal or fascist, supporter of 'mechanistic determinism' or individualism, imitator of Hegel or of Pascal. He answered many of these respectfully or sarcastically, angrily or with moderation, but all with scholarly and punctilious precision. His replies were so varied and articulate that, even after his death, he still provides answers with mocking irony or imperturbable detachment for those who try patiently to read his innumerable, many-sided, and complex works.

But who were his questioners and his critics? Let us begin by looking at those to whom he replied personally. We shall then see if these replies serve indirectly for those whom he cannot answer personally. Croce holds an important place among the first category. Their controversy was short-lived, but extremely intense, beginning soon after the publication of Pareto's *Cours*, and reaching its climax with the French edition of the *Manuale* – the after-effects of which lasted for some years. Important problems and themes were discussed, which in turn influenced some subjects rather than others to which Pareto later turned his attention. The young Croce reproached Pareto for having changed 'economic act' into 'mechanical act', and in an open letter to Pareto, published in *Giornale degli economisti*, he wrote: 'You talk of the 'unconscious actions' of man, but these cannot be the actions of a man in the form of man. Instead, at the most, they can only be the acts of man considered as an animal or a machine.' Accusing Pareto of having reduced economic acts to egoistic acts, Croce added: 'When the principle of egoism is reduced to the same thing as the principle of economics, instead of a distinction being made between economy and morals, the former is made subordinate to the latter and is denied any right of existence by being labelled as something completely negative, like a degeneration of the same moral activity.'[1] As we have already seen, Pareto replied to Croce in the same newspaper in a letter in which he claimed that value is purely a 'choice of quantity' in men, who, unlike animals, prefer quantity to quality.[2] Something else which Croce criticised in Pareto was methodological instrumentalism. An expression of this criticism is found in another open letter, where Croce wrote: ' . . . Even if I agree with you in supporting the rights of logical, scientific elaboration to make abstractions . . . I cannot believe that this elaboration carries anything arbitrary with it . . . You speak about dissecting a specimen from a concrete phenomenon and then studying it in isolation . . . but your 'dissecting a specimen' is already a solution of the *quid* which consists in the economic fact . . . It seems that your being a metaphysician is the least charge that can be brought against you. However, your latent metaphysical presupposition is that the facts of man's activity are of the same nature as the facts of physics; that for one, as for the other, we can do no more than observe regularities and deduce consequences, without, however, ever penetrating the intimate nature of these regularities and facts; that these facts are all phenomena of the same type. (This is to say that these phenomena would presuppose a noumenon which escapes us and of which they would be the manifestations.) So, while I entitled my work *On the economic principle* you have entitled yours *On the economic phenomenon.*'[3]

Not at all embarrassed by Croce's remarks, Pareto answered him in a letter in February 1901, stating his point of view. He said: 'We look at things from different points of view and it is therefore natural that, reasoning logically, we reach different conclusions.' He added, 'In the light of my poor – nay, very poor – knowledge, I am not able to find the difference between regularities among the facts of physics and those of man's activity . . . I do not in the least presuppose any noumenon. How could I presuppose what I am completely ignorant of? For my part, with modesty, I study only facts and concrete cases and try to find what regularities and what analogies they present.'[4]

But the real reply to Croce's remarks is contained in a note in the French edition of the *Manuale*. Here, he wrote: 'On the publication of the Italian edition, an author of great talent, Benedetto Croce, criticised me . . . He observed: "What is the imperfection of the human spirit? Do we by any chance know a *perfect* spirit by the side of which we can establish that the human spirit is *imperfect*?" I could reply that if the use of the term "imperfect" is only allowed when something "perfect" can be shown in opposition to this term, the word "imperfect" should be erased from the dictionary, as the opportunity to use it would never occur – perfection not being of this world . . . The fact that Croce is a Hegelian has evidently caused him to be offended when the ill-sounding epithet "imperfect" is applied to the human spirit.'[5]

In spite of their continual bickering and the fact that they spoke 'different languages', Pareto and Croce always behaved correctly towards each other. Pareto always spoke with great esteem of Croce as 'a man and historian', only complaining in a letter to their mutual friend, Vittore Pansini, that metaphysics divided them.[6] In another letter to Pansini, Pareto underlined the same feeling of esteem, almost repenting 'the vanity and inconclusiveness' of the controversy which he sustained until the *Manuale*, by saying: 'Croce, in following his way – and I, in following mine – are both logical.'[7]

If his relationship with Croce was muddied by a lack of comprehension, the same cannot be said about his relationship with Papini, another of his critics. In the same letter which we have just mentioned, Pareto was delighted that Papini had 'correctly assessed' his character. What had pleased Pareto was the article which Papini had written in *La Libertà economica* where he stated that 'the fundamental character of Paretian thought is that of being *non-religious*. But we should note, *non*-religious and not *anti*-religious . . . Pareto is almost completely alone in modern Europe, in not belonging to any religion – either old or new. He is the perfect, complete atheist confronting all these triumphant divinities.'[8]

With the exception of Croce's acute, even if polemical, arguments and the articles of his few but faithful admirers, Pareto's writings were more or less ignored by official Italian scholarship during their author's life, so that, perhaps not unreasonably, he considered himself to be persecuted. With great bitterness he wrote to Pantaleoni on 15 September 1917: 'It makes me laugh to read that Sensini is extremely lucky to have my esteem! This has caused him to be excluded from a university chair in this lovely Italian kingdom of ours . . . something in which we are partners in misfortune.'[9] But we know that Pareto never ignored Italian academic culture, whose chief exponents always found a place in Pareto's writings. The Italian academic culture of those times certainly found open criticism of its provincialism – even Croce was an outsider. It is understandable why Pareto used to speak about Italian university professors with extreme irony, and why he never missed the opportunity of letting fly pointed barbs against archaic culture impregnated with a positivism belatedly imported from France. One has only to remember Pareto's review of the third volume written by Lombroso, *L'Uomo delinquente*. He observed: 'But when Lombroso sees a child, is he really able to say whether or not that child will become a Boulanger or a Crispi? Anthropology of this sort seems to be very similar to astrology.'[10] The barbs which he aimed at another positivist, Loria, were equally sharp. He condemned him for thinking that 'not only is the economic theme the only one, but also that there is only one cause of all social phenomena in the end – the interest of the capitalist class'.[11] Later, on 31 August 1917, in a letter to Pantaleoni, he confessed that he had always been under the impression that Loria was 'a trained donkey'.[12]

But if Pareto was severe on the followers of an old-fashioned positivism, he was no less severe on the followers of the German school and neo-idealism – an example of which is found in the essay 'On the logic of the new school of economics' (besides the differences we have already seen with Croce). Neither of these remained an isolated phenomenon. The esteem which Pareto showed more than once for Labriola did not stop him from entering into controversy with him over the theory of value. Pareto stated: 'Professor Antonio Labriola, who is also well-versed in Marxist doctrines, says that 'the theory of value does not represent an empirical *factum*, neither does it express a simple *logical position* as some have believed, but it is the *typical premise* without which all the rest is unthinkable. It could be so, but if the *typical premise* is not a concrete, real fact, I abandon it and dispense with considering the rest.'[13]

Sometimes, however, Pareto's judgement on the dawning idealism was too drastic, and certainly hurried, as when, after having read Giovanni Gentile's 'Realismo e fatalismo politico',[14] he wrote to Pantaleoni on 3 July 1920: 'I have tried to read the article written by Giovanni Gentile and have not understood anything. There are people in lunatic asylums who reason as he does, and the poor things are kept there.'[15] On other occasions, however, his severe judgement was justified by the superficiality of certain of his critics. This was the case of Weiss who, in his review of Pareto's *Trattato*, wrote: 'In short . . . in his voluminous – nay, in comparison to the real content, rather long and drawn-out – work, Pareto expounds a rather limited number of ideas which cut a poor figure if set beside the inexhaustible wealth of intuition and development in the work of a Vico or a Hegel. Nor is this all, many of their ideas are presented in a much more persuasive, profound and scientifically correct form in the analogous pages of these two authors.'[16] On this occasion, letting off steam in a letter to Pansini on 3 July 1917, he wrote, 'I am glad to know that I have been discovered to be a Hegelian – even if rather an uncouth one. I should never have imagined it. Metaphysics has this much good about it – that by not expressing anything concrete it expresses everything. I shall have some visiting cards printed with the inscription: Vilfredo Pareto – Hegelian. I hope that someone else will discover than I am Platonist, Cartesian, Giobertian, etc., etc. I shall add these titles to my visiting cards.'[17]

During these years Pareto's irony became all the more sharp, because here was a man who had fought against customs protection all his life, and now found that the kind of cultural protectionism that united Italy was putting into practice was more offensive, and that it was making her more and more provincial. When still divided, Italy had enjoyed cultural cross-fertilisation from Europe – not only in the arts (Verdi for example), but also in sociology and politics (for example, Mazzini, Cattaneo, Manzoni, Pellico). United Italy seemed to have closed her frontiers not only to goods but also to ideas. Only if one considers this can one understand why Pareto's inquisitors – with the exception of Croce – were so few, and why, instead of a constructive exchange of ideas, it was so often a matter of sterile controversy.

During his life Pareto did not suffer only adverse criticism. He also had the good fortune to know enthusiastic readers and sincere friends, as is proved by his vast correspondence not only with Pantaleoni, but also with Sorel, Pansini, Pietri-Tonelli, Giacalone-Monaco, Sensini, Linaker, Placci, Amoroso, Barone and others. They give us another version of Pareto, perhaps something of an apologia but certainly extremely interesting and providing a clear picture of him. Although we do not possess the letters which they wrote to him (it seems that on the death of her husband, Madame Régis destroyed everything belonging to him, including the villa and the park of which no trace can be found), we do have different essays written by them on Pareto's work. Some of these essays were written for the *Giornale degli economisti* on the occasion of his death.[18] United in their admiration for him they differed in the reasons for this admiration. Some emphasised the purely logical and causal character of Pareto's work. This was the case with Pantaleoni, who wondered: 'Do human acts exist which are voluntary (that is, fruit of a will which is not conditioned by instincts, heredity, biological formation, education) and which are therefore not the result of past or present causes, simultaneous, or rapidly following one another? If the answer is no, there is no freedom of choice and there is no place for virtue or vice in the world. If the answer is yes, it must be demonstrated that, after causes and counter-causes have acted, and thus after the choice has been made, there still exists an internal tribunal which can override or overthrow that sentence through the exercise of free-will. Pareto would have answered no, denying himself every merit.'[19]

Besides Pantaleoni, Amoroso also emphasised the 'mechanistic' aspect of Pareto's work, criticising the 'non-Euclidean economics'; that is, those economics which 'would be expressions of acts which are not irrational, as they do not conflict with the formal law of logic, but *which contradict past experience* and, therefore, presumably the future as well'. He pointed out how Pareto's income curve 'gives a scientific form to, and explains the inner rationale of the age-old principle of *hierarchy*', concluding that 'the economic, and therefore social hierarchy, is indestructible'.[20] However he forgot the efforts made by Pareto to prove the difference between the social sciences and the other sciences, due above all to the subject-matter which it studies – man.

Barone's essay took a different line, however. He emphasised how Pareto had always tended to 'look for perfection, especially in considering not only the purely economic aspect of the various economic problems, but also integrating this aspect with all the others.'[21]

Another scholar who took an honest and objective interest in Pareto's scientific methodology was Alfonso de Pietri-Tonelli. In a speech given to *La Società Italiana per il progresso delle scienze* in honour of Pareto, ten years after his death, he stated that 'Pareto contributed towards the development of statistical methodology and its application.' He also emphasised how, although Pareto started 'from an absolute, scientific determinism . . . he then moderated his determinism . . . no longer stating the absolute necessity of uniformity and . . . in conclusion, reaching the point of attenuating his positivism as well: separating an abstract world, in which events happen according to deterministic laws, from a real world, from which one starts and to which one returns in building one's theories, but in which any forecast of future events is always affected by uncertainty . . . a determinism which is really not in absolute conflict with the concept of probability.'[22]

These discussions of Pareto's methodology which could have served as the starting point for further development and enquiry into his work, came to a standstill immediately after his death. The desideratum, foreseen by Borgatta, whereby Pareto's work – 'precious, not only for the substantial contribution on the uniformities of phenomena, but also for the methodological contributions to scientific problems' – which should have passed 'its most glorious life in future research where the elements and scientific germs of the hard work of thirty years would have been made fecund'[23] seemed to have been lost. But why? The answer is perhaps to be found by remembering that in the years immediately following Pareto's death fascism was being transformed from a government of order into an authoritarian government, and later into a totalitarian government. A worse fate could not have befallen Pareto – scientist, anti-metaphysician, anti-totalitarian, anti-colonialist, anti-militarist, than that of being quoted as the ideologue of a regime which was gradually losing all those characteristics to which Pareto had given his initial, incontestable support.

As long ago as March 1923 in an article, 'Forza e consenso' in *Gerarchia*, Mussolini had given the impression of having drawn his inspiration from Pareto. As Fiorot observes, another article on "The use of Paretian thought in a Fascist context' was produced by Vincenzo Fani, published in *Gerarchia* on 25 August 1923, and entitled 'Il Concetto sociologico dello stato'.[24] In Fani's opinion, the only parts of Pareto's work worth using were his ideas on the few who always command the many, and on force always deciding who must command. In a later essay, Fani defined Pareto as the Karl Marx of fascism, a title which was to be well received.

In a brief commemorative article written in *Gierarchia* in September 1923 another writer, Alberto de Stefani, affirmed that Pareto's chief merit lay in his having theoretically prepared the coming of fascism, and in 1924, Mussolini refers to Pareto as the most illustrious of his teachers.[25] In this climate, attention was shifted from Pareto as a methodologist of science, to Pareto as a virtual supporter of fascism. Many of his friends and pupils perhaps thought they were doing him a service by presenting him as a forerunner of fascism, thus increasing his fame. In the feverish epidemic of fascism – which infected the whole of Europe, from Spain to Hungary, from Portugal to England, from France to Germany – there were only a few farsighted enough not to involve Pareto. Among them must be mentioned Prato who, immediately after Pareto's death, wrote that 'giving in to a spiritual seduction absolutely foreign to his usual positivistic habits . . . Pareto gave this young movement his allegiance. But as the new situation developed, his logical, experimental faculties came to the fore again, expressing themselves in carefully considered judgements.'[26]

Another who was aware of the risk of using Pareto for propaganda reasons was Cappa who, praising the greatness of Pareto's work as an example of scientific method and the intelligence and energy it contains, wrote: 'Nothing is more disconcerting than seeing those who take just one aspect – the most striking – out of his work, and then sit back with the dull satisfaction of a professional.'[27]

Those sincere Socialists in whose service Pareto had fought with so much generosity, could be much less satisfied about his being used by the Fascists. In defining the *Trattato* as 'an original philosophy of history' Ciccotti observed, 'If it is true that the worth of an historian does not comprise his intellectual qualities alone – but that particular, moral qualities compete in its formation – then every time I read Pareto's works, I see silhouetted in the background his upright and manly figure, with that penetrating look, that word as sharp as a blade, that fierceness of thought, that caustic criticism – things which for me are another powerful comment on his work.'[28]

So the only ones who believed in Pareto as a supporter of fascism – while it suited them – were the Fascists. Then, as their totalitarian aspirations grew, their initial interest in him rapidly waned. Thus the majority of Italians remained in ignorance of his scientific work. His *Cours* was only translated into Italian in 1943. It was as if a shadow had been cast over his work. The new generations who had not known him at first hand began to criticise him. In one of his pithy, but wise, maxims in the *Manuale*, Pareto had written: 'If a man feels he is lucky, it is quite ridiculous to convince him that he is unlucky, or vice versa.' On re-reading all those who, for thirty years, obstinately saw Pareto as an evoker of the dark forces of irrationalism, we are tempted to repeat this maxim. And yet, in repeating it, we do Pareto no good, and we run the risk of not respecting his teaching – *all* his teaching.

NOTES

1 B. Croce, letter to Pareto, *Giornale degli economisti*, 15 May 1900.
2 Pareto, letter to Croce, *Giornale degli economisti*, August 1900.
3 Croce, letter to Pareto, *Giornale degli economisti*, 20 October 1900.
4 Pareto, letter to Croce, *Giornale degli economisti*, February 1901.
5 Pareto, *Manuel d'économie politique* (Paris 1909), p. 7.
6 Pareto, letter to V. Pansini, 7 April 1917, now in *Carteggi paretiani*, ed. G. de Rosa (Rome 1962).

7 Pareto, letter to Pansini, 23 April 1927, now in *Carteggi paretiani*, p. 11.
8 G. Papini, 'Vilfredo Pareto', *La Libertà economica*, 31 January 1917.
9 Pareto, *Lettere a Maffeo Pantaleoni*, vol. III, p. 217.
10 Pareto, 'Review of *L'Uomo delinquente di C. Lombroso*', *Giornale degli economisti*, November 1896, pp. 449–54.
11 Pareto, 'Del materialismo storico', *Zeitschrift für sozialwissenschaft*, pp. 149–53, now in Pareto, *Scritti sociologici*, p. 212.
12 Pareto, *Lettere a Maffeo Pantaleoni*, vol. III, p. 215.
13 Pareto, 'Proemio', *Biblioteca di storia economica* (Milan 1903), pp. IV–XIV, now in *Scritti sociologici*, p. 304.
14 G. Gentile, 'Realismo e fatalismo politico', *Politica*, vol. IV, 2, (1920).
15 Pareto, *Lettere a Maffeo Pantaleoni*, vol. III, pp. 269–70.
16 F. Weiss, 'Il nuovo verbo della scienza del Professore Vilfredo Pareto', *Critica sociale*, 16–31 May 1917, p 140.
17 Pareto, letter to Pansini, in *Carteggi paretiani*, p. 121.
18 *Giornale degli economisti*, Jan–Feb 1924. Sensini could not contribute to this number owing to 'a nervous breakdown ... in spite of a promise made to the editor of the review'. See G. Sensini, *Corrispondenza di Vilfredo Pareto*, (Padua 1948), p. 140.
19 Pantaleoni, 'In occasione della morte di Pareto: riflessioni', *Giornale degli economisti*, Jan–Feb 1924, p. 19.
20 L. Amoroso, 'La meccanica economica', *Giornale degli economisti*, Jan–Feb 1924, p. 8.
21 A. Barone, 'L'opera di Vilfredo Pareto e il progresso della scienza', *Giornale degli economisti*, Jan–Feb 1924, p. 21.
22 A. de Pietri-Tonelli, 'Vilfredo Pareto', *Rivista di politica economica*, Nov–Dec 1934 and Jan 1935, now in *Scritti paretiani*, ed. P. Pietri-Tonelli (Padua 1961), p. 101.
23 G. Borgatta, 'I rapporti fra la scienza economica e la sociologia nell'opera di Pareto', *Giornale degli economisti*, Jan–Feb 1924, p. 89.
24 D. Fiorot, *Pareto*.
25 *Ibid*, p. 314.
26 G. Prato, 'Corollari paretiani dell'ora presente', *Giornale degli economisti*, Jan–Feb 1924, p. 103.
27 A. Cappa, *Vilfredo Pareto*, ed. Piero Gobetti (Turin 1924), p. 84.
28 E. Ciccotti, 'Pareto e gli studi storici' *Giornale degli economisti*, Jan–Feb 1924, p. 119.

II   Pareto and his critics

By the end of the 1920s, the Italy in power had forgotten Pareto. The Italy in opposition had little time to worry about him – Gramsci and the most important Communist, Socialist and Liberal publicists had been imprisoned or exiled, if they had managed to avoid being executed. Not even Croce seemed interested in reading Pareto, and one or two of his pupils, like de Ruggiero, echoed the rather severe criticism made by the *maestro*, stating: 'I have read his *Trattato* with a sense of great sorrow, observing how a writer with such great historic learning, such as acute sense of politics, and such a winning scientific austerity, has managed to nullify his outstanding qualities in a work conceived in a mechanically abstract form.' The superficiality of this criticism and the extent to which it was tied to the fashions of the period can, however, be seen from the fact that de Ruggiero wrote a little further on: 'The behaviour of the author is very similar to that of the critics of science – Poincaré, Mach, and so on . . .'[1] But for the very same reason that Pareto was not taken seriously in Italy, he was beginning to be discovered by Anglo-Saxon scholars with whom, as we already know, he had had more than one exchange of opinion. The French edition of his *Trattato* was read and favourably reviewed. Speaking of Pareto, J.H. Robinson emphasised 'his aim to reduce sociology to the real "reasons" ' and defined this attempt 'as one of the several great discoveries of our age'.[2] In his *Contemporary sociological theories*, Sorokin firmly emphasised Pareto's logical, analytical method and his 'conceptual scheme'.[3] Talcott Parsons agreed with Sorokin in revaluing the methodological aspect of Pareto's work.[4] In the book written by G.C. Homans and C.P. Curtis, members of the seminar which Professor Henderson established at Harvard to study Pareto's work, Pareto's method was discussed once again: 'The characteristic of the *Sociologie générale* is that in it Pareto applies to the study of society the method which has been found successful in the maturer sciences.'[5]

The following year a book appeared by Henderson, who, for nearly ten years, had shown an interest in Pareto's work[6] and who was now so enthusiastic that he tried to attribute to Pareto conclusions that perhaps went beyond those which Pareto had originally envisaged. In underlining the fact that Pareto's scientific research was experimental, he rightly stated that Pareto 'demonstrated the abundant presence of certain kinds of residues and derivations in the writings of social scientists and explained how this condition interfered with the advancement of learning'. But then, perhaps not fully appreciating or not completely understanding the weight that Pareto had given to residues and derivations, he continued: 'He also held that the influence of these particular residues and derivations in the determination of public policy is disastrous.'[7] This is not true, for, as we have seen in his *Trattato*, Pareto held that 'the way of reasoning . . . in a scientific form . . . is often different from the solution which leads to an increase in the welfare of society. Therefore, it must only be used by those who have merely to solve a scientific problem . . . On the other hand, it is useful for social welfare among those belonging to the ruling classes who must *act*, in helping them to choose one of the theologies according to the problem they are facing: either that which desires to keep the existing uniformities, or that which wants them to be changed.' By a twist of fate, on the appearance of the English translation of the *Trattato*[8] the bad habit of entering into polemical argument as to whether or not Pareto was a fascist was debated outside Italy.[9] It was left to Henderson, who had already attempted a serious scientific appreciation of Pareto, to defend him from those who had chosen the easiest way to attack him: namely for alleged support of fascism.[10] Busino points out that 'the first intelligent and extremely subtle defence . . . was that of the physiologist, Henderson'.[11] Braga rightly points out that Pareto ended up by being the 'victim of a strange, historic circumstance: looked on with hostility in democratic countries for his fame as a fascist thinker, while in Italy the fascist climate prevented his teaching from being developed'.[12]

Until then, English-speaking scholars – with the exception of those like Henderson who knew French – had known Pareto either through some predominantly economic writing of his published in English at the time of the controversy with Edgeworth, Marshall and Fisher, or through essays written in English which Italian scholars published from time to time.[13] The English translation of the *Trattato*, therefore, threw other explosive materials on to a ground not yet ready to receive it, owing to its ignorance of Pareto's previous works. Some, therefore, found the *Trattato* 'an offence to ethics'.[14] Hook even

though he absolved Pareto of the charge of fascism which he categor-
ised as 'sheer poppycock', (this conflicts with Busino's view[15]),
condemned him nonetheless as a conservative. Hook's judgement was
founded on one sentence, as he himself said, 'tucked away in a long
footnote': 'the centuries roll by, human nature remains the same'.
From here he went on to say, perhaps somewhat arbitrarily, that
'Dewey's *Human Nature and Conduct* is . . . the definitive refutation
of this favourite theme – this song of all Tories.'[16]

Meanwhile, that aspect of Pareto's inquiries into residues which
seemed to have made such a negative impression owing to its 'vague
and arbitrary terminology' began to infect his critics, who tried to make
a post-mortem psycho-analysis. Bogardus rather conceitedly stated:
'He must have had "an error complex", for he discovers so many
errors in the thinking of the common people, of leaders and of scholars, that one wonders whether or not it is possible to avoid error in
thinking.'[17] Borkenau put forward the thesis that Pareto's theories
were the fruit of an 'oedipal reaction' against his father, and also
against all the 'ideals of his father' who was a fervent Mazzinist. In
this statement he did, however, forget certain things. Firstly, as
Finer rightly says, 'the correspondence shows that Pareto was proud
of his father and devoted to his memory'.[18] Secondly, as Finer again
points out, when Pareto's father returned to Italy after abandoning
his enthusiasm for Mazzini – the date is uncertain, but varies between
1848 and 1854 – Vilfredo had either just been born or was under the
seven years which Finer gives him. Thirdly, it remains to be made
clear what humanitarianism, the 'God Progress', and other 'Deities
of Mazzinism' which Pareto was supposed to have attacked to show
contempt for his father, mean for Borkenau.[19] Fourthly, it also
remains to be shown that 'a puritanical sexual morality . . . had formed
part of the Mazzinist creed'.[20] Fifthly, it is completely arbitrary to
describe Pareto as 'a rich man, desirous of enjoying the material and
the spiritual pleasures of life, leading, for instance, an intensive campaign against a rigorous sexual morality'.[21] Even admitting that with
this 'campaign against a rigorous sexual morality' Borkenau meant
Le Mythe vertüiste, we know that the work was not written in honour
of libertinism at all, but in contempt of false puritans and hypocritical
moralists. We also know how much Pareto admired Cromwell and the
real puritans, and all those who had created a moral system in which
they firmly believed. Borkenau's error of interpretation is pardonable,
however, if one remembers that later Braga too fell into the same trap,

and – neglecting the fundamental distinction which Pareto made between myth and myth – stated: 'Pareto conducts an often bitter campaign against what he calls "moralistic myth or rather sex taboos".' He went on to say, somewhat fancifully, that Pareto seemed to 'have realised intuitively that excessive sexual repression can result in psychological repression and a regression to infantilism and its consequent deficiencies of character'.[22] But this is not completely true either, as not only Pareto's writings, but also his life demonstrate. He lived an extremely retired existence, dedicated to work – and certainly did not give the impression of being a 'latin lover'.

Using the same psychological method as Borkenau, but from an opposite point of view, the method of inquiry into Pareto's work, adopted in Italy by Arcari, who stated 'he owed his puritan severity, which perhaps oppressed his adolescence, to the fact that his mother was a calvinist',[23] fails through its own inconsistency rather than from external criticism. Bousquet rightly observes: 'The life of Galileo is very intriguing and interesting, and his trial is still a subject of discussion. But even if nothing were known about it, the study of the problem of the validity of his theory to tides remains totally independent. And this is also true for Pareto.'[24] It is not that Pareto's life is irrelevant to a deeper understanding of his work, but rather that it should be considered not only in terms of the psychological influences of people and events, but also in terms of the degree of influence that his behaviour had upon the events of his life.

In examining Pareto's work, Morris Ginsberg also resorts to the psychological approach. He seems to follow the suggestion made by McDougall when he states: 'His neglect of psychology has resulted in an extremely vague use of such terms as *sentiments, instincts, interests,* which has made a proper understanding of his views more difficult than it need be',[25] and when he complains that 'Pareto does not undertake, as might have been expected, an analysis of such processes as repression, projection, aim, inhibition, substitution or sublimation, dramatisation, and the like.'[26] Ginsberg follows in Hook's footsteps when he points out that 'He is impressed by the fact that in moral judgements, for example, people are swayed by superstitions and prejudices which deceive themselves and others. But this applies to all human thought and action and if seriously pressed, would lead inevitably to the conclusion that there can be no logical thought or action at all.'[27] In conclusion Ginsberg too emphasises the conservative aspect of Pareto's work when he states: 'Pareto's denial of human

progress rests upon (1) his disbelief in any rational ethics; (2) his view
that history so far has disclosed no significant changes but only oscillations. As to (1) I do not find that he provides any reasoned justification for his disbelief. As to (2) it seems to me that he greatly exaggerates
the constant elements in human history, and that if there is no law of
human progress neither is there any law of cyclical recurrence. From
the point of view of politics in any event, if a choice is to be made
between persistent aggregates and combinations, I see no reason for
not choosing combinations.'[28] And yet, in these few sarcastic lines,
and perhaps quite unconsciously, Ginsberg reveals the essence of
Pareto's teaching and thought which comprises the individual freedom of choice to be a liberal or a reactionary, a revolutionary or a
conservative, each following the way he wants.

   Then the fashion of attacking 'Pareto the conservative' passed, and
a return was made to 'Pareto, methodologist of science'. Creedy
recognised Pareto's worth in having achieved through social analysis
the same results as Freud had reached through individual analysis.[29]
Talcott Parsons observed: 'Either Pareto's *Treatise* is really a hodge-
podge and does not contain a coherent theory at all, or the critics have
failed to penetrate to the deeper levels of the work. In my opinion the
truth is nearer the latter.'[30] Talcott Parsons, as if absorbing 'Pareto's
method into his own system' (as Meisel observed[31]) and proving
that he had understood the central point of Pareto's thought, claimed
that the '. . . relation may be that between a symbol and its meaning.
In so far the causal relation is always "arbitrary" but the symbolic
relation is none the less important to human life . . . What characterizes
logical action in this respect is that the systems of symbols involved in
it refer to or express systems of intrinsic relationships in the external
world. Their 'function" is that of intrinsic alteration of the external
world in the service of an "end".'[32]

   But at the time when Talcott Parsons wrote this, war in Spain was
imminent and the voice of reason was drowned in the thunder of guns.
Fate ordained that the approach to Pareto should once more be on the
lines of, for example, 'Ein theoretiker des fascismus'.[33] Aron was
retrogressive in accusing Pareto of having supplied fascism with a
philosophy. With hasty judgement, he demolished the *Trattato* as
'a gigantic derivation' and the aggressive tone used against Pareto was
almost that of personal animus, especially when Aron stated 'The
grand bourgeois turns fascist. This gentlest of men behaves like an
intellectual savage. And yet, he cannot quite deny his true nature: it

desires a violent élite but one intelligent enough not to begrudge genius its claim to leisure and the pleasures of the mind.'[34] Some years later Aron indulged in a form of exculpatory self-criticism when he wrote, 'We were in an age . . . in which the passions that roused us were different from those of today.'[35]

In fact the whole world, a prey to the craziest of passions, seemed to sink into darkness for nine long years – if we include the atrocities of the Spanish Civil War. During this time Pareto was not mentioned, and even immediately after the war his name seemed to have been forgotten. Italy still felt the effects of the demolition work carried out by Croce and de Ruggiero, but fortunately the war had parted some of the clouds of metaphysics. There was the will to reconstruct and to return to work, but work required technique and technique required method. So, some attention was directed towards Pareto, and his few faithful followers like Bousquet[36] and Giacalone-Monaco[37] who had never ceased to discuss Pareto's work now acquired more influence. But the work of these two, although essential to the historic reconstruction of the development of Pareto's life and thought, and useful in removing certain prejudices – such as the effect on the young Pareto of his mother's alleged Calvinism – began to show their inadequacy for a critical re-examination of Pareto's work. The generous, unemotional defence made by Giacalone-Monaco of a 'Pareto as pure scientist' when he affirmed: 'The author has no desire to leave any political teaching, since politics presuppose a faith, and faith necessarily blurs the intellect',[38] although useful when Pareto was accused of being an irrationalist, now fell short of what was needed. In the same way, approval of Pareto's reaction to 'socialist thieves', risked prolonging controversy along the same sterile lines of the past.[39]

It was, however, necessary to clear the field as much as possible of sentimental rubbish, and for this an historical reconstruction was needed to place Pareto in his age. It was Gabriele de Rosa who supplied this need by undertaking the laborious but scientifically profitable task, thus providing a completely fresh approach to the study of Pareto.[40] From this extensive correspondence an apparently contradictory Pareto emerges – thus proving La Ferla right. La Ferla had observed: 'Although he declared himself opposed to carrying out any political action – even the most direct – in reality he did so, persuading people of the inevitable decadence of the democratic-parliamentary system and the inevitable solution of the crisis through force. But all this in the name of, and with the language of a positive objective

science.'[41] The result is a Pareto who, although he had 'a fixed idea
... not to believe in ethics',[42] did, however, propose 'strong ideas
and moral vision'.[43] In truth, 'there is nobody who does not feel that
a high moral conscience inspires the whole of the work' of this
apparently cynical and cold man.[44]

That there is a two-sided Pareto, as La Ferla perhaps unwittingly
described him, is today becoming one of the best-credited hypotheses.
Aron deliberately worked on this thesis and, after having revised his
position, stated: 'Pareto is not necessarily a doctrinaire of the authoritarian regime as was believed or sometimes said. The fact is that he
presents different aspects to most, if not all, readers and can be used in
a variety of different meanings.'[45] Another eminent scholar, Bobbio,
reached a similar conclusion, stating: 'Pareto's thought was ambig-
uous, like that of Machiavelli, and gave different results according to
whether it was interpreted purely and simply as a wholesome lesson in
political realism (equally serviceable to either party in the dispute) or
interpreted as an art of making precepts for one or other of the
parties.'[46]

But this new way of interpreting Pareto, which those who had
supported him had intended as a re-evaluation, risks making him
appear a turncoat – something which he resisted so vigorously.

NOTES

1 G. de Ruggiero, *La Filosofia contemporanea*, Storia della filosofia, vol. IX,
(Bari 1962), pp. 494–5.
2 J.H. Robinson, *The Mind in the Making. The Relation of Intelligence to
Social Reforms* (New York 1921), p. 47.
3 P.A. Sorokin, *Contemporary Sociological Theories* (New York and London
1928).
4 See Talcott Parsons, 'Pareto's central analytical scheme', *Journal of Social
Philosophy*, April 1936, pp. 244–62, now in *Pareto and Mosca*, pp. 71–88.
5 See G.C. Homans and C.P. Curtis, *An Introduction to Pareto; His Sociology*
(New York 1934), p. 15.
6 See L.J. Henderson, 'The science of human conduct, an estimate of
Pareto and his greatest work', *The Independent*, vol. 119, 1927, pp. 575–7,
and 'Pareto's science of society', *The Saturday Review of Literature*, vol. 12,
May 1935, pp. 3–4.
7 L.J. Henderson, *Pareto's General Sociology: a physiologist's interpretation*
(Cambridge, Mass. 1935), pp. 57–8.
8 Pareto, *The Mind and Society*, ed. A. Livingston, trans. A. Bongiorno and
A. Livingston with the advice and active cooperation of James Harvey Rogers
(London 1935).

9 See R.V. Worthington, 'Pareto, the Karl Marx of fascism: a scientific sociologist', *The Economic Forum*, 1933, pp. 311–15, 460–6; M. Cowley, 'A handbook for demagogues', *The New Republic*, vol. 80, 12 September 1934; W. McDougall, 'Pareto as psychologist', *Journal of Social Philosophy*, vol. 1, October 1935, pp. 36–52, who as Meisel reminds us in *Pareto and Mosca*, p. 27, 'as a professional psychologist . . . was especially offended by Pareto's vague and arbitrary terminology'; F.N. House, 'Pareto in the development of modern sociology', *Journal of Social Philosophy*, vol. 1, October 1935, minimising Pareto's work, reminds us on p. 85 how Darwin, William James, McDougall, Sumner and Graham Wallas had a long time before had 'the idea that human behaviour is always and everywhere in large part non-rational'. Fortunately there were some like Talcott Parsons who, on the contary, recognised that 'in recent years Pareto's contributions, particularly to sociology, have been underrated rather than the reverse'. Talcott Parsons, 'Pareto's approach to the contribution of a theory of social system', *Convegno internazionale Vilfredo Pareto*, Accademia Nazionale dei Lincei, Rome 1975, p. 18.

10 Henderson, 'Comments and rejoinders, McDougall vs Pareto', *Journal of Social Philosophy*, vol. 1, October 1935.

11 G. Busino, 'Introduction' to Pareto, *Scritti sociologici*, p. 67.

12 G. Braga, *Forma ed equilibrio sociale* (Bologna 1959), p. xlix.

13 See: F. Burzio, 'The new sociology of Vilfredo Pareto', *Adelpi*, London, vol. 2, 1923; G.A. Borgese, 'The intellectual origins of fascism', *Social Research*, November 1934, pp. 458–85; B. Croce, 'The validity of Pareto's theories', *The Saturday Review of Literature*, 25 May 1935.

14 See J.H. Tufts, 'Pareto's significance for ethics', *Journal of Social Philosophy*, vol. 1, October 1935, pp. 64–77.

15 Busino, 'Introduction' to Pareto, *Scritti sociologici*, p. 67.

16 See S. Hook, 'Pareto's sociological system', *The Nation*, June 1935, pp. 747–8, now in *Pareto and Mosca*, p. 59.

17 E.S. Bogardus, 'Pareto as a sociologist', *Sociology and Social Research*, November 1935, p. 167–8.

18 S.E. Finer, 'Pareto and Pluto-democracy: the retreat to Galapagos', *The American Political Science Review*, vol. 62, 1968, p. 442.

19 See F. Borkenau, *Pareto* (London and New York, 1936), p. 11.

20 *Ibid.*, p. 15.

21 *Ibid.*

22 G. Braga, *Forma ed equilibrio sociale* (Bologna 1959), p. xxxiv.

23 See P.M. Arcari, *Socialismo e democrazia nel pensiero di Pareto* (Rome 1966), p. 7.

24 G.H. Bousquet, 'A propos de Marie Métenier, mère de Vilfredo Pareto, faits et réflexions' in *Cahiers Pareto*, no. 16, 1968, p. 223.

25 M. Ginsberg, 'The sociology of Pareto', *The Sociological Review*, July 1936, pp. 221–45, now in *Pareto and Mosca*, p. 90. Another, like Ginsberg, who has read Pareto only from a left wing point of view is Robert A. Nye. In *The anti-democratic sources of élite theory: Pareto, Mosca and Michels* (London 1977), he says, p. 47, that with their 'democratic élitism (they) have dirsegarded the timeless conception of democracy' and 'whose original

aim was the utter discredition of political equality and classical democratic aspiration.' He thus contrasts them with John Stuart Mill.

26 *Pareto and Mosca*, p. 96.

27 *Ibid.*, p. 94.

28 *Ibid.*, pp. 106–7.

29 See F. Creedy, 'Residues and derivations in three articles on Pareto', *Journal of Social Philosophy*, January 1936, pp. 175–9.

30 Talcott Parsons, 'Pareto's central analytical scheme', *Journal of Social Philosophy*, April 1936, pp. 244–62, now in *Pareto and Mosca*, p. 71.

31 See J.H. Meisel, 'Introduction 'to *Pareto and Mosca*, p. 24.

32 Talcott Parsons, in *Pareto and Mosca*, pp. 85–6.

33 See Ch. La Roche, 'Ein theoretiker des fascismus', *Neue Schweizer Rundschau*, April 1935, pp. 800–13.

34 R. Aron, 'La sociologie de Pareto', in *Zeitschrift für Sozialforschung*, no. VI, 1937, pp. 489–521, now in *Pareto and Mosca*, p. 119.

35 R. Aron, 'La signification de l'œuvre de Pareto', *Cahiers Pareto*, no. 1, 1963, p. 12.

36 G.H. Bousquet, *Vilfredo Pareto, sa vie et son œuvre* (Paris 1927). The book was later enlarged and elaborated on and published as *Pareto, le savant et l'homme* (Lausanne 1970). Also: *Précis de sociologie d'après Pareto* (Paris 1925); *The Work of Vilfredo Pareto* (Minneapolis 1928); 'Introduction' to Pareto, *Manuel d'économie politique* (Paris 1927); 'Introduction' to Pareto, *Les Systèmes socialistes*, 2nd ed., 3 vols, (Paris 1926); 'Introduction' to Pareto, *Cours d'économie politique* (Geneva 1964). He also wrote many essays, some of which have been quoted in *Cahiers Pareto*.

37 See T. Giacalone-Monaco (ed.), *Vilfredo Pareto, dal carteggio con Carlo Placci* (Padua 1957). Also: *Pareto, Lettere a Ubaldino e Emilia Peruzzi; Pareto-Walras; Pareto, riflessioni e ricerche; Pareto e Sorel.*

38 Giacalone-Monaco, *Vilfredo Pareto, dal carteggio con Carlo Placci*, p. 35.

39 See Bousquet, *Pareto, le savant et l'homme*. Having observed that the Socialists in Switzerland had proposed a heavy, progressive wealth tax, and that Pareto had moved to France for a few months until the proposal was rejected, Bousquet states on p. 84, 'One may or may not approve of this act of a bourgeois determined to defend his wealth from Socialist thieves . . . as for me, I admire my teacher whole-heartedly for having dared to show his feelings, and deplore the fact that we bourgeoisie no longer have the class instinct which would help us to survive without being a herd exploited by those in power.'

40 Pareto, *Lettere a Maffeo Pantaleoni*. Under his influence Pareto's *Lettere al Arturo Linaker, 1885–1923*, ed. M. Luchetti (Rome 1972) was printed. The articles which Pareto had written for *Giornale degli economisti* were also published under the title of *Cronache italiane*, ed. C. Mongardini.

41 G. La Ferla, *Vilfredo Pareto, filosofo volteriano*, p. 166.

42 See G. La Ferla, 'Nota su Pareto' in Pareto, *Mon journal* (Padua 1958), p. XLV.

43 See G. La Ferla, 'G. Sorel and V. Pareto, due spiriti inattuali', *Nuova antologia*, May–Aug 1963, p. 311.

44 See G. La Ferla, 'Nota su Pareto' in Pareto, *Mon journal*, p. XLV.

45 R. Aron, 'La signification de l'œuve de Pareto' in *Cahiers Pareto*, no. 1, 1963, p. 15.
46 N. Bobbio, 'Introduction' to Pareto, *Trattato di sociologia generale* (Milan 1964), p. xxx, now in *Saggi sulla scienza politica in Italia* (Bari 1969), p. 73.

III Reading Pareto

Reading Pareto is like following a road which branches off into fascinating, attractive by-ways. Letting oneself be charmed off the main road is like going along the blind alleys of a maze. But just as every maze has an entrance and an exit, so Pareto's work has its conclusions, and at every crossroads only the careless reader who lets himself be lured along them is disappointed and deceived. But what are the characteristics of the right road? Let us follow the instructions of the builder of the maze. Although initially arbitrary, his method furnishes us with two principles. The first is that propounded in 'An application of sociological theories', according to which in every sociological phenomenon it is necessary to distinguish a *principal fact* from a *secondary fact*. The second is that of verification by which 'scientific commonsensical statements', which Pareto called theories, can have a *logical nexus* both in relation to 'experimental matter' verifiable in practice and in relation to 'non-experimental matter' verifiable in principle – thus anticipating by many years the concept of verifiability of the Vienna Circle.[1]

Now let us pass on to discuss the principal facts and secondary facts of Pareto's work. As many have already pointed out, undoubtedly a primary fact is his technique of research – extremely modern in respect of concepts of verifiability and utility, setting him beside Pierce in respect of beliefs and ways of behaviour, and close to Dewey's pragmatism in respect of the fact that a situation and its circumstances limit our experience and actions, even if Sidney Hook thinks the opposite – as we have already seen.[2] But Pareto's universality is surprising in that, having meditated at length on classical thought, he managed to fuse it with modern thought. Hume's axioms which stated that 'induction cannot be assumed to lead to the truth' and 'that the sun will rise tomorrow is to be regarded as a belief rather than as an established truth', spurred Pareto on to seek not only logical constructions, but also the springs of the motivations of beliefs. He believed that he had found the latter in emotions and residues, which he showed to be long-lasting, but not eternal. He had often proved that there is a correlation between individual emotions and collective emotions and also between the level of wealth reached and the moral values current. Likewise, he had often warned that the infanticide and cannibalism of pre-industrialised and savage societies (which do not know what the accumulation of wealth is) – rather than being the effect of a morality untouched by the Grace of God – are psychic, social and economic, owing to an inability to save food supplies. Realising this, Pareto continually advocated higher production and the accumulation of more wealth, as in these lay the foundations for evolving higher moral values, because 'freedom is a luxury' which still has to be earned.[3]

Another primary element of Pareto's methodological teaching is that of equilibrium. When discussing Pareto's social equilibrium, Marill only speaks of the legal and constitutional equilibrium in the division of power and, criticising him for this, Bousquet says that the idea of equilibrium 'which has always attracted Pareto's attention . . . is that of the mutual dependence of the elements in a system'.[4] Pareto turned his attention not only towards the equilibrium of some social elements, but of all social elements: economic, psychic, religious, customary, and so on. This concept of equilibrium can be found in his very earliest writings when it is a matter of balancing the old and the new. Gradually the concept emerges as a matter of finding a meeting point between the individual and society, freedom and necessity, consent and coercion, rulers and ruled, production and consumption, wealth produced directly from work and wealth extracted from others, utility for the community (in the sense of a sum of individuals) and the utility of the collectivity (in the sense of an independent entity above the individual), centrifugal forces and centripetal forces. All this explains why this apparently simple concept of equilibrium is so complicated and that it is this which is the keystone of all Pareto's work, and reveals what he really is.

As we have already seen, Pareto has been accused more than once of being a conservative. Does the proper interpretation of his theory of equilibrium afford grounds for such an accusation? Almost certainly not, if one considers the equilibrium that he talks about is dynamic, not static, and if one also believes that amid all the infinite variety of life it is always man who uses his faith and reason, chooses between courses of action to build whatever type and level of civilisation he desires through a succession of approximations. It is not true then, that in the system desired by Pareto all innovation was banned. It is rather that the responsibility for man's actions was left to him. For Pareto being a heretic had an important social function: it is simply that there was no better proof of his really *being* the heretic he claimed to be than the sacrifice he was prepared to make. In this sense he believed in heroism and courage if they were *real*, and if the person involved was prepared to pay a price for them.

Pareto's 'Man' really is the arbiter of his own destiny – much more so than Comte's, Spencer's, Hegel's, or Marx's. More than once in the past he proved that he had read, digested and meditated on these authors' works. Both Hegel's dialectic of servant-master in *Die phenomenologie des geistes*, and Marx's dialectic of proletarian-bourgeois, can be found in his concept of the circulation of the élites. Unlike his successors, Pareto uses both of these, placing them in correlation and balancing them dynamically. His teaching is that any effort of man's will is made within certain socio-economic limits, and that no socio-economic organisation makes progress without myth and individual will. Thus, the view that Pareto was Hegelian is just as erroneous as the argument that Pareto followed in Marx's footsteps, especially because it is based upon an alleged affinity between the two which, after careful scrutiny, proves to be false. For example, it is not so easy to accept that 'Pareto loathed the bourgeoisie just as much as Marx had done',[5] as that Pareto had been 'an old man who aspired to be the Machiavelli of the middle classes'.[6]

Pareto's 'Man' acts psychologically like Hegel's 'Man', who from servant seeks to become master, but unlike him he finds himself immersed in the economic world of Marx. The result is to produce a sort of intellectual acrobat who can move forwards but who is unable to take steps which are too long because he might fall; if he wants to proceed, he must study the ground step by step.

In order to maintain equilibrium, it is not only necessary to know all the circumstances but also oneself and one's partners. The ancient maxim 'Do unto others as you would have them do unto you', seems to leave Pareto perplexed. For him, whoever chooses a way of life *absolutely* different from the way of life of the majority of people is automatically doomed to extinction. In this context, in his *Cours*, he states: 'If a man like Edison had invented the telephone in the Middle Ages, overcoming the material difficulties of execution, both he and his apparatus would simply have been burned.' This means that the degree to which the world can be changed depends upon what the circumstances allow, and that maintenance of one's standards of living or civilisation prohibits radical change. In this light his anti-humanitarian polemics and his thesis on the use of force gain a precise meaning. In a world in which the death penalty, polygamy, elimination of the weak, and infanticide are widespread, then to sustain a different mode of life as realistically as possible, it is necessary to use at least in part the instruments of those who do not accept this way of life. As Bobbio has so rightly remarked, massacres and genocide were not invented by Pareto, neither was 'human folly'. He is honest when he observes that if Pareto 'had lived for another ten years, he would have had to reproach himself for having made an understatement'. He continues: 'In spite of the irritation that his anti-humanitarian outbursts cause in the reader who only skims the surface, the key to the cynical Machiavellian Pareto – as he is generally viewed – in the end proves to be the wrong key.'[7] For Pareto, it was not really that the end justifies the means so much that the means are ends in themselves. From this springs Pareto's modernity and the influence which he has had on many of the sociologists and economists of our time. His influence on Schumpeter is self-evident too. Bouquet writes: 'Today, after the appearance of *Capitalism, socialism and democracy*, another approach is needed, even if the interpretation of the history of capitalism proposed by Schumpeter is inspired by Marx, credit is also due to Pareto.'[8] But if Pareto's influence on 'Schumpeter the economist' is undeniable, it is certainly wrong to believe that 'Schumpeter the sociologist' followed in Pareto's footsteps, even if he himself claims: 'We cultivate the subnormal and do our best to suppress whatever there is of strength and genius. In conditions such as these, Pareto's message . . . is a healthy antidote.'[9] Pareto had never supplied any antidotes. At the most he confined himself to indicating where one road or another would lead the men who took it. He did not advise, because he never chose for others. At most he invited others to choose. His science is not exhortatory precisely because it 'is no other than analysis made coherent only as an instrumental context which he himself has created for the most part, and which in its majesty gives an idea which leaves no doubt about the *relative* position of the author'.[10] All he does is to furnish different technical instruments which different people can employ with different wills for different ends. For example, he clarifies the fact that just as you cannot have your cake and eat it, so you cannot have humanitarians (people who respect the old, children and sub-normals) and destroyers of wealth. Another thing which he emphasises is that you cannot support a civilisation of mass consumption and at the same time oppose birth-control. It is not by removing the privileges of the few that the many will gain an improvement in their standard of living, because this only improves when the number of those who divide the wealth between them decreases, or when there is an increase in the production of wealth.

For Pareto, the term natural is not synonymous with the term necessary, and so the process of so-called natural selection which decrees that the weak must be eliminated can be modified by human actions. But to do this, those who want it modified must pay a price – that is, produce more. Thus beyond the neutrality of his science, now universally acknowledged as valid, the sociological moral value which underlies it must now be recognised, and the main demonstration of this value is provided by the *actions* of the 'Pareto Man' which become an example and an exhortation only to those who freely intend to follow that way of life.

Pareto has been regarded by many as a comfortably-off bourgeois who enjoyed life to the full, without taking into consideration the fact that he acted within the objective means which his life offered him, capable of sacrifice and even of accepting humiliation rather than bow to the arrogance of the victor of the moment. Neither did he give in to his illness. He managed to keep it at bay, and in this case too – within permitted limits – he managed to study and write with tenacity right up to his death, reminding us that in the struggle for survival the limits for man's development do not come only from his economic conditions, but also from his physical and psychological nature, which determine his position in the world about him. In this light, Pareto's work no longer seems to be the manual of a man who wants to rule, but begins to look like the handbook of a good citizen; not only able to aspire to power, but also to surrender what little power he has rather than barter it for his own integrity. On this principle, his way of life was always as single-minded as his writings which, on second reading give us new and useful answers to many of those questions which seemed to have no answer on first reading. To know Pareto's work, one must adopt the method which he himself used to understand man and society. Thus the words he wrote in his last essay come to mind: 'There are great currents of sentiments which never disappear, even if they only appear every now and again on the surface – for example the currents of faith, scepticism, idealism, materialism, positive religions, free thought. Whoever believes that he can eliminate them is deceiving himself.' So that, although throughout his work first one

Pareto appears, and then another, as Zuccarini says 'his opinions have always remained liberal and in favour of a system of democracy' even if this is sometimes below the surface.[11]

NOTES

1 On Pareto as a precursor of logical neo-positivism and the philosophy of language, see T. Giacalone-Monaco, *Pareto, riflessioni e ricerche*, p. 68 where he affirms: 'He substituted common terms with symbols to start off both himself and others with a neutral, expressive technique, thus unintentionally anticipating new tendencies.' Following the same line of reasoning on how to read Pareto, N. Bobbio in 'Pareto e il diritto naturale', *Convegno internazionale Vilfredo Pareto*, pp. 324–5, states that with his dualism 'between propositions that have a cognitive function and propositions that have a function which is exclusively persuasive or perceptive' Pareto adopts neo-empiricist ethics and it is so 'because the uniformities that a scientist discovers are completely dumb in reply to the question "What must I do?" '.

2 S. Hook, 'Pareto's sociological system' in *Pareto and Mosca*, p. 59.

3 Pareto, 'Il crepuscolo della libertà', *Rivista d'Italia*, February 1904, p. 19.

4 G.H. Bousquet, 'Pareto, l'équilibre social et M. Marill', *Cahiers Pareto*, no. 20, 1970, p. 135.

5 See J.H. Meisel, 'A question of affinities; Pareto and Marx II', *Cahiers Pareto*, no. 5, 1965, p. 173.

6 See Ellsworth Faris, 'An estimate of Pareto', *American Journal of Sociology*, no. XLI, 1936, p. 668.

7 N. Bobbio, 'Introduction' to Pareto, *Trattato di sociologia generale*, pp. XXXI–XXXII.

8 L. Bouquet, 'Vilfredo Pareto' in *Les grands courants de la pensée mondiale contemporaine – portraits* vol. II, (Milan 1964), p. 1211.

9 J.A. Schumpeter, 'Morphology and social psychology in Pareto', in *Ten Great Economists: From Marx to Keynes* (New York 1951), now in *Pareto and Mosca*, p. 127.

10 See T. Bagiotti, 'Del giornale paretiano e dell'unità analitica come criterio d'integrazione delle scienze sociale', 'Introduction' to Pareto, *Mon journal*, p. XXVIII.

11 O. Zuccarini, 'Ricordo di Vilfredo Pareto', *Nuova antologia* no. 1979, November 1965, p. 389. Raymond Aron in ' "Lectures" de Pareto', *Convegno internazionale Vilfredo Pareto*, p. 43, after having brilliantly synthesised the four ways in which to read Pareto – 'Fascist-Darwinian, Machiavellian-dictatorial, Machiavellian-liberal, sceptical-cynical' states that even if 'Pareto's style risks the encouragement of violence owing to its content, it could have taught the friends of freedom to be vigilant.' And if it has not done so, it certainly is not the fault of Pareto!

Select bibliography

WORKS BY PARETO
Battaglie liberiste, ed. L. Avagliano, Naples 1975
Carteggi paretiani, ed. G. de Rosa, Rome 1962
Cours d'économie politique, Lausanne 1896
Cronache italiane, ed. C. Mongardini, Brescia 1965
Fatti e teorie, Florence, 1920
Mon journal, Padua 1958
Lettere a Maffeo Pantaleoni, ed. G. de Rosa, 3 vols, Rome 1960
La Liberté économique et les événements d'Italie, ed. G. Busino,
    Geneva 1966
Manuale di economia politica, Milan 1906
Marxisme et l'économie pure, Geneva 1893
The Mind and Society, ed. A. Livingston, 4 vols, London 1935
Le Mythe vertüiste, Paris 1911
Œuvres complètes, Geneva 1964–
Pareto and Mosca, ed. J.H. Meisel, New Jersey 1965
Pareto e Sorel, ed. T. Giacalone-Monaco, 2 vols, Padua 1960–1
Pareto-Walras, da un carteggio inedito (1891–1901), ed. T. Giacalone-
    Monaco, Padua 1960
Scritti paretiani, ed. P. Pietri-Tonelli, Padua 1961
Scritti sociologici, ed. G. Busino, Turin 1966
Scritti teorici, ed. G. de Maria, Milan 1952
I Sistemi socialisti, trans. C. Arena, Turin 1951
Les Systèmes socialistes, Lausanne 1901
Trasformazioni della democrazia, Milan 1921
Trattato di sociologia generale, 3 vols, Florence 1916
Vilfredo Pareto dal carteggio con Carlo Placci, ed. T. Giacalone-
    Monaco, Padua 1957
Vilfredo Pareto, lettere a Ubaldino e Emila Peruzzi 1872–1900,
    ed. T. Giacalone-Monaco, Rome 1968
Vilfredo Pareto, riflessioni e ricerche, ed. T. Giacalone-Monaco,
    Padua 1966
Vilfredo Pareto: Sociological writings, ed. S.E. Finer, London 1966

OTHER WORKS

A. Antonucci. *Alcune lettere di Vilfredo Pareto*, Rome 1938

F. Borkenau, *Pareto*, London and New York 1936

G.H. Bousquet, *Précis de sociologie d'après Pareto*, Paris 1925
Vilfredo Pareto, sa vie son œuvre, Paris 1927. Revised edition:
Pareto, le savant et l'homme, Lausanne 1960
The Work of Vilfredo Pareto, Minneapolis 1928

G. Braga, *Forma ed equilibrio sociale*, Bologna 1959

A. Cappa, *Vilfredo Pareto*, ed. Piero Gobetti, Turin 1924

G. La Ferla, *Vilfredo Pareto filosofo volteriano*, Florence 1954

D. Fiorot, *Pareto*, Milan 1969

L.J. Henderson, *Pareto's General Sociology: A Physiologist's
Interpretation*, Cambridge Mass. 1935

G.C. Homans and C.P. Curtis, *An Introduction to Pareto, his
Sociology*, New York 1934

G. de Molinari, *Précis d'économie politique et de la morale* Paris 1893

Index of names

Agricultural League 37-8
Alexander I, Tsar 255, 258
Amendola, G.B. 260
Amman, O. 159
Ammon, C.G. 86
Amoroso, L. 283, 284, 287n
Andrae, P.G. 22
Annunzio, D. 242, 246, 253
Antonucci, A. 178, 188n, 189
Arcari, P.M. 291, 295n
Aristotle 4, 184
Aron, R. 292, 293, 294, 296n, 297n, 303n
Asquith, H.H. 121, 225
Avagliano, L. 177, 187n

Baccarini, A. 33, 34, 36, 38, 39
Bagehot, W. 25, 29, 86
Bagiotti, T. 303n
Bakounine, Alessandra 41, 139
Bakunin, M. 50
Barone, A. 283, 287n
Bastiat, C.F. 44, 113
Bebel, A. 124
Bernstein, E. 142
Bismarck, O.E.L. von, 47, 61, 109, 123, 183, 227, 275
Bobbio, C.N. 294, 297n, 301, 303n
Borgardus, E.S. 290, 295n
Borgatta, G. 285, 287n
Borgese, G.A. 295n
Borkenau, F. xiii, 290, 291, 295n
Bouquet, L. 301, 303n
Bousquet, G.H. 3, 5n, 100, 101, 105n, 106n, 145, 165n, 291, 293, 295n, 296n, 299, 303n,
Braga, G. 144, 165n, 289, 290, 295n
Bright, J. 44, 66
Buckle, H.T. 26, 51, 67, 69, 86

Burzio, F. 295n
Busino, G. 86, 99n, 105n, 111n, 134n, 189, 194n, 272, 276n, 289n, 290, 295n

Cappa, A. 286, 287n
Carnegie, A. 58, 59
Cavour, Count C. 194, 269
Charles Albert, King 113, 115, 116
Ciccotti, E. 108, 286, 287n
Cirillo, R. 101, 106n
Cobden, R. 10, 44, 66, 178, 244
Colajanni, N. 42, 80, 81, 93, 94
Coletti, F. 70, 75, 76
Comte, A. ix, 6, 7, 13, 24, 26, 28, 153, 154, 300
Cowley, M. 295n
Cournot, A.A. 83
Creedy, F. 292, 296n
Crispi, F. 47, 61, 71, 80, 81, 107, 173, 282
Croce, B. 74, 83, 99n, 108, 260, 279, 280, 281, 282, 283, 286n, 288, 293, 295n
Curtis, C.P. 288, 294n

Depretis, A. 54, 55, 57, 141
Dewey, J. 290, 298
Dreyfus, A.F. 112, 116
Durkheim, E. ix, xi

Edgeworth, F.Y. 83, 100, 289

Fani, V. 285
Faris, E. 303n
Finer, S.E. xiii, 144, 165n, 225, 228n, 290, 295n
Fiorot, D. 42, 53n, 225, 228n, 285, 287n

Fisher, I. 289
Free Trade League 10, 178
Freud, S. xii, 292

Galileo 154, 291
Gentile, G. 282, 287n
Giacalone-Monaco, T. 79n, 139,
    145, 165n, 176, 272, 283, 293,
    296n, 303n
Gide, C. 163
Ginsberg, M. 5n, 291, 292, 295n
Gioberti, V. 7, 13
Giolitti, G. 140, 166, 174, 252
Gladstone, W. 55, 58, 141
Grote, G. 182
Guesde, J. 70, 124
Guyot, Yves 41, 108, 112, 116, 244

Handel-Mazzetti, Mme E von 206
Hegar, Dr 126, 144
Hegel, G.W.F. 74, 157, 234, 279,
    282, 283, 300
Heisenberg, W. 176, 187n
Henderson, L.J. x, 288, 289, 294n,
    295n
Herzen, A. 50
Homans, G.C. x, 288, 294n
Hook, S. 289, 290, 291, 295n, 298,
    303n
House, F.N. 295n
Hume, D. ix, 234, 298

International Workingmen's
    Association 48

Jacini, S.F. 57
Jaurès, J.L. 70, 112, 116, 142, 174,
    225

Kant, I. ix, 234

Labriola, A. 108, 282
La Ferla, G. 77n, 293, 294, 296n
Lapouge, G. Vacher de 159
La Roche, Ch. 296n
League for Electoral Reform 10
Leo XIII, Pope 114
Linaker, A. 283

Lloyd George, D. 231, 238, 239,
    241, 249
Lombroso, C. 93, 94, 282
Loria, A. 98, 282
Luchini, O. 10, 12, 14
Luzzatti, L. 190, 194

Machiavelli, N. 184, 273, 294, 300
Malthus, T.R. 84, 88, 89, 190
Maria, G. de, 83, 99n
Marshall, A. 83, 100, 289
Marx, K. ix, 43, 48, 61, 62, 63, 64,
    66, 81, 94, 98, 124, 132, 133, 134,
    144, 145, 150, 157, 234, 240, 268,
    285, 300, 301
Massara, G. 115-17
Maury, L.F.A. 129, 130
Mazzini, G. 3, 61, 194, 283, 290
McDougall, W. 291, 295n
Meisel, J.H. 273, 276n, 292, 296n,
    303n
Métenier, Marie 3
Michels, R.W.E. xi
Mill, J.S. xiii, 13, 20, 22, 28, 32,
    34, 35, 51, 52, 57, 85, 86, 91
Millerand, A. 116, 131, 136, 140,
    142
Minghetti, M. 57
Molinari, G. de 41, 51, 52, 57, 66,
    67, 68, 72, 86, 91, 108, 116, 162,
    178
Mongardini, C. 78
Mosca, G. xi
Mussolini, B. xi, 260, 261, 262, 263,
    272, 273, 285

Napoleon I 178, 194, 253, 255, 258
Napoleon III 178, 220, 253
Naumann, F. 131
Naville, E. 22, 272, 276n
Newton, Isaac 96, 99, 144, 154, 202
Nicholas II, Tsar 167, 192, 225
Nye, R.A. 295n

Pallavicino, Marquis Trivulzio 20-3
Pansini, V. 281, 283, 287n
Pantaleoni, Maffeo 31, 40n, 41, 55,
    61, 69, 78, 80, 82n, 100, 107, 108,

121, 166, 234, 242, 251, 252, 254,
  261, 273, 281, 282, 283, 284, 287n
Papini, G. 4, 5n, 166, 281, 287n
Pareto, Domenico 109, 121
Pareto, Raffaele 3, 290
Parsons, Talcott x, xii, 288, 292,
  294n, 295n, 296n
Pascal, B. 128, 234, 297
Pasteur, L. 201-2
Pelloux, General Luigi 112
Peruzzi, Emilia and Ubaldino 3, 7,
  24, 31, 41
Pietri-Tonelli, A. de 283, 284, 287n
Placci, C. 195, 224n, 283
Plato 75, 153, 181, 219
Pliny 76, 123, 124
Prato, G. 285, 287n
Prezzolini, G. 166, 169

Régis, Jane 139, 283
Robinson, J.H. 288, 294n
Rogers, Thorold 71, 72, 86
Rosa, G. de 55, 60n, 80, 107, 111n,
  178, 188n, 234, 237n, 254, 273,
  293
Rousseau, Jean-Jacques 12, 153,
  158
Ruggiero, G. de 288, 293, 294n

Saint-Simon, C.H. de R. 163
Salisbury, Lord 55, 58
Saussure, Ferdinand de 86
Schumpeter, J.A. x, 301, 303n
Sensini, G. 272, 281, 283, 287n
Smith, Adam 27

Socrates 15, 181
Sonnio, Sidney 107, 141
Sorel, G. 100, 101, 105n, 182, 193,
  240, 283
Sorokin, P.A. 288, 294n
Spencer, H. ix, 29, 51, 57, 300
Stefani, A. de 285

Tarde, G. 142
Tocqueville, A. de 51
Todde, G. 68
Tortora, E. 72
Tufts, J.H. 295n
Turati, F. 108, 114, 116, 121

Umberto I, King 80, 107, 112, 121,
  135

Vico, G.B. 26, 27, 69, 282
Vidari, E. 136, 137
Viti de Marco, A. de 108, 166
Voltaire 58, 74, 134, 156, 234

Waldeck-Rousseau, R. 121, 131
Walras, Leon 61, 76, 83, 100, 101,
  103, 104, 176
Weber, Max xi, xii
Weiss, F. 282, 287n
Wilhelm II, Kaiser 123, 131
Wilson, W. 238, 241, 244, 255
Worthington, R.V. 295n

Zanardelli, G. 121, 140, 142, 166
Zuccarini, O. xiii, 303, 303n